DREAMING OF PORTUGAL

A Memoir

by Marianne Gilbert Finnegan

Marianne Gilbert Finnegan

White Horse Publishing
Saratoga Springs, New York

ACKNOWLEDGMENTS

Many thanks to the Writers Circle members of the Academy for Learning in Retirement at Saratoga Springs for their advice as the manuscript progressed, to Jane Mackintosh for sensitive editing, to Marion B. Renning for her encouragement and careful copy editing, and to my daughter Julia Cunningham for valuable suggestions for improvements. My thanks also to the good friends and fine people we knew in the Algarve. To protect their privacy, I have changed all names except those of my family. The events described in this memoir are as true as memory and the journal I kept during my years in Portugal can portray them.

Introductory quotation by José Saramago from his *Journey to Portugal,* translated by Amanda Hopkinson and Nick Caistor, 2000, Harcourt, Inc.

Cover photo by SoFOTO, Centro Cultural, São Lourenço, Algarve, Portugal

Photograph of Algarvian seacoast by Fulvio Roiter in *Algarve: Die Sonnenküste Portugals*, 1971, Atlantis.

DREAMING OF PORTUGAL

The journey is never over. Only travellers come to an end. But even then they can prolong their voyage in their memories, in recollections, in stories. When the traveller sat in the sand and declared: "There's nothing more to see," he knew it wasn't true. The end of one journey is simply the start of another. You have to see what you missed the first time, see again what you already saw, see in springtime what you saw in summer, in daylight what you saw at night, see the sun shining where you saw the rain falling, see the crops growing, the fruit ripen, the stone which has moved, the shadow that was not there before. You have to go back to the footsteps already taken, to go over them again or add fresh ones alongside them. You have to start the journey anew. Always.

José Saramago

DREAMING OF PORTUGAL

I
A Plot of Land

In 1972 my mother, Elke, who lived in Zurich for many years, bought a plot of land in the Algarve, the southern coast of Portugal, because a lawyer friend predicted that the gorgeous hundred-mile stretch of beaches would soon become the next Riviera. Elke paid the equivalent of fifteen hundred dollars for three acres about a mile inland from the Atlantic Ocean and adjoining a luxury beach resort called Vale do Lobo. She thought of the property not as real estate but as a paper investment to sell once it proved profitable. At the time, she had no idea how her purchase in Portugal would change our lives.

It is eleven years later and my mother is eighty-three, the same age as the century. While my husband Walter and I are in Zurich for our annual springtime visit for her birthday, she receives a letter and waves it with a gratified smile.

"Look at this. This is a hundred percent profit in just ten years. Isn't that wonderful?"

The letter is from the real estate firm of Rodrigues and Lopes, offering to buy back her property in Portugal for double her purchase price. Elke has enjoyed the idea of owning land with Riviera potential and was intrigued enough with the Algarve to buy several books illustrated with dramatic black and white photographs of sunny beaches, dazzling white villages, hillside farms with donkeys and almond blossoms, and rural people in traditional dress. Each time Walter and I visited her, we pored over the survey of her property and the books and photographs. We found the region starkly beautiful, but my mother wears pearls and high heels every day and likes Paris, London, or New York for vacations. When I was eighteen, she decreed that it was time I called her "Elke," explaining her reasons with, "You're grown up now and I'm your friend, not just your mother." My own sense was that having a grown daughter refer to her as "Mom" didn't suit her image of herself.

With her love of elegance, Elke never had any intention of traveling to a rustic patch of ground far from what she considered the basic amenities of civilization--art galleries, theaters, opera, fine shops and restaurants, and a good hairdresser. Walter and I, however, became ever more charmed by the lure of such a distant exotic place. At first we only pictured vacation afternoons on the terrace of a cool white villa under a distant blue sky, and saw ourselves strolling on beaches or through narrow sun-drenched village streets. By the start of the 1980s, however, Walter was facing early retirement from New York's State's Division of Alcohol Abuse and planned to open a private practice in psychology. I was executive assistant to the president in a college administration where rivalry often trumped cooperation. We were both in our fifties, making good money and not yet ready to retire, but each spring when we visited my mother and spoke of Portugal, we left behind bureaucracy and office politics and began to dream of life changes. Something about that undeveloped plot of land in a faraway place suggested that in a few years we could break out of our embedded lives and embark on something new.

"We ought to go see your land," we urged Elke each year but she wasn't interested and we had to content ourselves with the maps and picture books.

Now Elke hands me the letter, saying, "It's time for me to sell, don't you think?"

I read it and, not wanting to lose my vision of a foreign shore I say, "I think it's sad to sell before you've even seen it," and pass the letter on to Walter. He is a comfortably large man with keen blue eyes under bushy eyebrows, buoyant white hair and a short well-trimmed beard. As a psychologist, he usually listens more than he speaks, but I've noticed that when he does speak, people tend to pay attention.

He is curious. "Did you write asking them to quote you a price?"

"No, we've had no correspondence for years," Elke says.

Walter and I look at each other with the same thought that he says aloud. "If they're offering you twice as much, it must be worth a lot more." He suggests alternatives. "Maybe you can get a better price from someone else, or maybe you won't want to sell right away if land values keep rising."

Elke looks doubtful but Walter continues. "If you go there, you might even decide to build a house on it. Then you might sell for a whole lot more."

That's too much for her. "I won't build anything, not at my age."

"Let's at least go see it," I urge once more. "We've been talking about it for years and now seems a perfect time. Why not just see it before you sell? The three of us could meet there this summer for vacation. That wouldn't commit you to anything. You can still sell afterwards if you want to."

For our next few days in Zurich we talk back and forth about a visit to Portugal. Elke discusses the idea with her friends at an evening gathering. She expected laughter at our proposal, but one friend has actually heard of the Vale do Lobo resort and mentions a five-star hotel there. Reassured that she won't have to camp out in a patch of sand, Elke capitulates, but refuses to travel in the heat of summer. Before Walter and I leave Zurich, the three of us agree to meet in Vale do Lobo in early September to stay for ten days at the opulent Hotel Dona Filipa.

Our first sight of Portugal is at dawn as our plane circles over

Lisbon. We see red-tiled roofs, old buildings, winding streets, everything bathed in gray-gold first light of day, and a beautiful wide river, the Tagus, shimmering and dotted with boats. Walter and I hold hands, feeling that we are soaring through a fairy tale. Then comes the airport and the thump of reality. Air inside the worn terminal is hot and stale, and every square foot of floor space is crowded with African workers. They lean against walls or sit in groups among a jumble of suitcases, cartons tied with string, and cloth bundles, weary and numb as though they no longer expect to reach any destination, or even stir from the airport. We and our fellow transatlantic passengers are dazed from our long flight. Doggedly we haul our baggage and stumble over people to reach the outside. I wonder if this is an unusual day at the airport or if that mass of silent exhausted black workers is always there.

Seen from our rented car, Lisbon close up is disappointing, its streets and buildings crumbling and gray. Then we reach the great modern bridge across the Tagus River and the wide view opens up, blue, white, silver and sun-gold. On the other side of the river stands an enormous stone statue of Christ with arms outstretched to bless the harbor, a replica of the one in Rio de Janeiro. We pass it, heading south to the Algarve on the main two-lane road which is as disheveled and lively as a string of backyards. All along we see roadside stands with produce of oranges, grapes and melons shielded from the sun by makeshift roofs of dry reeds. Every clearing holds vans, tents, and campers surrounded by family groups of stocky dark-haired people wearing clothes in colors bright as the fruits they sell. At intervals we pass a cluster of small stucco houses and one or two cafés crowded with male customers.

Two hours out of Lisbon, we start seeing eucalyptus trees and orchards of cork oaks with bark peeled half way up so that they seem to be wearing orange stockings. Though the scenery is lush in late summer, driving through it is harrowing. Small European cars whiz by us at reckless speeds (usually passing on hills and blind curves), and then crawl with horns honking and lights flashing behind mule-drawn carts or open trucks heavy with logs or produce. Since everything shares the same road, traffic either creeps by inches or shoots ahead in frenzied bursts of speed.

Halfway along to the Algarve, we pass through Alcaçer do Sal, an old city of white and pastel houses with terra cotta tiled roofs and a church tower topped by storks' nests. The houses have tiny windows and narrow doorways; life is hidden behind walls. We continue on our way, past flocks of grazing sheep as we drive between vast fields that rise in easy slopes to a distant horizon. Then the road winds through the Monchique Mountains and leads us at last down to the Algarve's flat coastal landscape at the edge of the wide Atlantic. We drive along the coastal highway, past villages that are not the stark black and white of photographs we have so often looked at. Colors blaze all around us. The ocean is a silver dazzle. Houses have burnt orange tile roofs, many draped with cascades of red or fuchsia bougainvillea. Walls are so white in the sun they make our eyes squint. Walter and I are tired from our long journey but happy to have reached this place which has beckoned us for years.

Two days after our rendezvous with Elke at the Hotel Dona Filipa, the three of us are scrambling through underbrush in search of boundary markers. With the help of local maps and surveys, we believe we have located Elke's property on the Estrada Vale do Lobo, the road leading from the east-west coastal highway down to the ocean. Now we need to make sure. The local boundary markers are two-foot-high rectangular cement posts with painted initials of the owners. We walk along the road and after twenty minutes we find the first marker daubed with E. G. for Elke Gilbert. Shouts of triumph. Then we head inland through a flat sandy area covered by dried summer stubble and a few stunted trees. Elke, though dressed in city regalia as always, gets into the spirit and trudges along with us. We climb a hillside and reach a wooded area shaded by tall jack pines. At the top, we find the second marker. More cheers. We head across the wooded ridge of the hill and in a short while we've got the third one. Now we know we have the outlines of the property and stop to take photographs of Elke, her foot in a dainty white leather pump, planted on the marker like a hunter with her trophy. We head back down the hill toward the road, pausing for more photographs of each of us biting into fresh purple figs from a lichen-coated fig tree, and of Walter in the shade of a carob tree, smiling beneath an unaccustomed Panama hat over his thick white hair. I also take several views of the landscape. Though Elke's deed describes it as "poor sandy soil unfit for farming," its very unfamiliarity entices us. Then we walk further, poking cheerfully at shrubbery lining the edge of the road. It's been easy so far and we expect no problem discovering the rectangular plot's fourth corner. But our happy mood fades when we don't find the final marker and Elke grows ever more agitated

"They've stolen it," she declares while picking her way around some dried thistles with prickly points.

"Why would anyone want to steal just one boundary marker, Mom," I protest. "It's just a slab of cement. What good would it do them?"

"They've stolen it so I can't claim my property." Blonde head down, pearl necklace dangling, she keeps inching forward, poking with a stick at the tangle of dried thatch and thistles beneath the line of umbrella pines. She is outraged by the perceived attack on her ownership as well as by the destruction of her nylons.

An eighty-three-year-old woman in an agitated state on a hot day sets up a desire to murmur soothing phrases, provide comforting pats, iced tea, cold compresses or whatever else might restore calm. Walter's and my own attempts at soothing phrases, however, merely goad Elke toward frenzy. We watch helplessly as she beats on through the underbrush and mutters, "They're crooks and they've stolen it."

She searches on, as if convinced that the land itself will leak away through the unmarked corner. Then she sees us standing to one side. "Why aren't you looking?" she snaps, "We need that marker."

"Because we're way beyond the edge of the map. It's not going to be here." I try to keep irritation out of my voice.

"Well, maybe they've moved it somewhere else so I won't find it." She keeps going, stick in one hand, patent leather handbag in the other. When her mutterings grow faint, we can tell she is nearly exhausted.

"Come on, Elke, let's go back to the car. We can look again tomorrow," Walter coaxes.

"No. Tomorrow, we drive to Faro and talk to Rodrigues and Lopes and tell them the marker is gone," she insists, and we agree meekly to everything, cajoling her back into the car so that we can return to the hotel.

We are all tired, hot and thirsty when we enter the cool hotel, and quickly order iced drinks. Elke sinks onto a sofa, clearly relieved to be returned to the hotel's grand lobby with its white marble floors and Chinese Red lacquered wall panels. Islands of oriental carpets bear Peacock Blue upholstered furniture.

The Dona Filipa is an old-world five-star beauty with a Moorish look. Towering white walls with balconies and blue awnings overlook the Atlantic. Patrons may swim either in the hotel's own pool or walk a few paces to cabanas and blue chaises along the beach of fine golden sand and towering sandstone cliffs. Golfers are drawn to a twenty-seven hole course, with its sixth hole snaking around a notch in the cliffs. All this is part of Vale do Lobo, a resort complex of white villas adorned with bougainvillea and pink oleander. Multicolored lantana hedges, umbrella pines, and flowering trees bring precious shade from the dazzling summer sun. For tourists, a cluster of pseudo-thatched huts beside the beach contains cafés and shops that sell gifts, newspapers and sportswear. Long-term villa residents may buy provisions at a small expensive supermarket. And everywhere throughout Vale do Lobo, there is green green grass. The grass (as well as all the flowers, hedges and trees} is sustained by an intricate underground irrigation network without which none of the lush plantings would survive.

One kilometer inland from the edge of this cultivated greenery, Elke's property typifies the Algarve's real landscape, dry and scrubby like southern California before irrigation. The Mediterranean climate of long dry summers and short winter rainy seasons favors trees that can endure extreme contrasts and bear the region's main crops of figs, almonds and olives. The rainy winter months bring delicate flowers and beautiful almond blossoms in February. In spring the fields grow a thick tumult of daisies and poppies. But by June everything not watered by human effort dries into prickles and thatch.

Prickles, thatch and a few dusty trees mark Elke's land. Walter and I who have lured her to Portugal are now eager to venture beyond artful tourist luxury to explore the natural, to us exotic, countryside. But she has quickly judged the entire region rough and primitive and clings to Vale do Lobo as an oasis of civilization.

The next day, after circling for an hour through a maze of narrow one-way streets in the nearby city of Faro, we find the "offices" of Rodrigues and Lopes, Estate Agents. Our search might have been shorter if we had not expected some type of office building. Instead we at last determine that the address on Elke's correspondence is in a row of storefronts on a street facing Faro's harbor. Searching for house numbers in the late morning sun's brilliance, we pick our way past vendors' carts loaded with leather goods, Indian jewelry, and pirated audio tapes till we locate the right dust-streaked window and part a beaded curtain to enter the store. The dim interior holds a cluster of file cabinets, several ancient metal desks covered with high stacks of papers, and three shirt-sleeved men who respond with expressionless grunts to our greetings of "*Bom Dia*" (good morning) which, except for "*Obrigado*" (thank you), pretty well drains our pool of Portuguese phrases.

Lapsing into English (as they knew we would), Elke shows copies of her letters to and from the firm, introduces herself as a landowner, and asks to see either Senhor Rodrigues or Senhor Lopes to discuss her property, with particular reference to one missing cement boundary marker.

One of the trio before us, whose lower shirt buttons gape across his ample middle, introduces himself as Senhor Lopes and identifies a one-armed man with a black eyepatch, as Senhor Rodrigues. We don't catch the third man's name but observe Portuguese custom and shake hands all around murmuring our various versions of "how do you do."

Senhor Lopes returns to his earlier post, lounging against a file cabinet. "You have come to sell the land, Madam," he states, "and you have make so long voyage from *Suissa* (Switzerland)? Is not necessary. We would arrange through the post as we did do with your purchase. Save much trouble for you." He concludes with a sigh, implying that her trouble is nothing compared to his.

Senhor Lopes clearly assumes the resale is a done deal but Elke doesn't reveal her intentions. "I have not decided if I want to sell," she states. "I came here because I want to see the land for myself with my family." She points toward Walter and me and then glares at Senhor Lopes. "And now I can't even be sure where it is because someone has taken one of the markers."

Senhor Lopes' done deal might actually have succeeded but his condescending tone and the matter of the missing marker have put Elke on guard, and he doesn't reckon with Walter's and my vision of owning land in Portugal. We three stand stolidly in the crammed storefront. The heat, the dusty palm trees, the beaded curtain, the strips of fly paper hanging from the ceiling, the black eyepatch and the dour sweating men bring to mind old foreign intrigue movies starring Sidney Greenstreet and Peter Lorre.

"What you want with the land if you don't sell?" Senhor Lopes asks, looking at my mother's silk dress and high heels. "You don't want live here in Portugal."

I chime in. "She might want to build a villa, for vacations."

He gives a cinematic snort worthy of Sidney Greenstreet. All three men shake their heads. "Is difficult," they murmur in unison. Senhor Lopes continues, "You come here from another country. Know nothing, *nada,* about construction here. *Muito difficil...*" Elke seems about to agree but Walter, former school board president, is not intimidated. "We have built many buildings in the United States," he says. "We can learn to do it here."

"Ah, Estados *Unidos,*" they counter, "Is very different there. Is not the same here." There is a moment's silence. Then Senhor

Rodrigues joins the discussion.

"If you truly wish to build, we can help. We have fine villa plans." He rummages in a desk drawer and extracts several grayed photocopied sheets. Senhor Lopes takes them and presents them to my mother. "Three designs, very nice villas. You can choose."

We look at the smudged pictures without enthusiasm. "What about my marker?" Elke returns to her main interest. The men look baffled. "We know nothing about markers. When you build, we put in a new marker."

We seem to be at an impasse. Taking the photocopied villa plans, we promise to think about their proposal, shake hands once more, and drive back to our hotel for lunch beside the pool.

I leaf through the photocopies with disdain. "I certainly wouldn't build an ugly little house like those."

"I don't want to build *anything*." Elke states once more. "I still think I should simply sell."

"But you don't know what the land is really worth today," Walter cautions. "Let's at least try to find out that much."

The following day, with Elke's consent, he and I visit several storefront real estate offices in Almancil, the town nearest Elke's land. Photographs in their display windows show villas and condominiums rising like white trophies of wealth all along the Algarvian coast. More specifically, we learn that the five-mile road from the main highway to Vale do Lobo's beach is deemed a prime site for both commercial and residential development.

"Well, now we know why Rodriguez and Lopes want to buy back Elke's property," Walter says as we leave one agency. We still suspect their offered price is far too low and decide to investigate further. As we leave Almancil we spot a large sign announcing "*Roemer Construçoes, Lda.*" We turn into the driveway and stop in front of a sales office that is smaller than the sign.

Inside the one-room building we meet Joost Roemer, a tall dark-haired young man with a shy smile who turns out to be not Portuguese but Dutch, the son of the company's owner. We introduce ourselves and explain our errand. He seats us around a glass-topped table that bears photo albums of villas evidently built by *Roemer Construçoes* or, in the English version, Roemer Villa Construction. As we sip tiny cups of espresso coffee, Joost estimates that Elke's three acres are now worth not twice but six times what she paid eleven years ago. Walter and I are thrilled with this discovery which justifies our trip.

But Joost Roemer also informs us that the missing marker is the least of Elke's problems. Though she did indeed purchase the land in 1972, her deed is no longer valid. In 1974, Portugal had a revolution. The army, peacefully but adamantly refused to continue fighting to retain Angola and other colonies, thus ending the regime of longtime dictator Antonio Salazar. The populace supported the revolt, stuck flowers into soldiers' rifles, and declared the 25th of April the day of revolution. Portugal became a socialist democracy, more strictly socialist at first, then gradually more relaxedly democratic. As far as we outside the country noticed, nothing much happened after that, but some things did change. In its first zealous days, the new government seized records of all land purchases, confiscated some large estates owned by foreign corporations, and changed all numbers on records of deeds to smaller holdings. None of the former numbers remained valid, including the number on the deed Elke still holds.

At the end of this enlightening talk, Walter and I thank Joost Roemer for his help and he gives us his card as we leave. We are eager to impart our new knowledge to my mother and a little nervous about its potential effect on her.

"You didn't tell me that I need a new deed," Elke accuses Senhor Lopes when we return to his storefront in Faro the next day.

He remains calm, only the shirt buttons across his paunch are under stress. "Madam desires we build a villa, we will arrange for the new deed."

"No, I don't want you to build a villa. I want to sell the property."

"Then is simple. We pay, you return the deed, and all is complete."

"We believe we can get a better price," Walter states. "Quite a lot better."

"Then we have no more business." Senhor Rodrigues sinks back against his favorite file cabinet.

"Will you at least help us to get the deed corrected?" I ask.

Senhores Rodrigues and Lopes exchange pained glances, and protest that establishing clear title at this point is a matter of some difficulty. Much research is needed at Loulé, the county seat.

"Very difficult, taking much time. One must go to Loulé to find the land records, then look at many records to find the right one with the new number. Many hours, days, maybe even weeks." Senhores Rodrigues and Lopes have no extra time. They might agree to do it, certainly, but it is hard to say just when….

"We are very busy, have much work." Senhor Lopes waves in the direction of his two companions lounging amidst the clutter, and shrugs his fleshy shoulders to convey his helplessness. Perhaps Madame might better reconsider their offer, go back to Zurich, and not trouble herself further about a small plot of land of no use to her.

My mother is no fool. Even though she doesn't really want to keep the land, she can smell a scam when its odor is as strong as Senhor Lopes' eagerness to assist her by taking the property off her hands. We retreat to a sidewalk café beside the harbor where we first vilify Senhores Rodrigues and Lopes and then try to decide what to do.

"Maybe the estate agent we spoke to yesterday can help us find the deed," I suggest, hoping to persuade Elke. "He's a nice young man from a Dutch family. They build villas and also sell property. Maybe he would help."

"These people tried to cheat me on the price and didn't even tell me that the deed has to be changed. I won't trust them again," Elke says." I'm not going to deal with anyone here,"

I try to soften her stance. "Rodrigues and Lopes may be crooked but that doesn't mean you can't trust anybody in the whole Algarve."

Walter chimes in. "This is Portugal, after all," he reminds her.

"You might have to deal with someone who lives here, someone who knows the local rules and how things get done."

"I'll find someone in Switzerland who knows," Elke insists and though we return to the subject several times during our remaining days, she is determined not to speak to anyone else in Portugal about her deed.

As is her custom, Elke has her breakfasts in bed and spends the morning hours on her toilette. Meanwhile Walter and I spend time at the beach near the hotel or wander along the edge of the golf course near the cliffs. As we walk, Walter points longingly to a foursome in the distance. "I should have brought my clubs. Just look at those fairways! And all right next to the hotel!"

Everything is posh at the Dona Filipa, voices subdued, hotel guests dressed in designer sports ensembles and dining apparel. But when they go down to the beach, both men and women take off everything above the waist and keep on as little as possible below it. Whole families cluster together on chaises or blankets under sun umbrellas. I'm startled to see that among their men, children, picnic supplies and beach toys, the women are bare-breasted.

"I don't quite know where to look," I murmur to Walter.

"*I* know where to look," he says with relish, "but I'm not sure it's polite."

Further along the beach where women sun themselves at the base of the cliffs or stroll at the water's edge, the impact of their near nudity is diminished by boundless stretches of sand, ocean and sky. We learn the rules of etiquette. Discreet signs inform us that "topless" is OK at the beach but not at the hotel's pool or in the restaurants and, as Walter sensed, obvious staring is gauche. He quickly perfects his *un*-obvious staring and becomes an enthusiastic convert to topless bathing

"I think you should take off your top too," he urges.

"Oh, I don't know. I'm not sure I could do that."

"Why not? You'd do just fine in the bosom competition."

I say maybe someday but not just now. Though European women of all ages are clearly used to stripping down without a second thought. I need second, third and fourth thoughts and finally decide I'll just wait.

The Portuguese women seem to be waiting also. About a twenty-minute walk in either direction from the Vale do Lobo complex, we see beach life with few tourists. Portuguese young men play *futebol* (our soccer), families picnic, children race about, and girls with long dark hair sunbathe. We don't see a single topless woman, old or young, among these groupings. That reminds us that Portugal is still a Catholic country with traditional ways that probably disapprove of adults taking off their clothes in public.

Several times Walter and I drive back to Elke's property, getting familiar with its contours. Along the road's edge, a row of broad umbrella pines fronts a sunny brush-covered field dotted here and there with an indigenous tree—we count three almond, two fig, one carob. A scrub-covered hillside slopes upwards to a wooded area shaded by tall pines at the rear of the three-acre plot. We enjoy walking back and forth across the land and imagining the placement of a villa. Should it be near the front on the level ground, or should it be set back on the hillside?

On other mornings, nearby rutted dirt roads put our rental car to the test as we pass ancient stone aqueducts, rustic farmhouses and women carrying baskets of produce on their heads. Farther afield, small villages with cobbled streets are bordered by sparsely windowed walls of homes that turn their backs to public view. Whatever direction or road we follow, each morning offers new places we are eager to explore.

After our morning jaunts, we take time out for lunch with Elke beside the hotel pool and then we all retire to our rooms for rest during the hottest hours. I read paperbacks I have brought and Walter is happy with the *International Herald Tribune* which contains the daily crossword puzzles from the *New York Times*. In mid-afternoon the three of us gather again to sightsee. We drive through towns strung like white jewels along the coast: Quarteira with its fish and produce markets and colorful fishing boats on the shore, Albufeira built on hills that rise toward high cliffs, and Praia de Rocha graced by magnificent rock formations in the bay.

Elke is interested but not enthusiastic. She has come here to humor us but grows eager to return to her comfortable routine in Zurich. In contrast, Walter and I are ever more captivated. Why are we so drawn to this place? We have enjoyed vacations in Europe when we used our visits to Elke to branch out to other countries. But we felt no special pull until Elke invested in her piece of property here more than ten years ago. Since then we've become ever more intrigued with Portugal. Now that we are finally here, we've seen the friendly dark-haired people, the varied landscape, and the Atlantic nearby with miles of white beaches and warm ochre cliffs, everything suffused all day long by a dazzle of sun and at night by unexpectedly brilliant stars. This beauty has exceeded our imaginings.

But we also see new hotel and villa complexes, golf courses and gas stations. The region hums with a building boom that traditionalists view with regret but most native-born residents seem to welcome. Contrasts between old and new illustrate both gains and losses brought by our contemporary world. For centuries the region's economy subsisted on its fishing fleets and small inland farms. The magnificent beaches were not recognized as valuable assets until the twentieth century. By the time my mother first bought her land, farsighted speculators and developers were touting the entire area as a future Mecca for people seeking escape from wintry climates. Now those predictions are proving true and tourism is the major industry. The Algarve teems with energy, like an expanding frontier where pioneers can build a new future. Maybe that's why Walter and I, imbued with American frontier history, feel so welcome here.

For our dinners, Elke prefers the hotel dining room's hushed comfort. Since she has indulged our wish to roam each afternoon, we think it only fair to defer to her, though we do feel a bit frustrated at our luxurious remove from local life. But toward the close of our vacation, we do manage to coax Elke out to a nearby restaurant, a small lively place called "Mr. Freddy's." The owner and host is a tall handsome young Portuguese. We think at first that he himself is Mr. Freddy, but not so; his name is Oliver. Mr. Freddy is Fred Astaire, who was Oliver's boyhood idol. The restaurant is brimful of Astaire memorabilia—posters, autographed studio photographs, post cards, sketches, and of course, taped music and songs from movies. The mix is oddly charming, images of the super-sophisticated Astaire in top hat and tails dancing all around the homey, noisy Portuguese restaurant.

Elke is gracious, knowing that she has done us a favor, but has not adapted to our surroundings. When Oliver comes to take our order, she asks for lobster, the one shellfish that doesn't thrive in the warmer waters off the Algarvian coast.

Oliver is apologetic. "Madam, we do not have lobster this evening, but I can order it for you from Lisboa and get it in two days. You come back then and we will have lobster for you." Elke is gratified and gives him a regal smile but makes no promise to return.

We decide on *Cataplana*, the traditional dish of small clams and black mussels, sausage slices, pork and potatoes, stewed and served in a beautiful copper casserole with a hinged lid. When the lid is opened the aroma and the flavor are hearty and rich with garlic. *Vinho verde*, the young Portuguese white wine with a light fizz, washes it down nicely.

On the morning before our departure, Walter and I take our final walk along the beach between the blue Atlantic and the terra cotta cliffs. We walk on firm sand at the water's edge, enjoying the warm sun and the froth from the incoming tide on our toes, passing solitary strollers, sunbathers, young couples walking hand in hand, children building sand castles, the whole joyous beach panorama absorbed into a vast luminous silence.

I turn toward Walter as we pause to gaze out at the ocean. "This has been a pretty special vacation."

"That could be because we've thought about Portugal for so long."

"Maybe, but it would be nice to come back again, wouldn't

it?"

"Oh, we'll come back here." Walter says. "There's so much more I'd like to see." He looks past me toward the green slopes of the golf course. "And next time, I'll bring my clubs."

"Could you imagine having a place here to come back to every year? A villa of our own that we could build?"

He stays quiet for a few moments, then responds, "I bet we could do it. It would be a real adventure. The kids could come for their vacations, and I bet even Elke would like it once we added a few luxuries." He encircles me with his arm. "Let's hope we can persuade her not to sell right away, whoever she gets to work on the deed."

"I think I'll hold on to that nice young Dutch builder's card."

"Good idea," Walter agrees.

II
Mapping the Dream

Two years go by before Elke can find someone to clear the title to her property in Portugal. Then one Saturday her latest letter brings news. The lawyer friend who encouraged her original purchase has found a Mr. Gunnar Nielsen who emigrated from Denmark to the Algarve some years ago and now acts as a business agent for foreigners there. Elke writes that she has engaged Mr. Nielsen to get clear title and afterwards to sell the property.

Ever since our visit to the Algarve, Walter and I have liked the idea of someday building a vacation or retirement villa there. Elke's letter is a disappointment and I think about it all day. Next morning as Walter and I linger over our customary Sunday brunch, newspapers are spread across the kitchen table. I'm in my robe, he's wearing a plaid flannel nightshirt, and we don't look like serious entrepreneurs. As I refill our coffee mugs, I return to the subject of the letter. I've got to catch his attention before I lose him to the Sunday *Times* crossword.

"So Elke still wants to sell. Should we do anything?"

"Why don't we make her an offer?" He looks up at me. "Are you going to eat that other half of your English muffin?"

I pass the muffin onto his plate "You mean buy the land?"

He loads the muffin with raspberry jam. Before taking a bite he says. "No, I'm thinking we could propose a partnership. She provides the land, we provide the funds for building a vacation villa. We split the cost fifty-fifty." I ponder the idea as he dives into his puzzle.

In my next letter I ask Elke if she would consider a joint venture. I describe the increased profit we could share from improving the property and I also enlarge on the joys of future vacations together in the sunny Algarve.

Three weeks is normal turnaround time for our correspondence. I wait impatiently for her reply to arrive, but when it does, she makes no mention of our offer. Walter and I agree that it seems wrong to pressure her any more. If she wants to sell her property, she certainly has the right. But now that we've seen the Algarve, its spell has taken hold and we don't want to lose our dream entirely. We decide to start saving money toward buying our own piece of land there.

Things move slowly in Portugal. Another year passes. Elke is now eighty-six, and I have begun to telephone her every Sunday to make sure that she's all right. During one such call, Elke announces, "I've heard from Gunnar Nielsen. He has fixed my title. The number is corrected and the land is now definitely mine, title and everything."

"Mom, that's wonderful, how exciting," I start to burble.

Quickly she again cautions, "I don't want to build anything there."

I turn a bit stiff. "Well, congratulations. You must be relieved to have it cleared up after all this time." I restrain myself from any mention of vacations, villas, or building plans.

Elke says, "Can you imagine? Mr. Nielsen sent me a dozen roses for congratulations. That shows he knows the right way to behave. I was right to hire him."

"Yes, that's very nice." I find it hard to rise to her moment when all I can feel is the lost opportunity. Then I am stunned to hear her say, "How would you like the land as a birthday present?"

"Mom," I shriek into the phone, "You mean it?"

"If I sold it, you'd get the money anyway after I die," she says. "Now you can decide if you would rather have the land." I whoop with joy, thank her repeatedly, hang up the phone and whirl around the room. Walter watches me, solid and smiling, each of us thrilled that Elke's "paper investment" of fourteen years ago has come to earth and will soon be ours.

Now that we actually own a piece of Portugal, we start to think about it differently. It's one thing to fantasize about escape from humdrum dailyness, building a villa in a foreign place, and possibly retiring to a sunny climate; it's quite another thing to send the first letter, file the first form, risk the first dollars to arrive at an unknown outcome. Several times we turn to each other with the question, "do we really want to do this?" And it leads us to take stock of where we are and where we've come from.

Walter's boyhood was spent in New Jersey. Aside from his World War II stint in the Navy on a remote Pacific island, he rarely traveled; in fact, he never went to Europe until after we were married. Thanks to the GI Bill, he was the first of his family to go to college. There he found his calling as a psychologist. In graduate school, he rejected experimental research in favor of clinical work with patients. He married at age twenty-two, opened his practice, and had two children. The marriage later ended in divorce. When I first met him in 1964, he was chief psychologist at the mental health clinic in the county where we both lived.

His recovery from an alcohol problem led to his professional specialization in the treatment of alcoholism and substance abuse and in 1978 to his joining the staff of the newly formed New York State Division of Alcoholism at Albany. We married while he worked there. In 1981, he was called to Washington D.C. for a one year intergovernmental appointment. When he returned to his position with New York State, he found that the agency leadership had changed, and he felt as unwelcome as Rip van Winkle after his twenty-year snooze. Our first visit to Portugal in 1983 coincided with this low point when he had just decided to take early retirement from state service and open his own private practice. He did so and by this time two years later he has so many patients that I sometimes wonder if everyone north of Albany with a drinking problem shows up on our doorstep. Walter is devoted to his work, yet he often blue-skies about trying new things, some of which seem alarming or zany to me. He talks of learning to fly a plane, sailing to Florida in a small boat, exploring the outback in Australia. He seems to want some as yet unknown excitement in his life, and now there's the prospect of Portugal.

And I? How far have I come from that half-Jewish, half-Gentile child brought to America by parents fleeing from the Nazis? After the war, my parents returned to Europe because my father needed the German language to re-establish his career as a popular songwriter. I decided not to go with them because, at eighteen, I was greedy for independence and wary of becoming an immigrant all over again. But now so many years later when I think of Portugal, it doesn't feel like returning to the Europe of my early childhood; it feels like going forward into something new. My past personal history neither spooks nor entices me; the spur at my heel is the feeling of being stymied in the present. I feel I've reached a dead-end in my career.

I recently resigned from my administrative post at the nearby college to look for a new position with a better future. Against advice from wiser heads, I did so before I had that shiny new position. Therefore, I'm now slogging through the academic job search with applications, curriculum vitae, interviews, near-successes, near-misses. Walter, always an optimist, insists that something will turn up. I'm no longer sure. I'm an experienced administrator with good references, but I'm over fifty in a market pitched toward the hotshot young. Not getting a job when all about me seem secure in theirs feels like failure. Dutifully I study the want ads in each *Chronicle of Higher Education* marking those slots I might fit into. The odd thing is that I don't really want any of the jobs I apply for. None make me quiver but, after all, one must work and we need the income. Meanwhile, I'm piecing together a series of consultancies for various cultural agencies in Albany and New York. Like an academic gun-for-hire, I do research, write, and plan programs for causes and organizations that aren't mine. It's a pretty good living but I feel I've taken a wrong turn somewhere.

I've taken some wrong turns in the past. Two failed marriages were definitely wrong turns, but one of them left me with the great blessing of three beautiful daughters. Dropping out of college was another misstep, but in my thirties, with financial help from my parents, I returned and went on to graduate school. I earned a PhD in English and American Literature and afterwards landed an exciting job as director of a statewide humanities program. That helped me to support my daughters who became bright, responsible and loving adults. Then ten years ago I was lucky enough to find Walter. After our marriage I quit the job I loved to join him in upstate New York. Definitely a right turn personally but, as it has turned out, not a good career move.

Our marriage is stable, we have good friends, and we share a blended family of five grown children who accept each other reasonably well. We live in a roomy Victorian house within walking distance of the lovely downtown that attracts not only cigar-smoking summertime racetrack gamblers, but also a good number of year-round artists, writers and musicians. Except for five months of icy winter, Saratoga Springs comes close to small town heaven for many people. But after six years here, both Walter and I are a bit restless. The plot of land in Portugal has made us perk up like a hint of spice, a gleam on the horizon, something yet to be attained. I keep wondering is there a better path? Could we each uncover whatever feels submerged or unrealized? Could I still become the writer I hoped to be when I was young?

The biggest barrier to our going ahead with our building project in Portugal turns out to be our reluctance to be so far away from our children for extended periods of time. We know we would miss them keenly despite the fact that they are all grown up with their own lives. Walter's daughter Kathy and his son Terry are in their thirties, married with children. My three daughters are in their twenties. Julia is single, and works for a travel agency. Helen is also single, and works in a sports bar. My youngest daughter Sheila is recently married, and works at a hotel restaurant. None of the five live in our town, but all are within various driving distances and we exchange visits whenever we can. They are an essential part of our interior lives, we love them, are happy at their successes and worry about them when they stumble or are distressed. As parents of adult children who cling fiercely to their independence, we tread carefully, wanting not to interfere but help if we can, and most of all to be a part of their lives. When we talk about Portugal, we're surprised and touched to find that none of them are pleased that we might eventually decide to spend our retirement so far away. Their reluctance almost makes us scuttle our emerging plans but after many late-night hesitations, Walter and I decide to go ahead. "We'll have an ideal vacation place for the whole family," we tell ourselves. "And even if we do decide later on to retire there, we'd come back here regularly. We'd probably see them almost as often as we do now."

We don't know what we will find in Portugal, but I feel exhilarated when I think of it and so does Walter. "It's a good investment," he says soberly; but then his blue eyes sparkle, "and we could have fun." (I overlook the fact that he says the same thing whenever we pass a nearly collapsed country barn that might be restored, even though he has never even hung a shelf.) Whatever our individual qualms, we decide to go ahead on a practical basis of improving the investment, if this venture can in any way be considered practical. We will not expect too much, we tell ourselves. "One day at a time, one step at a time," as Walter says. This way, we will have the "fun" of turning Elke's patch of "dry soil unfit for farming" into a place with a nice villa where our family might gather for sunny interludes. And who knows where this adventure might lead?

In September, Walter and I return to Portugal. This time, because we may own a home in this country someday, we spend our first two days getting acquainted with Lisbon. We circle through the city by taxis to see landmarks recommended by guidebooks. We visit the restored medieval *Castelo de São Jorge* (the Castle of Saint George) at the crest of one of the city's seven hills, the Tower of Belém on the bank of the Tagus River, the large central city square of the *Praça dos Restauradores* (Plaza of the Restorers), and the famed Gulbenkian Museum established by Armenian oil tycoon Calouste Gulbenkian who lived in Lisbon from 1942 until his death in 1955.

Though Lisbon looks like an ancient and crumbling city, we learn that it is much younger than Zurich. Hardly any of the buildings predate the earthquake that devastated the city in 1753. The Marquês de Pombal, who directed the city's rebuilding, designed the new city plan with a central hub, now a large traffic circle. A huge statue of the Marquês with a lion at his side dominates the circle from which *avenidas* (wide boulevards) radiate like huge spokes of a wheel.

In between these *avenidas* is the older cityscape, mazes of narrow cobblestone streets nestled among the city's steep hills. Some streets are so narrow that people sitting on their front stoops must raise their feet out of the way when our taxi rattles past. Other streets are so steep that they have steps for pedestrians next to tracks for donkeys, wagons and, in this century, automobiles. Our taxi drivers chuckle at my typical tourist gasps as we plunge downwards at high speeds beneath lines of hanging laundry, past windows filled with flowers and bird cages, past young mothers pushing baby carriages, old women carrying net bags of groceries, and men clustered in café doorways-- all residents who, at the last possible moment, step calmly out of the way of imminent death.

At sunset we dine on the roof terrace of the Tivoli Hotel where we are staying. The setting sun casts a violet glow that turns worn city buildings a soft yellow. As twilight deepens we can see the lighted *Castelo do São Jorge* on a neighboring hill and, farther off at the city's rim, the shimmering bay of the Tagus.

After city sightseeing we again rent a car and head for the Algarve. This time, along with other vehicles, we are shunted onto a new north-south highway that can't yet be found on any map. Traffic moves very fast along its three or sometimes four lanes and there are no distractions, no roadside stands or camping families; the coziness of the old road we traveled three years ago is gone. Now we see only wide empty vistas under a huge sky. The change marks the difference of generations. The old road developed over a long time and its compatibility with village life made it gradually unsuited for modern commercial and tourist travel. The smooth new highway impresses us, but we're glad to have first traveled the old road that let us glimpse an earlier Portugal.

Walter and I have our first meeting with Gunnar Nielsen, who is now working on the transfer of Elke's title to me. We meet in his office on the *Estrada Nacional* in Almancil, the town nearest our property. Like many offices in Portugal it is a storefront, but unlike some, this is clean and modern. An attractive blonde young woman greets us as we enter and after a short wait, Mr. Nielsen, a bulky man of medium height with thinning pale hair and a florid complexion, emerges from behind a partition. As he approaches, I notice he has a slight limp.

"Mr. and Mrs. Finnegan, how do you do." he says, his voice jovial and loud enough to reach into far corners of the interior. We all shake hands and he leads us around the partition into his executive space, next to large display windows facing the street. The glass has a mirrored coating; passersby on the narrow cobbled sidewalk can see their own reflections but not anything inside; Mr. Nielsen can see everything outside and in.

He ushers us to easy chairs and takes his place behind a baronial desk. In back of him hangs a large portrait of Chiang Kai-shek, the Chinese Generalissimo from another era. On the desk itself is a mounted giant brass bullet. Near us, two coiled snakes sleep in an aquarium. I decide I'm not fond of Mr. Nielsen's taste in interior design.

We accept his offer of coffee, and the young woman brings two tiny cups of *espresso*.

"This is my daughter, Ingrid, she works here with me, as does my wife, who isn't here today." Mr. Nielsen points toward the back windowless area where we can see several metal desks and filing cabinets. We shake hands with Ingrid who smiles and then stands by, ready to assist. It's time for business. Mr. Nielsen speaks competent English in loud German-sounding tones.

"Now, to bring you up to the moment. The title is cleared, as you know from your mother, Madame Gilbert, a fine lady. But I will need more information to complete the transfer to you. This will be to Mrs. Finnegan only or to both of you?"

"Just to me, at this point. That's what my mother wants." Walter sends me a reassuring nod. We have discussed Elke's decision. She has been especially fond of Walter since he complimented her on her dimpled knees years ago but, because my father left her in 1955 and I have been married before, she places no bets that any marriage will last. To Elke, men may come and men may go, but inheritance is a matter of blood ties. Between us, Walter and I have agreed that the land and anything we may build on it will be our joint investment.

"Ah, yes, to you only. A fine lady, Madame Gilbert," Mr. Nielsen says again. Then with a volley of chuckles, he explains, "It doesn't really matter you know, everything here in Portugal is community property anyhow." He makes notes on a pad in a leather binder. "And what do you plan to do with the property? Your good mother indicated you may wish to sell."

"No we don't," I look at Walter again, hoping he will join in.

"At least not now," Walter says and leans forward to place his empty coffee cup at the edge of the desk. "We are thinking of building a villa for vacations, and possibly for our retirement later. And we're here to find out what we need to do to start the process. Can you help us with that?"

"No problem," Mr. Nielsen exudes confidence. "That's what I'm here for."

As we exchange documents and discuss steps required for residency, his "no problem," crops up whether there might be a problem or not. He clearly has no interest in long explanations. I suspect that he may at times have to go back to them whenever his first quick assumptions don't work. But for the present, he has the information he needs, and when we have finished with business details, I ask how he came to the Algarve.

"I came here from Denmark for a month ten years ago. My wife was ill and needed a warm climate. Here I saw many people from England, Germany, Holland, coming to buy property, but they didn't know how to get things done. I made it my business to learn the regulations. The official regulations, you know? The Portuguese government has regulations, this county has other ones, every city and village…and so on."

He crinkles his small pale eyes. "And then of course there are ways and people one has to know to get around the official regulations. The real ways to get anything done," he leans back and laughs and Walter joins in, men of the world sharing their expertise.

My guess is that Mr. Nielsen operates in a dimly lit borderland between the official rules and the other paths. Probably, if clients seem squeamish, he'll stay within the law. I suspect his first impulse is to bend it, hard to pinpoint why. Perhaps the large brass bullet on the desk, perhaps the snake aquarium behind us. Perhaps the air of many shady deals behind the smooth facade. But to give him his due, he has been effective at clearing Elke's title and is smoothly genial to deal with. His price seems high but without his guidance we would be lost in a maze of badly translated government regulations. We negotiate terms and when our meeting concludes, again shake hands.

As we leave, Walter admires the silver Cadillac, big as a boat, parked in front of the mirrored windows where Mr. Nielsen can watch it.

"The only Cadillac in Portugal," he claims with pride and then chuckles, "I don't really care, you know, but the clients know me by it. By now, zey expect it."

I ask if it isn't difficult to drive such a big car through the narrow Portuguese streets always crowded with people. "Zey get out of my vay," he booms, with evident relish at the thought.

Walter and I next go to Roemer Construction, the Dutch builders we visited on our earlier trip. This time, when we announce our building plans, our meetings are moved from the small roadside sales office to a large hilltop villa owned by the firm's founder, Jan Roemer. We deal with the eldest son, Joost Roemer, whom we met three years ago. Joost is a tall good-looking young man in his late twenties who moves with adolescent awkwardness and smiles as though eager to please. He seats us and picks up a clipboard, speaking English in a soft Dutch accent that reminds me pleasantly of my first boyfriend when I was a teen-ager. I fleetingly wonder if that is why I was drawn to this particular builder.

For some reason, Walter thinks I can deal better than he with the intricacies of foreign languages, even though I speak only German and a smattering of French and have tried to explain that this doesn't translate into understanding Portuguese. Furthermore, in this case we are speaking English, but when Joost turns to him, Walter as usual signals that I am the one to lead. I begin to outline our wishes for a villa with an open living-dining plan, two bedrooms and a third separate study for Walter.

Joost makes some notes on a lined pad, then looks up at us. "We could certainly design a nice villa like that for you."

Then, aware that we've not yet experienced the Algarve's winter climate, I ask, "What about central heating? Will we need that?"

"No, I don't think so. Central heating is very expensive, and our winter here lasts only six weeks. There's quite a lot of rain but it doesn't get very cold." Joost's pleasant accented voice is smooth and confident. "You will be fine with a fireplace, and maybe one or two portable gas heaters."

Walter is now ready to join in. "How cold does it get here?"

"Oh, never below five degrees. I think that would be about forty degrees Fahrenheit." Joost gives us a reassuring smile.

Accustomed as we are twenty below zero ice attacks in Saratoga, forty degrees in winter seems downright balmy to us.

We discuss building plans a bit longer and agree to spend the next day with Joost, showing him our property and seeing some villas the firm has built.

The following afternoon as Joost drives us through the countryside Walter and I look at Roemer villas with interest. All bear the whitewashed stucco walls ordained by Algarvian building codes. They have red tiled roofs with several tall chimneys, and most have verandahs with decorative Moorish arches for shade. With few exceptions, they are still bare of landscaping; an occasional garden is a welcome sight. At the end of the day, we agree that Roemer Construction will send us preliminary designs.

Back at the hotel from our day's jaunt, Walter and I begin to picture ourselves coming to live in Portugal after we retire. The prospect is exhilarating but also a bit scary. Immersion in a foreign culture seems attractive; the idea of an inactive life does not.

Maybe we should just stay with the idea of a place for vacations," I propose. "We're not ready to retire yet."

"Even then, I won't be ready just to sit around, or even play golf every day. Though there sure are enough great golf courses here."

"I think you'll always want to see patients. I wonder how you could do that here? "

"Honey, there are alcoholics who need help everywhere. Maybe I wouldn't have a full-time practice but I could work three days a week and play golf the other days," he takes a practice swing with an imaginary club.

"You're really not worried? "

"I'm not a worrier, Honey, you know that. I see this as an adventure. We could have fun here. Let's see how Nielsen does with transferring the title. After that, we've still got to figure out how we'll pay for building the villa. We can decide later if we want it just for vacations or for retirement. Elke might come for visits, and so would our kids. And if it doesn't work out, we can always sell it later on."

We keep on talking and speculating in the next days as we visit what will be our property, and become more familiar with the region. Our excitement at the thought of owning a home here keeps rising. Walter seems to have no fears, but I start to wonder, what would I do with my time if we came to live here after the villa is all built?

One Sunday afternoon he and I sit on a bench at the top edge of the Vale do Lobo cliffs and look out over the ocean, quietly absorbed in our own thoughts.

Then I happen to say, "You know, it's funny, everywhere else we've been, like in Zurich or London, I could always find a store that carried those orange paperback Penguin books, but here there's nothing like that. Only the kiosks with junky beach books."

"At least they have my *Tribune*."

"Yes, but I do wish I had something to read in the evenings. I've finished all the *New Yorkers* I brought from home." Without conscious design, I add, "This would be a good area for an English-language bookshop." Walter agrees idly and we say no more about it at the time. But in the next days the idea keeps buzzing. The area needs a bookshop; could I be the one to start it?

It seems crazy at first; I've never sold anything. But then I think after all why not? I could learn; I'm pretty resourceful and I've started and managed programs. This past year, my job search hasn't seemed seem to be getting anywhere. Walter and I have already agreed that we'd like to get away from Saratoga during the long icy winters and I do love being in Portugal. Maybe, I think, retirement could start a little earlier than we've planned so far. I begin to picture myself working with books, talking about books with readers and writers in my own place, me as owner and boss, no office politics. It starts to seem very appealing.

One evening, we revisit Mr. Freddy's restaurant. I've brought some photograph post-cards of Fred Astaire to give to Oliver, the owner, and as we finish our meal of shrimp and rice, he shows his appreciation by bringing us pony glasses of Portuguese plum brandy. Walter doesn't drink alcohol, but it would be rude to refuse. We settle back and as I sip the sweet brandy that smells like plums, I share my recent thoughts.

"I've been thinking more about the idea of a bookshop here."

"Oh yes?"

"What if we were to start one?"

Walter considers the prospect, "Well, we've got a good location, right on the road to the beach."

"It would give me something to do if we do retire here. You'll always have your work, but I've been wondering what I would do. I think I'd actually like running a bookshop."

"And you'd be good at it." With Oliver across the room and my glass is nearly empty, Walter smoothly exchanges it for his own full one. His blue eyes gleam as he keeps thinking. "A bookshop could be fun. We're building a villa anyway; no reason why we couldn't build a shop as well."

I start on my second brandy and try to temper my excitement. "The only thing is, neither of us has ever done anything like that."

"No, but that doesn't mean we couldn't learn." Then he adds a favorite ploy he uses on his patients, his children and me to counter fears of disaster. "What's the worst thing that could happen?"

"The shop could fail and we could be left with no money and a lot of books."

He laughs, "And then?"

"I guess we'd still have the land, and the villa."

"And don't forget, I have my pension from the state and as long as I keep a practice going we'll always have an income. You're good at organization and if this is something you'd like, I say go for it."

I find myself smiling. "Would you help?"

"Sure. It would be mainly your thing, but sure, I'll help."

We continue talking and planning, outlining ideas with rising enthusiasm. As I finish my second brandy in a plummy haze, Walter raises his water glass and offers a traditional Irish toast. "Shlanta morre," he says, "to Marianne's bookshop."

The next morning we return to Joost Roemer. This time we ask him to set the villa further back on the property and to place a second smaller building near the road, with large front windows appropriate for a shop.

III
Get Ready, Get Set...

We return to Saratoga, glad to have laid the groundwork for our Algarve venture. Now we must also prepare here for our eventual stay there. The first step, according to Gunnar Nielsen, is to apply for residency in Portugal. Walter and I make the three-hour train trip into New York City to file our formal applications. Near Rockefeller Center on Fifth Avenue, high up in a splendid 1930s skyscraper, we find the Portuguese Consulate, an office crammed with bureaucratic clutter. A dark-haired harried-looking woman steps forward, introduces herself as Maria Alves, and asks the purpose of our visit. We tell her we want to live in Portugal and she asks where we live now.

"Saratoga Springs."

Her eyes widen. "Such a beautiful place," she breathes and pauses for a moment before asking her next question. "Why do you want to live in Portugal?"

I am eloquent about that country's sunny climate, lovely scenery, warmth and friendliness of the people we've met during our vacations, our plans to build a villa on property we own in the Algarve, our wish to retire there to enjoy a pleasant later life...

"In Portugal?" She interrupts, wanting to make sure she has heard correctly. We nod. "In *Portugal?*" she repeats, her tone incredulous.

It occurs to me that as a woman she probably received low wages in Portugal with small hope of advancement. She must have greatly bettered her life by coming to New York and representing her own country at a comfortable distance. Our plans to leave our Saratoga home to her might appear like walking out of Elysium, and I try to explain.

"Saratoga is beautiful but we have very long winters. There's a lot of snow and the ice doesn't melt for months. The winters are hard." Maria Alves remains doubtful. She looks first at Walter, sturdy, white-haired, his blue eyes holding her gaze. Then she studies me, a trim middle-aged woman with brown eyes and brown hair, who speaks rationally. Both of us are apparently sane. Mrs. Alves pulls herself together and, mindful of her official duties, leads us through a list of official requirements for the residency process. We listen and I take notes. For the most part, the Portuguese government wants to know that we will have money enough to live on *there* and that we have been law-abiding citizens *here*. We leave the Consulate with a briefcase full of forms and instructions to satisfy these two avenues of inquiry. Maria Alves has told us that the approval will take about four months.

Completing our residency applications involves many letters back and forth, and even more documents—birth certificates, bank statements, police clearances, tax returns, business and personal character references, a copy of the deed to the Algarve property, multiple copies of passport photos and various additional supportive documents—many items needing to be sent again after the original mailings have disappeared into agency recesses. The reversals and repetitions call for dogged determination along with resolve not to let the process itself overwhelm us. Walter's clinical practice continues expanding and he now not only sees patients but also supervises two associates and an office manager. Since my consulting work is part-time, it falls to me to move Portugal-related matters along, pushing a little here, tugging there, making phone calls, filling out forms, writing letters, keeping in mind our eventual goal while staying involved with our accustomed lives here.

With the bookshop now a definite part of our planning, I decide that I'd better educate myself. I know nothing about being a bookshop owner. I've raised three daughters and earned a PhD. I've run a statewide program and managed annual budgets, but I have never owned a business, sold things, or worried about making a profit. Time for a crash course in entrepreneurship.

I begin by interviewing bookshop owners in Albany, Schenectady and Saratoga. They are kind and schedule time for me, but my academic credentials and love of literature seem seriously irrelevant, and my administrative experience brings pained smiles. "Do you like detail work?" asks one owner. "Do you want to work long hours for subsistence wages?" asks another. I'm not sure of my answers to either question. They show me around their stores with evident pride and I wonder, will I be able to do something similar? The only way to find out is to forge ahead. I follow the owners' advice and join the American Booksellers Association (ABA) and study its magazines and "how to" books where I learn about store layout, opening inventories, midlists, back lists and sales projections.

I also enroll in a community college for an evening course on small business management, sharing the commute with a young man who plans to open a combined pizza and video delivery business. I learn about L.L. Bean, and market research and I design an intricate business plan for my future shop.

To go beyond abstract charts of demographics and cash flow projections, I want a better understanding of actual business conditions and opportunities in the Algarve. For that, I return to New York City, this time to visit the Portuguese Chamber of Commerce at its office on 45th Street. There I meet with the director who listens politely from behind his desk as I outline our plans to build a retirement home in Portugal. When I get to the part about the English language bookshop, the director leans back in his leather chair and rotates it away from me so that he can study the mural map of Portugal on the side wall. As I finish, he rotates back towards me with somber attention.

"I do not think this will succeed. Is not a good idea."

"Why not? Lots of English speaking tourists visit the Algarve and those who don't play golf like to read on the beach. There are no bookshops for them, only a few paperbacks in the kiosks. I've been there and I couldn't find anything to read."

I do not persuade him. "Why would you open a book store for the English? They will not come." He speaks with authority. "The English don't read," he explains, "In the Algarve, what they do is get drunk and fall out of hotel windows."

He does not persuade me either. I can't credit his view of Shakespeare's countrymen. "Well, I'm going to try it."

He sighs at my foolishness and rises. He has given his advice; if I do not choose to take it, the onus is on me. To speed me on my way, he gathers up pamphlets and brochures and puts them into my hands. Then a promising thought strikes him. "Perhaps you can combine the book store with a café," he suggests. "If you serve some brandy, then they might come in and look at the books."

I thank him, stuff his pamphlets into my briefcase, and take my leave. I have read about negative reactions initially encountered by famous booksellers like Sylvia Beach who founded Shakespeare & Company in Paris and Frances Stelloff who started the Gotham Book Mart in New York. Contrary to his intentions, the Chamber of Commerce director has placed me among illustrious company and confirmed me in my enterprise.

In April I fly to Chicago for a five-day booksellers "school." In May I attend the ABA's national convention in Washington, D.C. accompanied by my eldest daughter, Julia. We have a good time garnering piles of free books and posters from publishers' booths. We hear lectures given by experts in store design, marketing, computerized inventory, anticipated best sellers, and reliable backlist stand-bys. A workshop about selling children's books turns out to be the only gathering where booksellers discuss the actual content of books. As we sit down, a young woman at the podium is introduced. She begins her speech:

"In an old house in Paris all covered with vines..."

To which the enraptured audience, as though intent on a litany, responds, "Lived twelve little girls in two straight lines."

Then speaker, panelists, audience, Julia and I, and possibly the custodians and window washers continue, smiling and chanting, "In two straight lines they broke their bread, and brushed their teeth... They went to bed at half past nine. The smallest one was Madeline."

For the rest of the workshop, these booksellers talk with zeal about books for children. They love and hate; they care what children read; above all, they *read* what children read. It is an inspiring hour.

Only at the end of the conference do I discover that this nationwide impressive professional support system will not be accessible to me when I open my bookshop in the Algarve. The ABA does not work with overseas booksellers.

On the last day of spring, June 20, 1987, Maria Alves from the Portuguese Consulate telephones to let us know our residency visas have been approved. Walter and I will be allowed to stay in Portugal for one year. After that, if we haven't disgraced ourselves, we can apply for annual renewals. Maria Alves told us last September that the approval process would take about four months. It has in fact taken nine months. That's probably a good rule of thumb for every part of this enterprise, a little more than twice as long as we're told to expect, and I wonder how many more steps still lie ahead. By the time we complete construction of an actual villa, we may be ready for the eventual retirement we talked about. For now, though, we must report to Lisbon within ninety days to validate our visas.

With this milestone reached, I decide to begin keeping a journal of our venture to build a villa and a bookshop in Portugal. This might make an engaging story to look back on someday. I caution myself that such a story would only be enjoyable if one looks back on something that has become a success. Who knows if that will turn out to be the case? Yet going into it, I have to believe that there *will* be a story, one I shall enjoy in the future. Keeping the idea of success dominant, as I hope to do, will be like a ninety-seven pound weakling modeling for Michelangelo's *David*. But recently, even before today's phone call, I've sensed a surge of new ideas and new energy.

Walter is exhilarated too. He decides to celebrate today's news of our approved residency by making steamed mussels for dinner. My role as *sous chef* is to supply the salad and garlic bread. As I wash lettuce, my thoughts hover around our plans.

"You know, I'd probably be getting discouraged about my job prospects if it weren't for Portugal, but I think about that more than about the jobs I'm applying for."

Walter is standing at the kitchen sink, carefully de-bearding mussels with a medical clamp. "It's never easy being on the job market. Once we get busy building the villa, maybe you won't have to do that any more."

"And now that we've gotten the approvals, we're beyond the idea stage; it's getting real."

Walter extracts the fuzz from the last mussel and sets the full pot on the stove. "We're going to have a great adventure; starting a whole new life. How many people get to do that at our age?"

"All because my mother bought that land on an impulse fifteen years ago."

Walter nods, pours white wine over the mussels and turns on the burner. "God bless Elke," he responds. "Get ready, you are going to love this dinner."

Now, after all my research into bookselling, I'm about to enter the trenches by working at the bookshop on Broadway in Saratoga. I will be an apprentice sales clerk during the summer tourist season, for three days a week in July and full-time in August when the racecourse is open and our city population triples. If I survive, by September I'll be ready-or-not for Portugal.

To clear my calendar for this job, I have mailed my last batch of work and final bill as a consultant for The College Board. This means I'm exchanging a series of freelance contracts that paid me $200 per seven-hour working day plus expenses, for a summer apprenticeship where I receive minimum wage of $3.65 an hour. Certainly this is a risky exchange and would be difficult without Walter's financial support.

The book *When Smart People Fail* identifies one trait of people who make successful new starts as their willingness to settle for lower incomes or more menial work, at least for an interim period while they rethink. One such person is quoted: "Sometimes, you have to go back to zero before you can even get to one." In my first week at my summer job, I figure minimum wage is about zero for me. Walter and I laugh about the fact that I now make less per hour than our cleaning lady and the man who mows the grass. Walter finds it more purely amusing than I; my own laughter has an edge to it.

The owner of the bookshop and my boss is Jack. He's in his thirties, slim, balding, with a sandy colored beard, and he wears jeans and a plaid flannel shirt. This description would fit four out of the five booksellers I interviewed last fall. If it's a required uniform, I'm already at a disadvantage both in gender and attire.

Each morning Jack greets me by reviewing what I did wrong during the previous day.

"Your totals didn't match the figures on the sales tape," he says the day after I first closed out last evening's cash register.

"You displayed the new books without making out file cards for them," on the morning I've just taken pride in my artful arrangement of the new arrivals.

These start-of-the-day rebukes are certainly justified but make my spirits slump before each new work shift. I'm sometimes tempted to suggest more energizing management techniques, but Jack didn't hire me as a management consultant, and I remind myself of his generosity in taking on such a grossly unqualified helper.

I work with two efficient young women who treat me gently as they would a child with learning disabilities. Their assessment is not far from the truth as I ask the same questions over and over. Though I've studied bookstore management in theory, in practice I might be among the least useful and most "extra" extra help that Jack has hired. I'm amazed that as a lifetime reader I can be so ignorant about so many books. I'm overly educated about a narrow sliver of literature and abysmally ignorant of everyone else's reading tastes. Ask me about the Victorian novel, Virginia Woolf, or theories of literary criticism and I may be able to help you. Ask me about cookbooks, horoscopes, murder mysteries, sports anthologies, gardening, hiking guides, good reading for three-year-olds or grandmothers who crochet, and all I can do is run for help. Needless to say, very few people ask about literary theory. And mastering the cash register, a computerized marvel, seems more difficult and mysterious than writing a thesis.

At the end of two weeks I still feel buffeted by tasks I cannot do. What *can* I do, one might well ask. I can find the filed index card for a book sold and subtract one from the total number of copies shown on hand. I can dust books. I can shelve new books alphabetically by author (if I'm told what sections they belong in). I can gift-wrap. I can put customers' purchased books in paper bags. With Jack's instructions in my ears, I can approach people with the proper greeting. ("Don't say 'may I help you'? The answer will be no. Say 'did you have a question'?") I have learned the store's layout well enough to guide people to the section they want. ("Never point; always lead the customer to the right section.") I can search out a likely title. ("Never just wave at the shelves; put a book in the customer's hand.")

So I reassure myself that I've learned quite a lot in my first two weeks. I also get a 20% discount on any books or calendars I buy for myself and, if I do that, it about takes up my pay check which means that my training costs Jack less in money than it must in aggravation. But every day I feel a little more secure even with a steady stream of customers. A clump of them, though, all waiting to be served, still makes me nervous.

My first day alone at the store is a Sunday. I thought it would be peaceful but I am busy from the moment I walk in. I manage to do a bit of everything, collate the Sunday papers and set them out, open the store, set up the cash register, handle cash sales, checks and credit card sales, take special orders, and gift-wrap. Four or five people are browsing at all times throughout the day. At intervals, I even give some minimal advice on what to read though I'm often nonplused when asked by people whose tastes I don't know. At the end of the day, I close up, cash out, and balance the take for the day. Finally, I lock the shop door behind me and deposit the money at the bank's night deposit window across the street. I feel quite satisfied, but I am also extremely tired and my stomach is upset because *nothing* as yet is second nature. Furthermore, I'm not at all sure I even *like* it.

When I first thought of a bookshop in Portugal back on the beach at Vale do Lobo, I pictured myself presiding over a cozy shop filled with books familiar to me, discovering new ones, learning the tastes of congenial customers, having stimulating conversations about world literature and spending peaceful evening hours reading the best newly published works. Now I'm finding the daily reality of my job at Bookworks quite a contrast from my pretty picture.

Closest to my aching bones is the fact that I find it unimaginably tiring to stand all day behind a counter. The shop has only one stool to perch on for the three people on duty at any one time. The two girls who work there with me don't seem to need to sit down, but I cling to that stool like a toehold on a cliff.

More worrisome for the long term is learning that the shop makes hardly any money for anyone associated with it. The wages paid to the sales clerks are so low as to be exploitative, but these wages are paid by owners who themselves live on the edge of poverty. And the work itself is an endless chain of petty details, never-ending and doubling back upon itself. Tiny operations are performed for every single book from ordering to point of sale or return, for a total of 15,000 to 20,000 titles. The part that I do goes on hour after hour, filled with those tiny detail beads of shelving, dusting, re-arranging, filing, tracking books in and out, wrapping, making change and smiling, always smiling. It is intensely busy work that leaves no time to think about or even read what one is dispensing right and left. I feel steeped in an ongoing, intense, but *wrong* relationship with books. Further, I suspect the part of the business I don't do yet, the behind-the-scenes work of book-ordering, returning, bill paying, payroll, bookkeeping and accounting, is a barrage of more details. One does want the sense of something larger behind all the pieces, the sweep of an idea or goal that the details fit into. I hope I can discover that larger scope when I actually own a bookstore. For the present, I try to keep learning and not think too much about greater meanings.

Fred Astaire died last week. I wonder if the news has reached Oliver, the owner of Mr. Freddy's restaurant in the Algarve. "America's greatest dancer," Balanchine termed him and everyone seems to agree. When I was a kid at Saturday movie matinees I didn't appreciate the dance numbers; now I have a better idea of the genius they took. And I especially like what Astaire said in an interview. "Dancing is a sweat job...you may go for days getting nothing but exhaustion. This search for what you want is like tracking something that doesn't want to be tracked." That last sentence haunts me. I wish I'd known when I was young that a writer's work isn't just hard and lonely; it resists. Unlike my father who wrote all the time whether or not he had an audience, I was too easily discouraged. Maybe if I'd had a better understanding of the struggle involved in finding the right words and the right readers... but Fred Astaire also said, "The thing I hate most is nostalgia," and I guess he's right. These days I'm tracking the vision of a bookshop in Portugal and that offers resistance enough.

I'm getting better at Bookworks in small ways. My fingers have learned to handle the money; handing out change in coins and bills is not the hurdle it was earlier when dropping parts of little cash bundles marked half my transactions with customers. I'm no longer so nervous at finding titles on microfiches while people are waiting. They know it takes some time to focus the screen, find, read and understand the information. I'm relieved to find that people don't erupt in irritation; they even appreciate the service. They wait. I realize that when I myself have to wait in line somewhere, I don't usually go crazy and start abusing the clerks.

I'm also learning more about the stock of books, though since they go in and out each day, that's still the largest skill to master. But the small maneuvers are getting easier. During these weeks I have gained deep respect for sales people everywhere who stand all day behind counters with good humor and who operate cash registers with such confidence. Writing an article, chairing a meeting or organizing a conference is child's play for me, compared to clerking in a retail store.

For months since we came back from Portugal we have exchanged drawings, letters and draft contracts with Joost Roemer, our builder, and have made all the adjustments we could think of. Joost has advised us that the zoning laws permit us to build one but not two structures on the property, and the Roemer design team has come up with an ingenious solution. Our house will be set back behind the shop building, which will front on the road. The two buildings will be connected by a small courtyard with a terraced arcade. That way, though they are in fact separate buildings, the plans show them as a single complex. The shop should be easily accessible to customers while also shielding the house in back for our privacy. Joost has also persuaded us to add a pool, assuring us that it will raise the potential resale value.

To meet the ninety-day deadline for validating our promised residency permits, we've booked our flights to Lisbon for September 9th. Elke will join us for a week at the Dona Filipa Hotel where we hope to see how our building plans are coming along. Official permission to actually build anything is taking so long that, after all my preparations, I sometimes grow uncertain about the enterprise

"What if I stayed on in Portugal for a while after our trip?" I propose one evening as Walter and I are reading in bed.

"Why?" He is startled and turns to look at me over his half-frame reading glasses.

"Well, everything is going so slowly. Maybe I could goose things along by being there."

He rubs his beard, newly trimmed and bristly, and waits to

hear more.

"I get discouraged when nothing's happening. Maybe I could rent a storefront to start the bookshop and I could also push the builders if I'm there on the scene."

"That would make good sense if there was a building, but there isn't yet. And that might take another year. I don't want you over there by yourself for a year, Patoot. We're supposed to be doing this together. Try to be patient. Just remember, one day at a time."

He's right. I don't want to live there by myself. And yet, as I try to resume my reading, I continue with nighttime worries. Walter is not as impatient as I am. He loves the dream of Portugal while it's combined with his full life and work here, with me taking care of home and daily life while also planning for Portugal. How will he like it when we are really there? How will I? Will we miss our children too much? Will we lose all our money?

When we turn out the lights, I move in close to him. "I've got heebie-jeebies."

"Just snuggle up," he murmurs. "The old heebie-jeebie chaser is right here," and I gradually relax. Walter has been the steady polestar, guiding me, maintaining his enthusiasm for the whole idea, while I, doing the day-by-day work of it, periodically waver like a quaking aspen tree. In part, the humdrum part of the process is good for me. It consists of putting one foot in front of the other, sending one letter after another, making one specific choice or decision after another. So long as I do that, I'm OK. It's when I step back and view the hugeness and strangeness of the venture as a whole that I get stymied and my determination falters.

To ward off such wavering, I decide that in September, after my stint at Bookworks has ended and we return from our Portugal trip, I'd better keep trying for a real job with a decent salary, at least for the present.

But I am keeping on with my journal and it's funny how the writing itself exercises a positive pull. This is supposed to be a *success* story after all, and I feel the impetus to make it that. The only way to do it is to do it. We'll discover the answers to our questions by living it through. The distance between Saratoga and Portugal is the difficulty but also the glamour. I fall asleep remembering what Fred Astaire said. "The search for what you want is like tracking something that doesn't want to be tracked."

IV
Unexpected Events

On August 9th in 1987, a month before our planned flight to Portugal, I am in a Saratoga Hospital room, watching Walter's uneasy sleep. He has been here since the night he woke up with intense abdominal pain a week ago. A few days later, the doctors diagnosed diverticulitis and said they would try to avoid surgery by treating it with intravenous antibiotics. All he's had since then is that bed, countless tests, injections and IV's, and pain, pain, pain. He gets shots for the pain, which make him sleepy, so he can talk, only in brief spurts before dropping off again.

So many procedures and machines. Disposable stuff everywhere—tubing, needles, packages of gauze and tape. Beeps and flashing lights. Instruments and wheeled carts. But they still haven't taken away his pain. What happened to people a hundred years ago, without all the paraphernalia? Was it better, worse, or just the same? Walter has been brave and sweet through it all, never crabby, pleasant to the nurses, loving to me. But he's not getting better. Now the doctors say the surgery can't be avoided. Last week it seemed ominous and fearful, but now we just want it to happen so that he'll get some relief.

To keep my promise to my boss, I'm still working at the bookshop during the daytime. My daughters Sheila and Helen, and Walter's son Terry, have come to take turns staying with

Walter in the afternoons, and I spend evenings and nights with him in his room where the nurses have kindly set up a cot for me. My daytime shifts at work keep me a bit distracted, but at night I keep waking up saying "Please God, let him be all right." He's so full of energy and life; it would be terrible if he were cut down. I would so hate it if he died.

Walter is in the operating room now and I'm waiting. This crisis has come after a period of years when we were both strong and healthy, and now I feel we didn't make good enough use of the time together. If he recovers from this bout, I hope I remember how fragile everything is at this time of life. I want more good years with him—years when he's strong and active, so he can do some of the things that intrigued him—sailing, learning to fly, going to Australia. Because I had no interest in those things myself I held him back. Now I wish I hadn't. I want him to have a full measure of everything he'd like. He deserves that. He doesn't at all deserve so much pain.

The doctor has just come to say that the surgery was successful but he warns that Walter's still not out of the woods. I think of how lost I'd be without him.

When he awakens, I tell him I'm sorry for having hurt him ever, and he squeezes my hand, saying, "Oh, honey, we get on— we get on—.and we love each other." Then he drifts back into his druggy sleep. I'm not really sure what he meant, that time goes on, or that we get along together. The ambiguity makes it richer; both are true.

Another Sunday morning. The days at the bookstore seem very long. For one thing, I'd rather be at the hospital with Walter and for another, our whole Portugal enterprise that led to my job has now become problematic. Walter and I are going to have to rethink everything, including starting a bookshop. If he recovers fully, we might still go ahead with our plans, but if his health is precarious we may not want to risk moving to another country, especially one with dubious health care. Jack at the bookshop says, "If it were me over there, it would be, 'don't take me to the hospital; take me to the airport'." Exactly! I have canceled our September plane reservations and asked Gunnar Nielsen to petition the Portuguese Consulate to extend our residency permission due to illness. Ironically, the permit to build our villa arrives in the next mail. I think wistfully of how thrilled we would have been a few weeks ago, and quietly file it with the other residency papers we've accumulated. For the time being, Portugal is on hold.

With the close of the Saratoga racing season at the end of August, my temporary job has come to an end. Walter is getting stronger. His color is better, his blue eyes are clear under their bristly brows, the tubes are gone and he's hooked up to only one IV on a pole that he pushes along during short walks down the corridor. We both pay careful attention to the nurse who gives us instructions about how to care for his temporary colostomy. The doctors say he can come home in a week.

A few days before his scheduled discharge, when I return from my morning shower at home, I ask him about Portugal. He pulls himself up in bed and reaches for the New York Times I've brought. "Oh we have to go," he says without hesitation. "We've been looking forward to this for so long and no way do I want to miss out on our adventure." His enthusiasm brings me new energy, as though he has given back our dream.

Walter wants to fly to Lisbon as soon as possible to confirm our residency so that villa construction can get started. I make reservations and, though he is still somewhat weak, we make the trip in mid-October. Elke joins us at the Dona Filipa. She has attached this stay to her other previously planned activities. First she spent one week in Munich to visit friends and store her mink coat with her favorite furrier for the winter. Her next week was devoted to the annual Frankfurt Book Fair. She has been translating books from English into German for twenty years and enjoys renewing acquaintances at the enormous fair each year. In the past, the workshops and cocktail parties energized her, but this time when we meet her at Faro airport I am shocked to see how frail she looks. During our two-week stay together in the Algarve, she continues to seem exhausted from her travels.

Walter also needs more rest than usual so we do very little sightseeing on this trip and focus on business. Several times we confer with Joost Roemer on the final details of our construction contract. We also meet with Gunnar Nielsen and study the plaques on his office wall. As President of Blue Ribbon Services, Algarve Tourist Promotion, Foreign Resident Assistance, and Golf Buggy Manufacturing, Limitada, plus various subsidiary and lucrative enterprises all founded and directed by himself, Mr. Nielsen's eggs are in many baskets and he does not hesitate to move them about. He does things as they are needed, or rather, smoothes the way for other people to do things they want to do. Among his many other responsibilities, he has also become "our man in Almancil."

Elke has no interest in taking part in our meetings. As before she spends most morning hours in her room, but now she doesn't walk down to the Vale do Lobo beach plaza for a mid-morning coffee as she did during our previous stay. This time she spends the entire day in her room. I visit her there each afternoon while Walter rests. Toward evening, she takes a long time dressing for dinner at the hotel. To spare her energies, Walter and I don't even suggest dining somewhere else. Even so, when we walk down to the dining room, Elke is often short of breath. We try to persuade her to see the hotel doctor but she refuses with her customary distrust, "I'm not seeing a Portuguese doctor." I make her promise to see her own doctor as soon as she gets back to Zurich.

While we three are still in the Algarve, the foundation is laid for our villa and shop. We are glad to see that we've not lost any mature trees. The row of stone pines still screens the property from the road, and the large carob tree remains near a corner of the foundation. Walter and I pace around the new footings in the dry red soil. What with two buildings and a connecting arcade, the ground plan appears immense, like an archaeological dig. "Looks like we're building a village," Walter comments, and we are both a bit awed by what we have set into motion. "I wish we didn't have to leave just as all this is starting," I say, knowing we both feel the same way

The following morning, on the way to the airport for Elke's flight home, we pause to show her the start of the villa that will stand on land she bought so many years ago. She looks politely but doesn't get out of the car.

"With a room and a bath for you, any time you want to come," I say, wishing her to share our enthusiasm.

She nods but that isn't quite what she wants. "I think it's better if you build a separate guest house," she advises with her old authority.

We have been over this before and I try not to be impatient just as we are about to say good-bye but I don't quite succeed. At the airport, Elke adamantly refuses a wheel chair and as we slowly walk to her gate, she carries the cane she doesn't like to use and leans on me instead. I feel remorse for my earlier curtness, especially now that she seems ill. We kiss in parting and I remind her of her promise to see her doctor. Then she's gone.

Two days later, Walter and I also start on our journey home. In Lisbon, where we must change planes, I telephone Elke. She says, "I slept for two days and I feel much better," but still sounds a bit breathless.

"What does the doctor say?"

"I see him tomorrow morning. But right now I have to go, I'm getting ready to go the opera tonight." I am relieved that she feels up to that and am somewhat reassured about her health. I hope her tiredness had just been from traveling to too many places in a short time.

It is October 19, 1987, as Walter and I fly from Lisbon to New York on TWA flight 901. From two stockbrokers seated behind us we learn that the stock market has taken a huge plunge. The brokers have left their wives vacationing in Portugal while they themselves are flying home because of the crisis. All during the flight, they take turns walking up to the cockpit to get the most recent market quotes. Each time they slide back into the seats behind us, they announce the latest bulletin. "Down a hundred... Up eighty-five points....Holding steady at eleven fifteen..." It sounds like a bedside vigil with temperature readings or white cell counts for a patient in danger. Walter listens intently. By the end of the flight, the situation still sounds alarming. Many people seem to have lost a lot of money, at least on paper. The men behind us predict a falling dollar. We wonder if the crash will affect our Portugal plans.

Upon our return home, I am surprised to find a letter containing the offer of a job as speechwriter and editor for the Acting Chancellor of State University of New York. I feel buoyed by the prospect, but a little hesitant. If I take on a full-time job, we'll again have to rethink our schedule for Portugal. Then I reason that since my new boss is interim rather than permanent chancellor, my job tenure might not outlast his. Meanwhile, we can have time to make sure of Walter's health, and to be nearby for the birth of my daughter Sheila's baby. My salary will also help our villa budget, which keeps expanding. And there's no doubt that being personally recruited brings a heady fizz to my ego. I agree to begin the new job in November, ten days after Walter's scheduled second surgery to repair his colostomy.

Walter's insides are reconnected and he is spending another week in the hospital to make sure the hookup is working. The great moment indicating success arrives one morning when Walter's announcement "Finnegan's First Fart," sends nurses giggling through the corridor. A few days later he is well enough to come home, and I report for work at my new job in Albany.

Then Elke starts telephoning every day, something she hasn't done in all the years she's lived in Switzerland. Her voice is weak and she says she's frightened because she can't eat and is losing weight. I am very concerned and telephone Zurich to speak to her two close women friends, Lydia and Ursula, and to her doctor. All tell me that she is suffering from exhaustion and needs rest and care but the doctor assures me that her heart is good. Her friends *say that she has refused to enter a hospital to recuperate and they are trying to arrange for home care which she also refuses. I'm relieved that her heart is sound, but I want to see her and persuade her to accept help at home. I arrange to fly to Zurich over the long Thanksgiving weekend.*

On November 20, three days before my scheduled flight, I receive word that Elke has died suddenly of congestive heart failure.

I am at work when the telephone call comes. After the first shock, all I know is that I have to get to Zurich right away. I telephone the chancellor to ask about a leave of absence. Within three minutes, he is in my office, hugs me in sympathy and offers me the use of his car and driver to take me home. I'll always remember that spontaneous rush to bring me his condolence in person. That kind of swift response is not studied, it comes before thought. And I find it even more touching since I've only been at work for three weeks and we still hardly know each other.

When I get home I call my eldest daughter, Julia, who is on a business trip in Florida. The news has her in tears almost at once. Julia says that her "Omi" (the German word for Granny) has been such a vivid personality in their lives she can't imagine her not being there. I feel sorry that I shocked her with the news at work, so I wait till later in the day to call my youngest, Sheila, at home. She has always been especially fond of her grandmother even though they only met during Elke's annual visits to the States. As I expected, Sheila is heartbroken and keeps saying " no? no?" through her tears, as though pleading with me that since I've given her this awful news I could take it away again. In a second call we talk about Elke's active and good life and I say I think she had a good death and would have hated illness and weakness for months or years. Sheila agrees, but then says, "It's just that she said she was going to live forever. And we believed her."

Both girls and I telephone back and forth in the next hours. We haven't been able to reach Helen, my middle daughter, and leave messages with several of her friends asking her to call any of us. Many other calls go to my aunt and uncle in Maine and to Elke's

---

friends in Zurich about our arrival and funeral arrangements.

Elke had evidently been dressing to keep an appointment with her doctor when she was stricken. When she didn't show up, the doctor phoned Lydia and Ursula and they went together to her apartment and found her lying on the floor in front of her closet. The end appears to have been quick and without suffering. I hope so. But periodically throughout these days, I picture it as if I were her. I know she would have hated it; she didn't at all want to die. But she also didn't want to restrict her life in any way; fought limitations to the last moment. Maybe she thought she would always triumph over them; she believed so strongly in will power. I keep wishing that she hadn't been alone during these last weeks and that I'd known more clearly, earlier, what to do. And then I think that she tried to spare me because of Walter's surgery and because of my new job. She told me that her doctor assured her she'd be fine in two weeks. I guess I wanted to believe that.

Walter, though still not fully recovered from his second operation, flies to Zurich with Julia and me for the funeral. Afterwards, friends gather for a meal at the Ascot Hotel, where Elke often had dinner. We say it has been a nice ceremony and reassure each other, "she would have liked it; she would have approved," speaking of her as though she were still nearby watching over the proceedings with interest, and we feel comforted.

But at night, wakeful, I picture how we went through the funeral in tentative memory of what she would like, trying to be in keeping with her taste, because of our own needs. But all the while she is out there, cold, vacant, everything over, beyond liking or not liking anything at all. And I hate that thought, hate the thought of her death as the ending between us. Absence was all right so long as our lives continued. Separation was often better, more peaceful, less disturbing than close contact. But death leaves a void; insensate coldness is too dreadful to think of. Yet I keep imagining her last moments _as if she felt them_. I feel her frailty, her being struck from within, her falling dead to the ground, as if she sensed every relentless blow. Probably, it was more like my auto accident when I saw it coming and then, after I hit my head, *saw and felt nothing at all. Elke is not suffering, I tell myself, she does not watch. She simply is not. Only we are, and we imagine her still. I even live through the moments of her death as if there were an afterwards.*

We spend many days attending to legal matters, sorting through Elke's effects, putting her furniture in storage and closing her apartment. My feelings are jumbled: sorrow at Elke's death, worry about Walter who is still quite weak, pleasure at my daughter Julia's company, and tiredness from the long series of necessary tasks. Each time we ride the elevator up to Elke's apartment, I picture her in her doorway. After she pressed the buzzer to open the main downstairs door, she always stood there waiting for guests or for me. And now not there, not ever again...

But it is not at all bad being in her apartment. Aside from the incredible welter of papers and correspondence, everything is in attractive order. All the rooms are tidy. Elke's clothes and personal things are tightly packed in cupboards and drawers in her stunningly complicated neatness--underwear and gloves in individual plastic cases, shoes with shoe trees, a hundred small boxes and chamois bags for sundries. In the freezer, her favorite rolls individually packaged in plastic wrap and fastened with rubber bands. In this place where she lived for thirty years, we feel her presence fondly and call to each other at intervals to "come see this," or "remember this?" And we find among all the sophisticated paintings and books and elegant furniture, a sprinkling of funny little toy birds and straw animals, trinkets that a child would like.

I haven't cried, wonder if or when I will. But I think of her all the time. And when people here in Zurich describe her as "a great lady," and say how they admired her, I wonder why being with her was so difficult for me. I tried all my life to please her and to love her as much as she wanted but I never could. Perhaps, now that she is gone, I will be able to.

A month later, I return to my new job in Albany. I have a magnificent office in a pseudo-gothic confection of a building renovated for the central administration of New York State University. My office is on the eleventh floor of the tallest tower; the chancellor's office is on the floor above. I see him mainly at meetings, which I am expected to attend so as to be informed of university issues. My sole function is to draft speeches for the chancellor's many public appearances. I bring each draft to his executive assistant, and do not see it again. How the speech is edited, whether or not it is given, I never know.

On February 23, Sheila has a beautiful little daughter, Stephanie Elizabeth, my first grandchild, balancing our sadness at Elke's death with the joy and hopefulness of new life.

On our drive home from Connecticut where we were visiting mother and child, Walter says, "It's been quite a year," as we pass through the winter landscape of the Berkshires.

I put my hand on his knee. "Yes, and I'm just glad you're here."

"I'm still here and we're in pretty good shape. The practice is growing, you've got a good job, we have no real financial worries, and the kids seem to be in pretty good space."

"Mmm, yes, we are OK." I look out of the window for a while. Snow covers the hillsides and the sky is gray but calm. Then following our taking stock, I venture, "You know, we don't really have to do this Portugal thing."

Walter glances at me in surprise. "What do you mean? Why wouldn't we do it?"

"Well, maybe we started to think about it when things weren't going so well, remember? You had just gotten back from Washington and weren't sure what you'd do; and I wasn't happy with my job. Maybe five years ago we needed the idea of Portugal, more than we do now. And now Elke's gone and we've had the whole health thing with you. I was so scared I'd lose you. Maybe we shouldn't risk going so far away."

"Oh Honey, I'm here and I'm fine now. We can't live being scared. I don't think Portugal was an escape; we would have managed without that. In fact, we did manage. And you're right, we don't need it, but it adds something, doesn't it? —excitement? adventure? the new and unknown? I like thinking about it."

"So do I."

"And if we stop now, wouldn't we be disappointed? We'd always wonder..."

"Well, that's true; we'd never know if it was a good dream. If we never make it real it would be just a...a figment."

"I say we go ahead," says Walter.

"We go ahead," I echo, reassured by his resolve and once again exhilarated.

My days in the tower wear on. I sit solitary, reading newspapers and journals to remain informed about higher education and books to stimulate thought. I draft speeches on the computer. At lunchtime, in good weather I take walks on the nearby path along the Hudson River. For exercise in bad weather I walk from one end to the other of each long lower floor of the building. One day I open a door behind a picture in my office and discover an unused circular staircase in the turret. I prop the door open, descend the dusty stone steps for several stories but, fearful that I might be immured there, I return to my office. I feel kin to Elaine, the lily maid of Astolat, high in her tower waiting for Lancelot. When the announcement comes that the permanent chancellor has been named and will begin in July, I submit my resignation. Being chosen for this job has restored my ego and helped our finances, but the daily tedium confirms my sense that I have better uses for my returning optimism and energy.

The lure of Portugal glows brighter than ever.

V
The Vila Bonita

It's May, and the mail brings the latest packet of Polaroid snapshots Joost Roemer sends us each month to show progress in building our villa. I take the photos to Walter's study where he's making notes at his desk, sit down in the patients' chair and announce, "Dr. Finnegan, I need an appointment."

Still writing, he glances at me slyly. "Yes, Madam. I think I can fit you in. Do you need it right now?"

"Yes I do; it's an international emergency."

"Ah hah," I wait for him to finish writing and then put the pictures in front of him. The rough ceramic-block walls pictured in January appeared the same in March and April, and are still unchanged in these latest photos.

Walter studies them for a moment, then says, "Haven't I seen these before?"

"Well, you'd think so, but these just arrived and they're exactly the same as last month's. We've got to do something."

"It does seem to call for some direct supervision."

I press on. "We're going there in August for vacation anyway, right? I think we should try to stay longer."

"I'd like that," Walter responds quickly, then pauses. "But I don't think I can. My staff people have their own vacations in August and September."

I'm disappointed but not really surprised. "Well, if we can't both be there, maybe one of us will do. I could stay, at least for a few weeks longer after you fly back home."

"Let me think about that," Walter studies the photographs again. "I'm not crazy about the idea but maybe we can work something out."

Over the next days we discuss possibilities and then settle on our plans. In August we'll spend three weeks in Portugal together. I will stay on for six more weeks, while Walter flies home to run his practice. In mid October he'll rejoin me for the promised completion of our villa. Then we'll both return to Saratoga to prepare for our actual move early next year.

As we talk about that move I sense some hesitancy in Walter and try to bring it into the open. "You don't really want to close the practice do you?"

"I'd like to keep it going," he admits. "It's doing well and that way if anything goes wrong, or if we change our minds later on, it would still be here. And it would keep the money coming in." He looks at me with a placating smile.

My dream train seems to have hit a wall. "Are we back to the idea of keeping the villa just for vacations?"

"No, not at all. I just want keep the office going here a while longer. And it would be bring in some income till the bookshop is up and running."

"But how can you live in Portugal and have a practice in Saratoga?"

"I've got good associates. They can handle the day-to-day and I'll spend most of the time in Portugal with you. I'd come back for a couple of weeks three or four times a year to check up, do clinical evaluations, and see my own long-term patients."

Over the following days I reluctantly accept Walter's reasoning. As he says, his practice is insurance in case anything goes wrong, and we've both learned that things can go wrong. With his recent illness still in our minds, we agree to keep our connection to Saratoga, at least for the first year or two. Walter will come back regularly to check on the practice, and once a year we'll come back together for the Christmas season with our family. During summers, we hope they will visit us.

I wonder, is this is the way older people can get themselves ready to launch into the unknown? Step into the shiny new boat, but keep a long rope tied to the dock?

Though I am nervous about the prospect of the coming six weeks alone, I'm the one who persuaded both Walter and myself that I can do it.

"If you get too lonely, you can always come back home," he says and I agree. It's a safety valve, but I don't want to come back home for that reason. It would be giving in to fears and turning tail before we've even begun living in Portugal. Though I know I will miss Walter, I can look forward to his return. Meanwhile I have to find solutions to two worries about my time alone. First, that I will feel lonely and isolated in a strange new place where as yet I have no friends. To avoid that I need some "pegs" on my calendar, occasions for meeting people and going places. My second worry is that aside from watching over the villa construction I won't have anything to do. I need to fill those days alone with some work that interests me. Without such supports in view, I'm prone to see the time looming before me like a vast desert through which I myself will wander, parched and increasingly loony. I give myself pep talks to stay on course.

I decide to arm myself for solitude by carrying along two projects to ward off the willies. One has been floating about in my mind for some time. I want to write a short story grounded in memories of my youth in Woodstock, the artist's colony in the Catskills. Six weeks alone will be a good amount of time to start that. My other project aims toward the exciting future; I will decide on the bookshop's opening inventory. The materials needed for both these projects, as well as books for bedtime reading (after all, the lack of a good bookstore was a major motive) have filled five cartons. I pack two more cartons with our clothes for cooler fall weather and send everything off air freight, care of Gunnar Nielsen's address.

Because our combined stay will last ten or twelve weeks, we need to avoid the steep tourist prices of Vale do Lobo and reserve a modestly priced hotel room in the nearby coastal town of Quarteira. That done, and with our children kissed good bye, our friends promising to write and our Saratoga house to be cared for by a sitter, we embark on the by-now-familiar trip to Lisbon and from there to the Algarve.

The brochures advertised Quarteira as a "quaint fishing village," but when we arrive there after our transatlantic flight, we find that it is no more quaint than Miami. Instead we quickly see that Quarteira is a prime destination for bare-bones package tours for sun-starved working class vacationers, mainly from Britain and Germany. Two long parallel roads along the beach are crammed from end to end with high-rise hotels and condominiums, many still unfinished. They not only dwarf older small homes and shops behind them but also seal them off from their age-old views of the ocean. No longer can residents see fishing boats out on the water or back on shore with each morning's catch.

We stroll among the crowds of young vacationers. At street level, the tourist trade has spawned a string of bars, restaurants, mini markets, souvenir shops, ice cream stands, newspaper kiosks, and racks of beachwear and plastic beach toys. We find our hotel and check into a room with just space enough to walk around the bed. As the sun sets we discover that the sunburned tourists who swarm everywhere in daytime also rock the bars with music and shouting at night. We seem to have landed in a round-the-clock block party in the midst of a construction site.

After a sleepless night, we load our luggage into our rental car and drive inland to search for a place more suited for a middle-aged couple's summer. We reject several motels as too expensive and continue on our way. Just before noon, we see a sign announcing "*Quartos*" (Rooms) with arrows pointing to a side road. We turn into an uphill gravel driveway to find the Vila Bonita (in Portugal the word "villa" is spelled with a single "l"). A cluster of small buildings surrounds a swimming pool. Flowers and shrubs bloom everywhere in brilliant reds, pinks and yellows. We pass a row of tall poles bearing the flags of Portugal and the nations of most of the Algarve's tourists: England, Germany, Holland, France, Belgium, Switzerland and the United States. We follow the driveway to a parking area shaded by a trellis of blossoming pink oleander. A slim dark-haired man wearing jeans and a T-shirt is grilling fish on a small outdoor barbecue in the open doorway of a garage. We say our *"Bom dias"* and muster our Berlitz phrases to ask if any *Quartos* are available.

The man smiles at us and approaches. In accented but good English he asks, "What are two Americans doing way down 'ere in the Algarve?"

Relieved at the English, we tell him "We're here to watch over the building of our house," expecting no special attention since no one except our builder has shown any interest in our venture.

To our surprise, our new acquaintance smiles again and extends his hand, "I'm Mike Moreira, welcome to the club," the first words of welcome to us as potential residents of the Algarve.

We all shake hands and Walter's attention is diverted to the grill. "What kind of fish are you cooking there?"

"Oh these are *sardinhas* (sardines), you'll see a lot of those around 'ere. But they smell too strong to cook inside." Even in the open air the smell is pungent, like a dozen open cans of the sardines we're familiar with. These fish, however, are as big as trout. Walter is clearly entranced. Mike crouches over the grill and scoops the fish onto a platter. When he straightens up I see that he is tall and slim for a Portuguese, with brown hair just beginning to be tinged with gray and dark eyes squinting from his cigarette smoke. When he smiles at us, his good looks are somewhat marred by a missing bicuspid tooth. Missing teeth are common in Portugal, but never cease to jar our American expectations.

"OK now, Mr. and Mrs. Finnegan, if you come along I introduce you to my wife and she can show you the rooms." He leads us to the reception area in the main house where his wife, Odette, is working at the desk. She is sturdy, with green-gold eyes and golden tones to her skin, and greets us pleasantly in accented

English somewhat different than Mike's.

While he carries the tray of grilled fish into their kitchen, Odette shows us around the property. In addition to the reception area, the two-story main building contains the owners' living quarters, several small guest apartments and a breakfast room. A second villa has more apartments and rooms, and a smaller building beside the pool serves as snack bar and social area. The garden setting appeals to us far more than the crowded beachfront hotels. Odette shows us a compact one-bedroom apartment with its own terrace bordered by a grape arbor and geraniums. We are ready to move in on the spot.

As Mike helps us take our suitcases from the car, I compliment him. "So many different flowers, your garden really is beautiful."

He is pleased. "There is a saying," he recalls, "A Portuguese house without flowers is like a woman without a smile."

Our small apartment suits our needs perfectly. We'll be comfortable for our first weeks together and then while I'm here alone the hotel's guests and its friendly owners will keep me from feeling isolated. We unpack, congratulate ourselves on our find, drive back to Quarteira for some groceries to stock our tiny refrigerator, and settle in.

During our first days, we adjust to the rhythms of the Vila Bonita. Every morning, before the sun gets too hot, we savor our first coffee on the apartment's terrace and watch Mike coast his battered blue station wagon down the driveway. He doesn't turn on the motor till he gets out to the road, so as not to waken sleeping hotel guests. Fifteen minutes later, he returns with two Portuguese maids and large paper sacks of the crusty rolls served for breakfast throughout Portugal. The clear early morning, rolls with fresh butter, orange marmalade, and a second cup of coffee, give each day a lovely beginning. We gaze out over the rolling landscape and even Quarteira's high-rise towers, so congested close up, gleam like white obelisks in the distance. After breakfast we drive inland to the town of Almancil to check for mail at our new *apartado*, the mailbox rented from the post office. We buy the *International*

Herald Tribune at the *papelaria* (newsstand) and a few groceries for lunch at the mini-market. Our purchases completed, we nudge along preparations for settling in Portugal.

Every few days we visit our building site. Progress has indeed been disappointingly slow. Joost Roemer tells us that the past winter, always the Algarve's rainy season, was simply too wet for building. Our house is a mostly empty shell with plumbing pipes laid in the cement slab foundation. Under the nearby carob tree stands a shed about eight feet square made from roughly plastered ceramic blocks and roofed with palm fronds. It serves to hold tools and a fuse box that draws electric power from a nearby pole. A large hole behind the house indicates where the pool will be. That's all. It's now August and hard to imagine this project completed by October. Though we can't say much to the workmen beyond *Bom dia*, we hope that frequent visits will speed things along.

We meet with Gunnar Nielsen to expedite our residency permits. We ask if he can obtain our identity cards while Walter is still here. He says, "Normally not so quickly, but I can do it."

Then I state our plans for a bookshop and ask what regulations might govern that. He tells me I will need to apply for a business license and an import license for the books.

"Can you help us to apply for those licenses?"

He says, "No problem. I can do that."

And finally, because getting a new telephone line here can take up to two years, "Can you help us apply for a phone before our house is finished?

Again he says, "I can do that." Our man in Almancil!

But the seven cartons we've sent ahead, care of Gunnar's address, seem to have disappeared somewhere over the Atlantic.

I plead, "Can you trace the boxes?"

"No problem. Zey vill show up," Gunnar assures us.

After our morning errands come my driving lessons. Because rental cars with automatic transmission are not available in Portugal, Walter has been our driver during our earlier stays. Now, as I anticipate six weeks by myself, I must learn to drive a stick shift or be stuck like a shrub wherever I'm planted. After twenty-five years of driving smooth automatic cars on wide American highways, I'm struggling to master a two-cylinder standard shift Citroen on a secluded dirt road and I can't believe how hard it is. Whenever I get as far as third gear, the slightest movement unnerves me: a stray dog, an Algarvian woman all in black beneath a black umbrella, a motor bike roaring past in dust clouds, even a carob pod falling from a roadside tree, and I stall the car. Then I can't start it again.

Sometimes I manage to turn the key and shift into first. I wait for motion but nothing happens.

"Take your foot off the clutch or you won't move," Walter says.

I try but my left foot feels nailed to the pedal. The motor roars as the car jolts forward, then stalls for the third time. Walter looks very large in the passenger seat, his thick white hair brushing against the roof of the small car, and he endures the lurching with remarkable patience.

"After a while, you'll know when to shift. You'll feel it."

What he doesn't know is that I think I have to downshift through every gear to stop the car in a mirror image of starting it. Picturing a quick stop with this procedure makes any speed, even six inches an hour, seem wildly reckless.

"You'll get to feel it," he keeps trying to reassure me but I don't believe him. I can't feel anything I'm supposed to feel. Every lesson ends in despair. Either I shout at Walter, "You don't explain so I can understand," while he calmly waits for my outburst to pass, or I put my head down on the steering wheel and sob, "I can't do it, I'll never learn."

Then we change places and he drives back to Vila Bonita while I try to compose myself. There we often find Mike at his small barbecue grilling lunchtime chicken or sardines for his family. "*Ola*, Mr. and Mrs. Finnegan, everything OK?" he asks in innocent good cheer, and we smile and say everything is just fine and go inside for our own lunch and some calmer hours.

In August at midday in the Algarve, the sun blazes white-hot, making metal or plastic surfaces too hot to touch. A standing car heats up like a roasting oven and the steering wheel can only be held through gloves or a towel. By one o'clock the shops and offices close, the restaurants are full, and no one stirs out of doors again until three. We are happy indoors with our lunch of farmers' bread, a round wheat loaf with a light brown crust; the pungent pale yellow cheese of the region; and unbelievably delicious red tomatoes. We finish with sugar-sweet purple grapes. Afterwards, we read or nap in our shaded bedroom. These hours of rest in the middle of the day, so unlike our routines at home, feel like a real vacation.

In the afternoon we either relax at the pool with other hotel guests or walk twenty minutes through a forest path to the nearest beach. The woods are filled with Portuguese families picnicking on blankets and plastic lawn chairs under the shade canopy made by umbrella pines. The picnickers surround themselves with bottles of water and wine, round loaves of bread, melons and oranges whose juicy fragrance wafts toward us, as do the stronger odors of sausage links in waxed paper and open cans of sardines. As the season wears on, our walk through this homey woodland scene becomes less picturesque and more littered with greasy papers, plastic wrapping, and empty bottles and cans.

We voice our dismay to Mike after a particularly messy afternoon late in August.

"Long time ago," he says, "people come to picnic and leave their garbage, peels from fruit, pieces of bread or sausage, bits of paper. The winter rains or wild animals, they take care of it. Now it's plastic. Doesn't go away." We nod; the problem is familiar in the States also. Mike brightens, "In springtime every year, they come from Quarteira to make a clean-up."

"It's such a beautiful place when it's clean," I say.

"Is a nice beach," Mike agrees absently, looking toward the setting sun that burnishes the trees and the red tile roofs of white villas. "But when I was a boy growing up in my village, Marianne, you should see... this Algarve was just fields and fields of poppies and daisies as far as you could see or walk, and no fences anywhere. You could sleep at night with the doors open. No one to fear, nothing to worry about. Just little villages 'ere and there, and open fields of daisies."

Mike and Odette share equally in the work of the Vila Bonita. Odette manages the house, the guest rooms, and the breakfast service with the help of two maids. Mike takes care of the bar, the pool, and the garden, supervising an aged man who wears a black fedora to ward off the sun. Bonita, their pretty teen-aged daughter who has glossy brown curls and her mother's light eyes, helps out in the snack bar in the afternoons.

Mike's native language was Portuguese and during years he spent working abroad before returning to Portugal he gained some rudimentary German and a good command of English. Odette, a native-born Haitian, speaks fluent French, competent English, and Portuguese she learned from Mike's mother. Between them, the couple can converse in most native languages of guests from the countries whose nine flags wave above their pool. Travelers from other countries usually speak enough English to make themselves understood. Both Mike and Odette seem to enjoy their seasonal parade of visitors. They host a poolside barbecue each Saturday night, with guests, mostly pairs of young friends or couples with children, placed at long tables with those who speak the same language, while Mike and Odette circulate among them to encourage all to get acquainted.

On evenings without barbecues, Walter and I explore the region's restaurants either by ourselves or with compatible hotel guests. We sample elegant and expensive fare at resort hotels on the coast, and simple meals at local bistros with checked tablecloths in Almancil, Faro, Quarteira, or Albufeira. In the hotel dining rooms, tall and sleek northern Europeans murmur to each other over crystal, silver, and white linen. The crowded bistros hum with noisy talk and laughter among dark-haired Portuguese families, all savoring the strong garlicky Algarvian dishes, followed by *sobre mesa* (dessert) of flan or almond cake so sweet that it stupefies the tongue. Each environment has its charms.

Around 5:30 each afternoon, Mike changes from gardener and handyman into bartender and host for the cocktail hour. He goes inside, removes jeans, T-shirt and baseball cap, showers and then emerges in a clean sport shirt and slacks. While Odette cooks their evening meal in their apartment, Mike serves drinks at the snack bar and chats with guests at several small poolside tables. Sometimes he sits with Walter and me and tells us about himself. As a young man, he tells us, he was conscripted into the army and served in Angola. Afterwards, to earn more money than he could at home, he worked in Germany and France and then in America where he was a truck driver for seventeen years.

"I grew up near Estoi, where they have the big market every month, you know? My family have a farm there, but was a hard life, very poor."

"We were poor, too," Walter says. "My father was gone and my mother worked for the telephone company. But she didn't earn enough to support us kids and I had to help out. I caddied at the golf club on weekends. And if I carried double bags, I could earn more money than she did all week."

Mike leans closer across the table. "We were so poor, Walter, that we couldn't afford the half-penny fare to ride the bus to town. The whole family have to walk."

Our presence here does seem to give a push to progress on our house. The well-digging machinery arrives and several men assist the motorized works to make the hole by taking turns manually pushing the bore up and down. Other men set iron struts into the swimming pool excavation. August days are hot and the work proceeds with frustrating slowness but it does inch forward. We keep visiting the site as Walter quotes from management principles. "It's not what you *expect*, it's what you *inspect* that gets things done."

We get to know the chief mason at the site, Senhor Viegas, a small barrel-chested man who always wears a dark blue sailor's cap. Since everything is made of ceramic bricks or tiles that need cementing, Senhor Viegas works at all levels. Sometimes we find him on the ground stoking a small motorized cement mixer, sometimes down in the unfinished swimming pool, sometimes up on the roof. Whenever he sees us, he bobs his head, smiles, and tips his cap. Our communication is limited to such smiles and nods until the day I overhear him say a few French phrases to a fellow worker. From then on my limited French can serve to ask simple questions about day-to-day building activities and if he speaks slowly, I can understand his answers. He tells us that Portuguese children study either French or English in school for six years. During lean times, Senhor Viegas and many young men emigrated to work in France for several years. Now there is a building boom and they find work at the local construction sites.

One day, the tiles for our roof arrive at last. We've chosen traditional individually- crafted tiles, each about a foot long with a curved top and flat edges that allow for layering. These tiles are now made only by a few factories in the north of Portugal and we are thrilled to be on hand when, without advance notice, the factory truck lumbers into our rough driveway. The truckers work a mechanical lift to unload several large crates and then drive away. At that point, the age-old Portuguese system takes over. Senhor Viegas climbs a ladder to the wooden supporting roof. Another workman opens a crate with a chisel and begins flinging tiles, one by one, up to him. Senhor Viegas catches each one and stacks them into neat piles. The two men perform the unpacking, throwing, catching and stacking of each roof tile like a sturdy ballet. Their rhythmic synchronized pace can go on for hours.

The slow progress on our villa parallels my ever-so-slow progress in driving. I'm better on back roads but still terrified by the main ones. Most motorized Portuguese are first- generation drivers in love with speed. Moreover, they travel on paved roads and highways superimposed on older mule-tracks or footpaths and now carrying every form of vehicle. During a typical trip on the *Estrada Nacional 125*, the nearby coastal highway, we may see Portuguese families crowded onto wooden platforms affixed to motor cycles; German tourists flashing by in high-powered

Mercedes; red-tasseled donkeys pulling carts filled with gypsies; drunken young men racing each other on motor cycles or in dented Fiats; farm women walking at the highway's edge with baskets of produce on their heads; ancient trucks loaded with chickens or melons; huge oil vans lumbering slowly up hills and plummeting down them; and the local fish peddler who stops his rattling station wagon at each intersection and sounds his musical horn to market the day's catch.

This mismatched transport is enlivened by the European male's driving code that treats the most casual automotive errand as a combat sport. Portuguese men, genial, slow-moving and frequently late for appointments, treat cars as missiles to shoot them ahead of the pack, though they may have no place special to go. Even Walter, who drove quite sensibly in the States, here narrows his blue eyes, clenches the wheel and joins the competitive sport with macho glee. He has quickly learned to tailgate, blow his horn, and whip in and out of lanes to pass slower vehicles. As for me, though I've outgrown my imaginary reverse shifting routine, the geographic and human unpredictability of the roads makes even defensive driving feel like a suicide mission. But with Walter's departure date approaching, I keep at it.

My worries about his leaving are somewhat eased when Gunnar Nielsen is proven right and our seven missing cartons arrive at Faro airport. Once they are transported to our hotel apartment, I feel fortified for the coming weeks alone. To celebrate, Walter and I drive to Almancil where we buy a state-of-the-art IBM typewriter for me, with a keyboard that, with the flick of a switch, can be converted to any one of twenty-three languages. We set up this electronic marvel in a corner of our living room near the kitchenette with its gas stove that we must light with matches. Such discrepancies in technology remind us that Portugal is still an emerging country.

In the snack bar beside Vila Bonita's pool hangs a framed photograph of the hotel in its first days, with the main house plunked down bare and new in a field of rubble.

"How long ago was that?" Walter asks waving toward the photograph with one of the packaged ice cream cones we have extracted from the freezer. We're perched on bar stools while Mike stands behind the counter and polishes glasses.

"Five years," Mike answers.

We gaze at the single naked structure in the photograph. All the rest, the other buildings, the pool, and the profusion of flowers, trees, and shrubbery have come about in just five years. We feel better about the barren waste that surrounds our own stark villa.

Mike points across the pool to a slope on the other side. "And up there is where we'll put the next villa," he keeps wiping a glass. "But I'm not sure, I'm thinking to sell the place."

Walter and I exchange startled glances. Nothing in the cheerful bustle around us has led us to expect Mike's announcement. We're disappointed, wanting this good place to be here for a long time, not to change when we have just found it.

I look at the groups of convivial vacationers clustered at tables around the pool and the children splashing in the water. "Why do you want to sell? It's so nice and seems to be doing so well."

"Yes, is doing well, but is a lot of work all the time," Mike puts down the glass and takes a deep puff from his cigarette. "It would be different if I had sons. They could learn the business and help around the place. Then I could leave it to them. But I have only the one daughter, you know, and Bonita don't really care about it."

"She's awfully young," Walter says, "Wait and see, maybe in a few years..."

Mike is thoughtful. "This is a good time for the tourism. I think maybe is better to sell now. The prices are high; everybody look for good property."

We're all quiet for a moment. Then Mike puts out his cigarette and comes out from behind the counter with a change of mood. "I advertise and I wait and see. And if I don't get my price I don't sell. Then next year we make the new building. Come, I show you where."

We follow him out of the snack bar and up an incline toward

one side of the property where we stop by several stacks of ceramic bricks.

"You see? I'm ready to start. But I have to get a loan from the bank." Mike turns toward Walter with a grimace. "You know how that is. The bank will give you a sausage if you give them a nice fat pig."

We watch as Mike paces the outlines of the prospective added building and uses his arms to indicate the placement of guest rooms and apartments. After we admire his plans he says "I like to see your place, too. Why don't we drive over there tomorrow?" We are pleased and agree upon a time. Then Mike picks a ripe purple fig from one of his trees, splits it open to display its plump pink flesh and presents it to me with a flourish. It is luscious.

Mike's visit turns out to be uncomfortable. He walks through the partly finished house and bookshop buildings with a serious, almost pained expression. "Is large," is his only comment. Then as we get ready to leave, he points to the blue and yellow painted tiles on the risers of the two steps between the living and dining areas. "Those tiles are old fashioned now," he remarks and then apologizes, explaining that he prefers the newer factory tiles, which are plain with only an occasional mass-produced flower design.

In his pride at being modern, Mike is like many Portuguese who are emerging from an older culture. For them, modern often means factory-made products, roof tiles prefabricated in sheets, aluminum doors, and other efficient features that for us lack the charm of traditional handicrafts. We Americans used to be just the same, years ago tearing down the fine old buildings and wanting only new new new. Today we regret the loss. Now we restore, renovate, try to keep the lovely old things, even imitate them if the real ones no longer exist, like new houses built to look Victorian or simulated gas lampposts. I am sorry Mike doesn't approve of our choices, but I still love the colorful hand-painted tiles on our steps.

On our way back, he takes us up a side road to the top of a steep hill. We get out of the car and walk to the edge of a rise where we can see spread out below us the whole gorgeous panorama of the rugged Algarvian landscape at the edge of the sea. Quarteira's towers rim one side of our view, the golf courses of Vale do Lobo lie far off on the other. We are higher and more inland than Vila Bonita which we can just make out far below.

"Up 'ere is my place for dreaming," Mike says.

"Is this your land?" Walter asks

"No. But I buy it if I can. An old lady owns it but she don't want to sell. I don't blame her, but she's old and has no children." Mike flashes a conspiratorial grin. "I keep working on her. Maybe someday she sell to me...who knows?"

"Is this where you would live if you sell your hotel?" I ask as I gaze outward, almost hypnotized by the terrain.

"Up 'ere is where I would build another place. Bigger with more rooms. A real hotel with a restaurant, and over 'ere..." he guides us to a level grassy area, "I would put a terrace, with a dance floor so people could dance under the stars."

On the way back I wonder how many of us, like Mike, dream of the same things we have now, only somewhat more elegant, on a higher hill.

Early the next morning, Walter and I drive to Faro Airport. As we wait in the lounge for his plane, he puts his arm around me. "You know? I'd like fifteen more years. Building our villa here, going back to watch our kids doing well, being with you."

I know that his recent illness has made him newly aware of his mortality. "I'd like you around longer than that, " I say. "Your mother lived to be eighty-five. So I think you should ask for twenty-five more years."

Walter laughs. "Sounds good," he says as the flight is announced and I kiss him goodbye. My immediate challenge is to survive the automotive blood sport on the EN 125 and get back to the hotel. With as much confidence as I can muster, I drive out of the airport and edge into highway traffic. Portugal's record of "the highest automobile fatality rate in the world" spooks me as impatient drivers behind me blow horns, flash lights, glue their cars to my rear bumper, tear loose to pass me on hills and blind curves, and give me the cross-cultural finger as they speed by into oncoming traffic. I grip the wheel, stay on the right, keep my eyes focused on the road, and shift gears only when I must. When I finally turn into Vila Bonita's driveway I am trembling but proud. I have made it back alive, ready for six weeks on my own.

VI
Autumn at Vila Bonita

In the next weeks during Walter's absence, twice each day I leave the quiet of my terrace apartment at Vila Bonita and force myself to drive somewhere. I go to the bank and the post office in Almancil, inspect progress at our building site, meet with Joost Roemer to discuss changes and costs, and follow his directions to find stores for countless adjustments in tiles and fixtures. Twice each day I learn that the little red Citroen can alleviate boredom by transforming it into terror. Often I come home gasping, but I am mobile. I do wonder how long terror will sit beside me as I drive but I no longer worry about being stuck in a picturesque isolated Algarvian villa. I am regaining driving competence and along with it the independence I've been used to.

I miss Walter keenly, especially alone in bed at night. During daytime, though I spend many hours alone, I feel secure and cared for at Vila Bonita. I can chat with other guests at the pool if I feel lonely, and Mike and Odette are always nearby. She advises me which *supermercado* (supermarket) in nearby Quarteira has the best prices and where I can find peanut butter and chocolate chip cookies, both scarce in Portugal. And when Mike drops off my breakfast rolls he always takes an extra moment to ask, "How are you, Lady, everything all right?"

Every afternoon, I walk, exploring country roads that curve

in all directions. I walk past vacation villas with irrigated lawns and gardens into older scenery of farms and orchards with low boundary walls made of boulders and cactuses or other spiny plants. The reddish soil is dry from the summer's heat but orchard trees with wispy leaves bear olives or almonds, and occasionally I pass a fig tree or a large cork oak. I notice that no matter how small or primitive the old stone houses may be, whether neatly whitewashed or neglected, each has a television antenna perched on its tile roof. And every household has at least one dog. That explains why at night I hear dogs barking to each other in the distance. Most Portuguese love their dogs but not all are well treated. On my walks I pass a number of snarling hounds, crazed and ferocious from having been chained up their entire lives. Even friendly dogs, who are silent when cars pass, bark loudly when I walk past their domains.

Like a solitary child, I create my rituals. On back roads I notice many heaps of building rubble, each containing some pieces of the painted tiles, called *azulejos* that embellish Portuguese buildings. The beauty of this traditional art form intrigues me and I mark my days here by bringing home one tile fragment of a different design from each walk. At first this is not difficult; the profusion and variety of *azulejos* is remarkable. As weeks pass, I have to walk further afield to find new designs, but I never come home empty-handed.

My week becomes marked with the "pegs" on my calendar that I wished for. Wednesday and Saturday mornings bring the markets at Quarteira and Loulé. On Monday and Thursday afternoons, I drive to the Almancil post office to telephone Walter. This is an intricate not always successful process. Since most homes in the region do not yet have telephones, the post office's four booths are usually surrounded by a dozen people waiting to make calls. They wait their turns not in lines but in clusters. All seem to know who is next and stand beside and around that person, watching and often assisting in the business to be transacted. When that is completed, the next person is nudged forward by common consent. Overseas calls are especially precarious, with circuits often busy and connections broken off without warning. Sympathetic bystanders watching my attempts sometimes comment, "Not AT&T, is it?" I don't have the heart to tell them that AT&T, which they consider telephone heaven, is at this moment being dismantled.

Each conversation I successfully complete and pay for is a triumph. The entire procedure demands skills I still lack: confidence to seize my turn to be served, vocal power to shout my request in Portuguese for an overseas line, ability to dial at high speed and explain to foreign operators when things go wrong, presence of mind and heart when I reach Walter and my daughters to express my thoughts and feelings, and to concentrate on their words while people cluster around me. When the call is finished, I need competence to understand the clerk who states the charges, and skill to count out the proper amount in foreign bills and coins. That amount is painfully high by American standards. The post office's rate for a phone call to the States is about five times what it costs in the reverse direction. And the rates in hotels, even small ones like Vila Bonita, are double those for public or home telephones.

On Sundays, Walter telephones me. Odette finds me when the call comes through at the hotel's only phone in the reception area. With a nice sense of discretion, she retires from sight behind the beaded curtain that leads to the family's kitchen. The curtain keeps out flying insects and also serves as a visual barrier but in no way hinders transmission of sound. Throughout phone calls, I'm always aware of presences behind those strands of pink and gray plastic beads, the family finishing their mid-day meal, Odette cutting up vegetables or washing dishes, Mike having his afternoon coffee. Whoever is there and however uninterested they might be in the words I shout across the Atlantic, the lack of privacy inhibits me and makes my responses stiff and unnatural. "I love you, baby," Walter says, "It's lonely here without you."

"I agree with you," I answer primly.

"Do you miss my warm body in the bed?"

"Yes, I have noticed a difference, the nights are definitely getting cooler."

At times I am simply homesick. My homesickness isn't crippling, more like twinges when I worry that life for my children and my friends will go on and they'll forget me. At the same time though, I find this enterprise more interesting than anything I've done for years. And the loneliness is turning out to be manageable. I'm working on the first draft of my Woodstock story and each morning, while sipping my coffee on the terrace, I write in my journal.

"Life begins in the morning," Mike says one day as he stops by on his way to skim leaves from the swimming pool. "What are you writing every day out 'ere?"

"I write about what I do here, about people I meet, like Odette, and Bonita, and you, Mike."

He ponders this for a moment. "You know what I think? I think someday you write a book about the Algarve," he says dreamily. "And I have the title for you. You call it 'Daisies Fields.'"

For my journal I am here in the present as I write about this new place. But I am also *not* here when I work on my story about Woodstock. For some hours each day I am back there where I was a girl. I guess being taken out of Europe to safety in America as a child laid the groundwork for who I became, but that essentially was the continuation of my parents' story. My own story started with my love for Nicky, the young soldier who lived in Woodstock and died of cancer after the war. Now I am trying to transform my memories into a story. It all happened long ago but whenever I enter into that time, the people I knew in Woodstock are as alive as they ever were and I am there with them. The story's sad and troubling close coincided with my parents' return to Europe when I was eighteen. How odd that forty years later I am here alone, once again learning to manage independence.

As my driving gradually improves, I travel greater distances. I visit the lovely church in nearby São Lourenço with its golden altar and the interior walls covered from floor to ceiling with antique blue and white tiles depicting the stories of Portuguese saints and martyrs. I go to a concert at the São Lourenço *Centro Cultural*, an art center fashioned from adjoining old houses by a German expatriate couple. There in a lovely room hung with brilliantly colored abstract canvases and open to a courtyard bleached white by moonlight, I listen to Mozart and Hayden played by a dark-haired Portuguese pianist and his blonde English violinist wife. He is elegant in a tuxedo and she wears a lustrous red satin evening gown over slim bare feet. During intermissions, which the British call intervals, I wander through the rooms looking at the paintings. People gather in small groups according to language and carry on spirited but separate conversations in German, English, Portuguese and Dutch. I'm not brave enough to join in but enjoy wandering through the language snippets.

My shopping excursions also expand. With clenched teeth I drive for half an hour on the narrow walled road up to Loulé, the county seat, in the foothills of the Monchique Mountains. Because of its distance from the coast, Loulé has so far been spared the tourist boom and still looks like a traditional city. It has a wide tree-lined main *Avenida*, a dense grid of side streets and numerous small city squares with old stone fountains that once provided community water. City buildings are painted in pastel colors and have ornate wrought iron balconies. Loulé's central square features the city market, a pink and blue fairy-tale building with turrets and scrolled stonework and an impressive arched entrance above wide stone steps. During morning hours, farmers idle on these steps while their wives sell produce inside. On Saturdays, there are added outside stalls with regional cheeses, sausages and great gray slabs of *Bacalhão*--the dried salt cod that is a staple of many Portuguese dishes. A few blocks away, a gypsy market in a sandy field sells clothing, plastic kitchenware, tools, and pirated audiotapes.

In the last week of September, a month before the similar shift in the States, Portugal shifts to standard time, the evenings grow chilly and the Saturday night barbecues cease. The number of hotel guests declines and people no longer linger by the pool in twilight. I take my afternoon walks earlier. The sun, a fierce cauldron in August, becomes a warming pan in late September when it gets dark by 6:30. Indoors, I write letters to my daughters, listen to BBC news or music on my small short-wave radio, or to Portuguese language tapes on a cassette player. Evenings start to feel very long. They seem even longer during electric power outages, which are frequent. I may be sitting at my electric typewriter or reading by lamplight, when in an instant everything goes dark. I light a candle and step to the outside door. From my terrace I can see if all lights in Quarteira are out, or just those nearby, or perhaps only those in the hotel itself. If the latter, Mike soon appears, walking in and out of apartments and rooms to open electric boxes and adjust circuit breakers till the lights return. If it's all of Quarteira, we have to wait, sometimes for hours. On balmy evenings, we gather on Mike and Odette's terrace, to chat in darkness while looking at the stars and listening to distant barking dogs. By October, evenings gradually grow too chilly to sit outdoors. Then I read for a while by the light of several candles on my kitchen counter and hasten the close of day by going to bed early.

One evening after my supper when I feel lonely, I go down to the bar where I sometimes watch TV reruns of "Streets of San Francisco" with Odette. This time I find Mike there instead. He omits his usual friendly greeting, just nods at me and continues glumly wiping glasses. I ask if anything is wrong.

"Today is my birthday. My mother makes a cake. Odette and Bonita, they give me presents. My brother came with his family." His tone is funereal.

"That sounds nice. Happy birthday, Mike." I wait to hear more.

"Yes, was nice," he continues gloomily moving bottles and glasses. "Forty-eight years old!" he shakes his head in disbelief.

"Do you feel old?"

"Sometime I feel like eighteen, but I had a friend from the old days in Estoi. He dropped dead a few months ago. Same age as me."

To cheer him up I decide to tease him. "Oh Mike, I sometimes think if you were just a little older, you'd be an attractive man."

He is flustered. "Hah, that's a good one! A little *older*. I don't know if that's a compliment or not." He shakes his head and suddenly seems the genial Mike we all depend on. "I *would* be attractive..." he wonders, "How old would I have to be?"

"At least over fifty."

"Well, I'm sorry, Marianne, but I don't want to be over fifty." We both laugh.

"Oh, it's really not so bad, Mike, life goes on pretty much the same."

Mike keeps wiping glasses but no longer seems quite as glum. A bit later he thinks aloud, "You know, I don't really feel so old myself, but I like the old ways, the way things were when I was young. My wife says I live in the past, and maybe I do, but it's because I have such good memories of the past."

I understand Mike's yearning for the past, his own and the Algarve's. Everywhere, I see signs of change in the midst of age-old traditions. On the beaches, dignified Algarvian matrons, dressed head to foot in black and carrying black umbrellas to ward off the sun's rays, walk past girls, topless or in bikinis under the same sun, stretched out in rows on the sand like glistening young sardines. In the nearby harbors of Quarteira and Albufeira, small fishing fleets ply their ancient trade in deep-bottomed boats with pointed prows, brightly painted hulls of red, blue, and green, their decks littered with worn tackle and nets. Between these two expanding old towns rises the planned resort city of Vilamoura with a huge marina of gleaming pleasure yachts whose occupants come ashore to gamble in the new casino. And vacationers who shop, sun themselves, sail, dine and get drunk in all the recently overbuilt towns strung along the Algarvian coast are served by hundreds of young Portuguese men and women who have been drawn from rocky inland subsistence farms to the tourist gold-mountain by the sea.

Those young workers leave behind older relatives who cling to traditional ways, but even they are changed. On one of my walks, I pass by a field where an elderly man tilling the soil looks like that Millet painting, "Man With a Hoe." The timeless beauty of the scene enchants me. Except, I notice he is listening to pop tunes from a transistor radio he has set on a box under a nearby tree.

When we visitors look at all this we often regret destruction of the centuries-old culture we find so picturesque. But that old man in the field may feel differently. I remember Chekhov's portrayal of the unrelieved, unending boredom and isolation of rural life as it used to be. I know that I love my short-wave radio with its crackling "BBC World Service" that I hunch over each evening, feeling like a spy out of a World War II movie. I even appreciate my two-cylinder red Citroen that gets me out and about, even though my stick-shift clumsiness still makes many a trip an experiment in terror. Walking is safer and better exercise but I don't get as far. Neither did the Portuguese farmers; it's understandable now that, as soon as they can afford them, they buy motorcycles. And even Mike, though he longs for the vanishing open landscape, would not want to relive the poverty of his boyhood. Instead, he gains his income from summer tourists.

Mike is not the only one at Vila Bonita who thinks about the past. Many times I think about my mother. Every now and then I have a pang when I see her name on her stationery I use for writing drafts, and when I realize that she will never see the villa we are building on her land here. Such moments bring pain and sadness. And above all, regret that it couldn't have been better between us.

My mother was my advocate and my ally. She took charge of me when I was a child and continued to care about me long after my father's interest had shifted to his son from a late second marriage. I called her "Elke" as she wished, though I never entirely dropped the "Mom." For me, she remained my mother, especially as I never felt the easy camaraderie of friendship. But I was always aware of how much I owed her. Elke--my mother—saved my life.

When I fled without money or prospects from my children's alcoholic father in 1964, she came to my rescue. My father had just had a huge theatrical and financial success with his German translation of *My Fair Lady*. Thanks to Elke, they together supported me and my three little girls for four years. After I finished college with their help, fellowships helped me through graduate school, and the PhD I earned brought me good jobs so that I was able to build a new life and support my daughters until they were grown. I was always grateful to both my parents, but especially to my mother. It was my father's money, but my support was due to her.

Sadly, during our annual visits back and forth I felt stifled by her vehement opinions. It was always a relief when the time came to say goodbye...except here, last year when we took her to the airport and she could hardly walk. When I asked her why she kept resisting a wheelchair, she leaned closer and whispered, "Because I don't want you to see me in it." Then I was pierced with pity for her and shame at my cold heart. She got her way and I never saw her in a wheelchair. Did she suspect that it might be my last glimpse of her? I'll never know. But now tears sting as I think of that parting.

Work on our villa continues. The roof is fully tiled and I'm excited to see the completed exterior of both villa and shop, still raw but definitely in place. The ground water for the well finally comes in at ninety meters down. Now Senhor Viegas works busily down in the pool applying its second layer of cement in preparation for filling. I begin to enjoy going to the site. For such a long time it always seemed as though somewhere along the way we could say, "Let's forget it; it's too fanciful an idea." Now our minds and imaginations have caused results "out there" in the world and those results will generate further changes both mental and actual. The difference between dreaming and doing lies in the execution of a hundred small steps

One Sunday, I go to the reception area to wait for Walter's

weekly phone call. Odette is at the desk doing the weekly hotel accounts.

"It's a lot of work running a place like this," I observe.

"Lotta work," she agrees, "But finally it begin to pay. Now people know about us and come back every year, and they tell their friends."

"You make everybody feel welcome, almost like a big family."

"That's what we want. And we get to know what happen to them every year, a new job, a new baby...sometimes they get sick and can't come that year. Or they go some place else for a change, and then come back and tell us all about it. Is nice to know the people, but is lotta work."

"Mike says you're thinking of selling."

Odette stacks some papers and then looks up at me with a weary smile. "Partly Mike want to sell, part want to make the place bigger. He think of selling every year when we get to the end of summer. Every year we get tired and say we can't do it no more, take care of all the people seven days every week all these months. But then in winter we say it's too quiet and when spring come, we get happy to start again."

I can well understand their fatigue after months of keeping the place running smoothly and being constantly cheerful and pleasant to one and all. Just as the Moreiras look forward to quieter days, my thoughts turn to my children and our friends in Saratoga and I am eager for Walter's return. As Odette resumes her paperwork, I wait for the phone to ring and gaze out of the window. The nine banners of visiting nations are a bit faded now from months in the summer sun.

On October 11th I pick Walter up at Faro airport. We load his bags into the car and then, with some pride, I whip smoothly around the airport's ramps and out onto the 125. Walter whoops with surprise. His last image has been of me timid and tearful behind the wheel and my new competence amazes him and pleases us both. "Look at this!" he keeps saying with each new maneuver I make, " I can't believe it." Then he says proudly, "My Babe!" and pats my knee, momentarily threatening my new equilibrium.

We drive first to our property. We now have a villa and a shop, each with a roof, doors and windows. We also have a covered arcade connecting the two buildings, terracing around them, and a pool. I have been intent on watching each step of these developments, but as I walk around with Walter I see through his eyes. A great deal is still undone. We pick our way gingerly through the interior spaces. The cement under-flooring is untiled and littered with boards and piping not yet connected to water. Walls are an unfinished gray stucco; there are no interior doors. Here and there a cluster of wires protrudes from walls and ceilings; none have been hooked up to electricity. We walk out to look down at the pool which is completed but filled with black water and construction debris. To complete the picture, the entire complex stands in the center of a moonscape of mounds, pits, and rubble.

"They'll never get this finished by the end of October." Walter says and I have to agree. No way can this project meet the promised completion date. Subdued, we return to Vila Bonita to find on our table a vase of spectacular pink roses that Mike has picked from his garden to welcome Walter. Over coffee we cheer up, decide to hurry things along as best we can in the three remaining weeks of our stay and then put everything on hold till we come back early next year.

All is quiet now at Vila Bonita; we are the only remaining guests. The snack bar is closed and the pool untended; bougainvillea petals float like bits of tissue paper on water become murky green. Walter and I spend hours each day tending to "last things." We visit local, county and regional offices to obtain necessary permissions and licenses. We meet once more with Joost Roemer to discuss fixtures and to make the fifth villa payment of ten percent, leaving only a final five percent still to pay upon completion.

On a gloriously sunny morning, I drive Walter to his last golf game of the season at the posh club in Quinta do Lago, another nearby resort. On our way there, a truck lumbers by in the other direction. In the open back, standing tightly packed against the truck's high sides, are about a hundred black men, construction laborers from Africa. I remember the hundreds like them we saw at Lisbon airport on our first landing in Portugal. I have also learned, from reading I've been doing, that fourteenth century Portugal was one of the first countries whose explorers captured black Africans and sold them in Europe, starting four hundred shameful years of the international African slave trade.

The men we now see are not slaves; they have come to work in the Algarve's construction boom and to send money home to their families. Mike has told us they come each summer, and go back to their own countries during winter rainy seasons. But their transport disturbs us. Those at the edges steady themselves by holding on to the wooden slats of the truck's sides and back; those in the center are jammed together so tightly they can't fall. We are still sobered by this glimpse of their working conditions when we turn into the manicured driveway of the country club. A few minutes later we watch foursomes of jovial golfers rolling by in their cushy golf carts.

In the afternoon, we pay a last visit to our house, which is humming along like a little factory with work proceeding in every room. Two men are installing roller-blinds on the windows, a man and a woman attach kitchen cabinets to the walls, a master painter and two assistants are staining wooden closet doors and, ever at his post, Senhor Viegas stirs cement in the small mixer. Everything is proceeding apace and we almost hate to leave.

As we have done toward the close of every stay in the Algarve, we go for a farewell walk along the Vale do Lobo beach. We see a few isolated sunbathers and several walkers like ourselves, but the chaises and beach umbrellas have been put away and beach restaurants and bars are shuttered. Clearly, the season is over. And so is our long stay at Vila Bonita. Our days as hotel guests have been a carefree time despite all the frustrations at the slow progress of building and the glacial pace of government agencies. Whatever obstacles we faced during the day, we could come back in the evening to friendly people in a pleasant place. On our last evening, we invite the Moreira family out for dinner at a nearby restaurant where Walter expresses our thanks.

"We would have had a hard time without you," he says. "Especially Marianne would have been very lonely here alone. You've made our stay a real pleasure."

We all hug and promise to keep in touch. Early the next morning we fly home for the Christmas season with our own family.

VII

Moving In

It's January, we're back at Vila Bonita and I'm huddled next to an electric oil heater (the kind that looks like an old-fashioned radiator on wheels), waiting for heat to reach my fingers and toes. I don't understand how it can be so pleasant outside and so frigid inside. Perhaps the cold is caused by these stone walls that radiate dampness like a mist. It makes me wonder how we'll manage in our own unheated house between now and springtime.

Outside the contrast is amazing. White roses bloom beside our door; red bougainvillea, geraniums and calla lilies fill Mike's garden. Little yellow flowers dot the roadsides. Woods and fields, which were brown and sandy in summer, are now green. In January this is confusing. The green and blossoming landscape makes us think about our bare plot of ground and we remember Mike's saying, "a Portuguese house without flowers is like a woman without a smile."

From the beginning, when our villa was still just a big hole in the sand and we imagined its white stucco walls, filigreed Algarvian chimney, and terra cotta roof, our picture always included blossoming hedges, exotic trees, and tropical flowers. "Our home will smile with a thousand flowers; we will make the desert bloom," we promised ourselves, having little idea of what that process would entail.

Now it's time to find out. We ask Mike if he knows any landscapers. He mentions two who work nearby and we invite them to our property. The first to come is a burly Portuguese gentleman who represents a prosperous firm that specializes in hotel and golf resort plantings. Severe and unbending, he is trailed by his assistant, a pretty young woman who carries a sketchpad and does the actual design. Walter and I follow them as they march back and forth.

"We won't need any work done on the back hillside," I explain, "We like the natural pine trees and wild shrubs."

The landscaper keeps walking, murmuring to the assistant who takes notes. We file across the front half of the property with its craters and rubble piles. Here and there stands a young umbrella pine or a lichen-coated fig tree, which I see as precious tokens of a greener future. The construction workers are far less sentimental. They heap building debris at the base of our puny trees and fling jackets over their branches when the sun grows hot. To them, one small pine more or less makes no difference.

"I hope your plan will keep these young trees," I say, "and add some other plantings, the bushes and flowers that grow in this region."

"Maybe a bit of grass," Walter adds, "but not a big lawn. And I like the succulents they use for borders here."

We continue describing our hopes as the gentleman and his assistant pace on, intent on their own impressions. "We'd like to keep most of it as natural as possible," we say several times and they nod politely. When they have seen enough, they promise us a garden plan and speed away in their black sedan.

The second landscaper arrives a few days later in a battered green van. She is Gillian Field, an affable English lady who has migrated from the Canary Islands. Her smile is pleasant and her hair floats in blonde tendrils like a halo above her roly-poly frame. I judge her to be about forty years old. After she greets us warmly, Walter and I accompany her she trudges up and down the rocky hillocks. We repeat our mantra, "We'd like to make the garden as natural as possible."

"Right," she nods, her round blue eyes alert and eager as she surveys the barren terrain. "Did you know that the front part of your land was once a riverbed?" She notes our surprise, then gestures to indicate the front half of our property. "Yes, all along this line where the land is flat. In heavy winter rains the riverbed flooded and the water would rush down across this area."

Walter looks toward the thick tangle of winter daisies that cover the neighboring field. "Does that still happen?"

"Oh, not for years. As you see, these are all fields now, no sign of any river. But there was one once." A breeze ruffles her light hair as Gillian turns to consider our own denuded ground. "A mimosa here would grow quickly and shield you from the road." She moves on toward the house. "Two palm trees would be a nice feature here against these archways. Some bougainvillea here, trailing over that wall." She curves her arms and flutters her fingers, making us see flowering vines adorning our bare buildings.

I am charmed. "Could you make a sketch for us?"

"Of course," says Gillian and waves a graceful good-bye from her van as she rattles away.

Within a week, the golf resort firm delivers a design in a handsome leather portfolio. A neat pastel painting shows our house standing primly in the middle of a large green expanse. A military row of trees and shrubs parade along each boundary.

"I could hit golf balls on that lawn," Walter says, "but it's an awful lot of grass to mow."

"And grass isn't natural here," I add, forgetting that perfect green lawns aren't natural anywhere.

The golf course design isn't quite what we've hoped for. Still enticed by Gillian Field's lovely descriptions of trees and flowers, we wait for her version of our future garden.

"Do you think it would be wrong to use an English landscaper instead of a Portuguese one?" I ask Walter." Maybe we're just drawn to Gillian because she seems more like us."

"I think we should use whichever design we like better.

Besides, how much like us is an English woman from the Canary Islands?"

One afternoon we are in Faro shopping for a teakettle in an appliance shop and I spot a large square box with the words "*Cobertor Electrico*" (electric blanket).

"Walter, Look at this!" I grip his arm, excited at the prospect of keeping warm inside our Vila Bonita apartment. Walter agrees that we should buy it, knowing this will not be an easy enterprise since the Moreiras watch electric current usage with razor-sharp attention. We hide the blanket in our car till dark and then smuggle it into our temporary home. When we take the blanket out of its box, we see that it has some odd features. Though sized for a double bed, it has a single control panel connected to one corner by a short electric cord. I plug the cord's end into the socket near the foot of our bed, and set the dial to high to give the blanket time to warm the sheets before we get into bed. When we do, we are happy.

"Doesn't this feel wonderful?" I sigh with contentment.

"Yes, much better." Walter agrees, but in a little while, he starts pushing covers down. "It's getting awfully hot. Can we turn this thing down?"

Yes we can adjust the temperature, I discover, but not easily since the control panel is on the floor beyond the foot of the bed. I step out onto the icy tiles, turn the dial down, dart back under the covers and we turn out the lights to sleep. An hour later, I have also warmed up and must step out again. This time I disconnect the blanket.

The next night we decide to try plugging it in near the headboard with the control easily near my hand. This time, when Walter starts tugging the blanket down, I gag and flail.

"What's the matter?" he mutters.

"I'm strangling." The blanket's short cord is now across my neck. I pull the blanket away from Walter's side and we settle down again. Later in the night, I wake up in a sweat, feeling like an egg being poached and I am pinned down by the cord. Fortunately, I can reach over and pull out the plug. From then on, we use our precious blanket mainly to pre-heat the bed before we get into it. Every morning, we bundle it into a suitcase and hide it in a closet to avoid its possible confiscation. Getting into a warmed bed is worth the trouble, and we are ever so grateful to exchange icy clammy sheets for ones still clammy but warm.

We have signed on for Portuguese lessons. Like the ad for foreign language tapes for "people who smile a lot," smiling is all we can do so far which makes us feel pretty stupid. So we have arranged for ten lessons with an elderly Portuguese man who lives in the neighboring hamlet of Vale D'Eguas. A lady I met at a concert at the *Centro Cultural* recommended him. Following her directions we drive up a hilly road with a mule track in the middle till we reach the crumbling house of our new teacher, Fernão de Melo.

"*Bom dia*, Walter. *Bom dia*, Marianne," he welcomes us and ushers us past a cluttered living room into his kitchen because, like most of these old stone houses (as we have come to learn), this one is very cold. The three of us cluster at one end of the kitchen table near a gas heater; the table's other end holds a jumble of old wine and brandy bottles. Fernão wears a tattered brown sweater. His thinning brown hair is long but combed back neatly. An ancient foulard around his neck makes him look like an old roué gone to seed. He has a large bulbous nose and I try not to focus on a mole at its tip, because he regards both of us with delight as he begins our lesson. First he helps us to pronounce his name correctly, a lingual adjustment for us that takes half a lesson in itself. (Not Fernand *à la* the French mode, but Fernãoun with sort of a nasalized yelp at the end.) When we have mastered that, we learn that today is *Terca Feira* (Tuesday) and we move on through the other days of the week. Fernão then directs us to buy an instruction book, a notebook and some blank audiotapes, and gives us a homework assignment for next time. Throughout the hour, he smokes many cigarettes and coughs alarmingly but he seems kind and eager to make us comfortable.

"A brandy, Walter? Marianne?" he points to a bottle at the table's corner nearest him. It is eleven in the morning, and we refuse with thanks. Fernão looks a bit disappointed but maintains his good humor as he tells us that he is married to Daphne, an Englishwoman who teaches at Faro University and turns out to be the lady who recommended him to me. They have two teen-aged children, a boy and a girl, and all four members of the family live in this tiny cluttered house.

As we take our leave we enjoy the prospect of knowing some simple phrases when we meet Portuguese people who live and work here. Fernão escorts us to the door. "In ten lessons, I can teach you what you need to get along. Then if you think you need more, I can give you another ten. But after twenty," he says, "You're on your own."

No word from Gillian Field for some weeks. Walter and I are back in the swing of nudging things along with the builders—a bit here, a bit there each day and always a little more money for this, an extra payment for that. Our main problem seems to be drainage. Each rainfall floods the septic system and we haven't even flushed a toilet yet. During heavy rains, water flows across our scarred landscape and has made deep gullies especially in front of the shop building. When Joost Roemer comes to inspect, we pick our way across the muddy terrain. With some suspicion, we convey Gillian's information.

"We've heard there used to be a river here."

"No, really? I never knew that," Joost raises his eyebrows in mild surprise at this bit of local geography.

"Seems like that might have been important," Walter remarks with heavy sarcasm.

Joost nods unperturbed. "Well, we will have to lay down some drainage pipes to redirect the water." Joost points along the path of the long ago river. "Then it will flow below the ground instead of on top." We agree, knowing that the pipes are needed, knowing also that the "redirection" will cost more money. We really are two innocents abroad!

Despite the outside debris, the house itself looks good and we are eager to move in. Though Mike and Odette have been very kind to let us rent our summer apartment in winter when they usually keep the hotel closed, we long to settle into our new home. It won't be long now; we expect Elke's furniture to be delivered from storage in Zurich in about a week.

On January 25th we are in our own villa at last. The movers come in the morning and we spend the afternoon moving furniture around till things seem pretty much in place, except for the cardboard cartons, which will take time to unpack. The furniture from Elke's apartment brings memories of her. Mostly, I'm happy at how nice everything looks in these new surroundings. I think she might be pleased that her things have come here to Portugal where her investment has now become a lovely new home.

I do feel an unexpected pang when I see the oval umbrella stand with two of Elke's umbrellas still in it and her black cane with the silver handle she didn't like because it wasn't real silver. So small a cane and she fought against it for so long. Her doctor advised her to buy it, but the only time I ever saw her actually use it was here in Portugal. Even then she wasn't sure how to walk with it or which side it went on and, still hating it, she frequently hooked it over her arm like an umbrella, or handed it to me when she carried her purse. Seeing that cane again brings back our last week with her here at the Dona Filipa, and the sudden sharp awareness that she is gone.

We are a bit disconcerted that houses here come equipped with so little. We've known about the outside: no plantings, no driveway, no fences, just bare lumpy ground left by the bulldozer. But the inside brings surprises. During the building process, we paid extra to have kitchen cabinets, an oven, stove and sink installed, and we knew that we must buy a refrigerator and other appliances. But now we see no electric fixtures of any kind except bare light bulbs dangling on single wires from the bedroom and living room ceilings. And the bathrooms are a surprise.

"Hey, Hon?" Walter calls, "There's no mirror in here. Shaving is going to be interesting." He emerges and we walk around to assess the situation.

"No mirrors or medicine cabinets in any of the bathrooms," Walter notes.

"No towel racks, no shelves for even a toothbrush," I add to the list. And a while later, "Not even a roller for toilet paper."

Lots more work to do while we camp out inside, but we love it. Are we crazy?

I continue unpacking. So far I have found thirty-six glasses for champagne among Elke's belongings but none for water or juice. Nor have we found her tool kit, a plastic box I remember containing delicate screw drivers, dainty pliers, and a tiny hammer and saw, everything miniature but functional and we could use some of those tools now. But the box might be in any one of forty-seven household cartons left to unpack (not to mention fifty-six more of books and papers which are stored next door in the bookshop building). My energy fades at the thought of opening them all to find it, but I tackle one more before the day ends.

Though it is winter, a young Portuguese man comes every now and then and stares into our swimming pool. The water is black with sand and silt from autumn winds and rains and clogged with debris left by our construction crew. After several such silent visits, one day he knocks on our door. He is quite handsome with typical Portuguese coloring of dark brown hair and eyes, but taller than men of older generations, and unlike them, his smile shows white even teeth with none missing.

"Pool very bad," he says. "You need pool man. I am Louis. I clean, take care many pools. We make contract, yes?"

Walter and I stare at Louis, speechless for a few moments while we mentally review our situation. February has continued rainy and cold and we're working hard to settle into our new house. Our long-time dream of a sunny retirement seems to be snagged on a tangle of thorny details. Our lovely white villa with its picturesque red tile roof holds the penetrating cold of a medieval dungeon. We have inadequate heat, no hot water, precarious electric power, and our property is a moonscape of sand and construction rubble. In sum, we are not prepared even to think about the pool.

"Come back in April," we tell Louis.

We look forward to the day we have a working telephone. Three separate phone company teams are responsible for installation. Team number one puts up the pole and runs a wire to the house. Team number two brings the telephone and hooks it to the wire. Team number three makes the connection to the switching station that gives life to the inanimate instrument. We have had teams one and two who left a bright red new instrument in our care, but we have yet to be blessed by team three.

A similar pattern governs the acquisition of water. First one group digs a well, then another group connects the pump to the well so that it can fill the *cisterna* (cistern). A third contingent brings the water into the house. So far we have reached the cold-water stage. A plumber has come to install the water heater, but someone else will have to come to hook it up so that we actually get hot water.

Indoctrinated now to think of progress in stages, Walter and I have decided that we need three stages of domestic service (necessities, that is, not luxuries like a telephone). They are, in order, heat, light, and hot water. At present none of the three is adequate. We have three electric oil heaters, one each in our bedroom, bathroom, and kitchen, making these the only spaces one can bear to be in unless one is doing gymnastics. All the other rooms are frigid. Our terra cotta tile floors are attractive but so cold that even with two pairs of socks and Reeboks I feel the chill creep upwards toward my knees. My nose runs all the time and I wear as many layers of clothing as I can assemble and with all that I can only stay inside if I move about. I now understand why Algarvian women look so square and muffled up: they are wearing everything they own.

"Do you remember the time when Joost talked us out of

central heating?" I ask as Walter and I huddle at the dining room table for the quickest lunch we can eat before dashing back to the bedroom for our midday siesta when we read in bed under our electric blanket.

"I do. He said we wouldn't need it because of the Algarve's short mild winters." Walter has looped a woolen scarf around his neck.

"Well, now we know better. Does this feel short and mild to you?"

"It is a little nippy," concedes the master of understatement.

I'm having a little trouble managing to eat while wearing gloves. "He talked us out of central heating because they don't know how to install it," I snap. "It reminds me of the Greek myth of Tithonus."

"And what is that?" Walter always enjoys a good story.

"Tithonus asked the gods for eternal life but never thought to specify eternal youth. He got his wish, but grew ever older and became a dried-out cricket chirping on a hearth."

"Well, you look like a cute cricket, not dried-up just yet." Walter tries to jolly me along.

"Thanks, but that's not the point. I wanted a short mild winter without Saratoga's long freeze. It never occurred to me to make sure about being warm inside." I gain control of my utensils and conclude that there's too much leeway in the world of wishes. One has to dream in specifics.

In the evening, as we huddle in bed reading, I wish aloud specifically. "I'd love some milk and cookies."

"That would be nice. Why don't you get us some?"

"I thought you might do that."

"It's too cold out there. Anyway, you suggested it." We read a while longer but the seed has been planted. Walter slides out of bed and picks a coin from the dresser. "Let's flip for it. Heads you go for cookies, tails I go." I win. He puts his slippers on over his socks and a sweatshirt over his flannel nightshirt that is over his T-shirt, and heads for the icy kitchen.

We are having the heaviest spring rainfall in Algarve history.

The *Algarve News* tells of roofs caved in, roads flooded, houses and shops awash. We long for sunshine but spring is slow to arrive. So are most other things. Progress on our house and grounds is at a standstill. No workmen show up because of the rain and we keep hearing the "next week" promises we no longer believe. Everyone says that to live in Portugal you need to be patient, which is an understatement. Actually, you need to be comatose.

We finally receive a sketch from Gillian Field showing our future garden and we are charmed by it, as we are by Gillian herself. Flowering shrubs and plantings in front of the shop and beside the house. Bougainvillea vines on the pillars in front of both buildings. A rock garden of succulents around the pool. A modest lawn curving from our bedroom side of the house around to the back with a slate path leading to the woods on the hillside. Lantana hedges along the planned boundary fence. Two palm trees to accent the house's front entrance. The existing umbrella pines will shade the shop from fierce afternoon sun. The drawing seems like a promise of our dream fulfilled. We ask few questions of Gillian, and sign the agreement with the understanding that she will begin planting as soon as the rains cease.

Our three heaters have two power settings each, 750 and 1250 amps, totaling 2000 amps per heater when both settings are used. But if we try these combined higher settings, all three heaters go out, as well as the house lights, the oven, the new refrigerator and the electric water pump. Then Walter must go outside to trip the main switch in the muddy little shed that houses our temporary electrical connection. Coming back in, he must either remove his shoes which have collected half an inch of orange mud, or track it across those attractive tile floors. We hope that someday soon our temporary one-wire power supply hooked to the construction shed will be converted to three permanent wires within the house. Earlier today, deluded by that hope, we pictured the villa adorned by soft outside lighting and bought a dozen decorative fixtures for light points in the outside walls where there are holes with bare waiting wires. But tonight, as I am cooking, the power goes out and everything is pitch dark. We're experienced by now and I light two candles ready on the kitchen counter. Walter pulls on his rubber boots, grabs a flashlight and gropes his way out to the shed, while I carry a candle over to a heater and lower the setting. Soon the power goes back on. Walter comes back, pulls off the muddy boots by the kitchen door, and I reach into the electric oven to stir the stew I'm trying to heat. A few minutes later, the power goes off again.

"What the hell…" even Walter's patience is fraying.

"I'll turn off the oven and heat this on top of the stove." For the first time I understand why our builders advised an electric oven and a gas-fired stovetop. Electricity is erratic while butane gas, though it makes me nervous, is dependable. I relight the candles, turn off the oven and place the stew over one of the gas burners, which I light with a match. Walter pulls on his boots again and opens the door. By this time it's raining. He takes his windbreaker from a hook, holds it over his head, and plunges back into the darkness. The power goes on, Walter returns, takes off the boots and drops the sodden windbreaker in a corner. With the rain, the orange mud has made splatters on the legs of his chino pants. His hair is standing up in damp white spikes.

I hurry to finish cooking and in a short while, we sit down to eat.

"How we could even think of adding outside lighting to this?" I wonder.

He munches silently for a few moments, then waves his fork at me. "I have an idea. We could sell the place."

"Oh sure, to people who want to be surrounded by mud and live in the dark." We continue eating while the warm meal and continued light gradually calm us.

"OK. This is just temporary." Walter is restored to good humor. "When the full power is hooked up this won't happen anymore. We'll get our outside lighting yet. And this stew is delicious. Is there any more?"

Combating the constant winter chill in our house is tiring

and we seek warmth elsewhere. Almost all local restaurants are warmed by large gas-fired space heaters. Unlike in the United States, restaurant meals here cost only a little more than preparing food at home, and we begin to eat dinner out regularly. On a side road just a short distance from our villa we find a small restaurant named *Pituxia*, its entrance adorned with a string of Christmas lights. The simple dining room is inviting with rustic furniture and white tablecloths and, best of all, two heaters keep it pleasantly warm. A heavy curtain inside the front door helps to keep the heat inside. In addition to convenience and comfort, we are happy to find that the food is good. *Pituxia* becomes a welcome respite for two or three evenings a week or on some weekends for our midday meal.

One afternoon, when we have finished our lunch, we leave *Pituxia* and stroll further along the side road before returning home. We walk up a hill and just past the top we see an empty house on the right. It is a solid structure but clearly deserted, with only bare rectangles where there had been windows and doors. The once white stucco walls have turned black from years of neglected mold and mildew.

"Let's see what it looks like inside," I say. We pick our way along the weed-filled driveway and clamber up stone steps to enter the house. The tile roof appears undamaged, but the rooms are bare of all woodwork and fixtures. It is a skeleton of a house.

"It's been pretty thoroughly stripped," Walter says. "Open like this, anyone could just come in and take what they wanted."

"What would make people simply leave a place like this and let it get ruined?"

"I guess we can't really know that." Walter says as we walk out to the road and turn back for a last look. "It looks well built; you'd think they could have sold it."

"It looks ominous, black like that. Maybe somebody got sick…or died."

"Or it got caught up in a family quarrel over an estate. We'll never know."

We walk a while further and are pleased to see that other

houses along the road are well maintained with pleasant gardens. The blackened house is an anomaly; we can't know its story but we don't forget it.

We pass two weeks waiting without results for plumbers, electricians and carpenters to come to fix or install things. Finally we declare our independence, buy an electric drill and wield it for many days, putting up towel racks and curtain rods, even a medicine cabinet. We look up words for things we need and write them down or bring samples. When I walk into the hardware store with a sample molly bolt in my hand, I'm amused to learn that some connotations may be international. The owner generates quite a few snickers among his customers when he shouts to a clerk at the back of the store, *"A Senhora queri um parafugo"* (The lady wants a screw). Actually, I want a dozen.

Once a week or so, Louis, our hopeful pool man, leaves his battered blue Fiat beside the road and walks past the house to the edge of the pool. As he stands there looking down at the murky water, he is a slim dark reminder of all we still have to do before we can even think of swimming. This morning, Walter has gone to the fish market for our dinner, the hardware store for some picture hooks, the post office for our mail, and the newspaper store for his *Herald Tribune*. Meanwhile I keep on with the unpacking. When Walter returns and settles down to read at the dining room table, I cut open another of the seemingly endless cartons. In among great waddings of paper are dishes. So that I don't step on them by mistake, I start to stack the dishes on the only clear surface left, the table where Walter is doing his crossword. The next box I open contains more dishes. Soon I'm competing for space with the newspaper.

"Could you move?" I'm holding a stack of plates.

"Sure," he helpfully folds his paper into a smaller square. "What's an eight letter word for an eastern operatic princess?"

I'm annoyed that he can't see my problem. After squeezing two more stacks onto the table I insist. "I really need you to move."

"What? Right now?" He finally looks up and sees that he is surrounded by dishes. "Can't you find another place to put these?"

I point to the kitchen counter, which is already loaded with bowls and jars. Walter moves over to an easy chair. We maintain a chilly silence for a while.

Then he puts his puzzle aside and watches me as I kneel on the floor furiously straightening the packing papers. "You know, we don't have to do everything all at once," he says. " Why don't we take some time out?"

By mutual consent we drive to the beach. We take off our sneakers and amble along the water's edge dodging waves and picking up seashells.

"This is how it was before we moved here," Walter puts a perfect scallop shell into my hand.

"We were on vacation then, but it's good to remember." We walk on a ways. The beach in February is nearly deserted with only one or two people silhouetted in the distance. The sky roils with gray clouds shot through with silver. The huge quiet makes our squabbles seem petty and we shift our focus away from tasks yet to be done to congratulating ourselves on all we have so far accomplished. The house isn't decorated yet, but it looks a lot better than a month ago. When we leave the beach, we feel restored.

"Turandot," I say.

"What?"

"An eight-letter eastern operatic princess."

VIII
The Thaw

Suddenly, all across green meadows and hills, the almond trees are in bloom; old gnarled trees bear pink-white blossoms that float like lace across the landscape. A legend often told here says that long ago, when the Moors occupied Portugal, a princess from northern Europe came to the Algarve as the bride of a Moorish prince. As the months passed, she grew ever more homesick for the changing seasons of the northern lands of her girlhood. The prince, who loved her ardently, ordered almond trees planted on the hillsides. The following February, the princess looked out from her castle window and saw white blossoms covering the landscape like a mantle of snow. From then on, her homesickness ceased.

Maybe the almond blossom cure will also work for us. We too miss our faraway northern land. No doubt we could have continued living in Saratoga quite pleasantly without upheavals, yet we chose to make this complex and far-reaching shift for reasons we now find hard to explain to others or to fully understand ourselves. When we first faced our bare plot of land in the Algarve, we felt that we could cultivate it, make a new home, perhaps even a new life. Many others have come from afar with dreams of their own. Everywhere we go, we hear their stories. The two young Englishwomen from London who own the nearby Bistro sought greater opportunity here. The man who owns the launderette in Quarteira came from

Australia to start his own business. The German couple bought an old farm in São Lourenço and converted it into the *Centro Cultural* for art and music. Despite our discomforts while settling in, we are energized by their example.

February is *Carnaval* time in Portugal. We're told that nobody works from Saturday through Ash Wednesday. There are parades and festivals, people drink a lot, eat special treats and hold dances in the streets. After all that, everyone needs to rest up on Thursday, and nobody starts a work week on Friday, so we don't expect to see any diggers, plumbers, or electricians during *Carnaval*. We decide to do as the Romans do, and drive to the parade in Loulé. We mingle with the festive crowds on the main A*venida* and enjoy the spectacle. Floats pass by carrying beautiful girls who throw confetti and candy to the spectators. Walter makes sure to catch one candy for me and then another one for himself. Marching bands play popular tunes. Street corner stands sell sticky sweet deep-fried cakes. Brightly colored streamers hang from the trees, and excited children run about dressed in costumes like American children at Halloween.

Our Portuguese lessons continue three mornings a week with Fernão who repeats his offers to warm us with wine or brandy from the jugs in his picturesque and crumbling kitchen. We always decline to his disappointment, but Fernão is a good teacher. Our progress is slow, but we understand a bit more as time goes by. I have some advantage over Walter since he knows only English whereas I have German and rudimentary French as well. I find many similarities to French, at least in the written languages. Speaking Portuguese, however, feels like carrying on a conversation with a mouth full of porridge. Everything, regardless of spelling, seems pronounced sh, j, or zh. The word for the beautiful blue and white decorative tiles seen everywhere in Portugal is *azulejos*-- with "z" and "j" spoken like "sh" with a hum, and the final "s" spoken like a "sh" without a hum--for us a one-word emblem of our tongue-tying difficulties. But we are learning basic phrases for greeting people and purchasing goods, which help to make us feel more confident. We can communicate, at least at a "me Tarzan, you Jane" level. We find nouns and names for things in our English/Portuguese dictionary. Verbs still give us trouble so we avoid them. This gives our talk when shopping an infantile tinge. "Hello." Big smile to signal good intentions. "Sweater, please. Red, please. More big. How much cost? More others? This one. Thank you. Good bye." Not too smooth, but a lot of progress since the time when all we knew was hello and thank you.

Our little red two-cylinder Citroen is also doing well, though it does lose power on highway hills where everyone passes us. We've named it "John Henry" because it chugs bravely in all kinds of weather through rutted dirt roads using very little gas, and only protests by dropping the rearview mirror into the driver's lap every few days. We stick it back onto the windshield with duct tape which holds till we get more of the dealer's super glue.

Now that the house is pretty well furnished, I'm starting to work on the bookshop. Design and layout come first, uncharted territory for me but one I must penetrate. Before we came here to live, I saw an ad for a British book-shelving company and wrote to request design ideas and a layout plan, a service they advertise. My letter included photographs, a floor plan of my shop, and copious descriptions of the Algarve, my needs, hopes, etc. Now, three months later, they have sent me an enlarged photocopy of my floor plan, asking where I'd like to put the shelves. This strikes me as less than adequate assistance. As with so many services one would like others to provide, it turns out that they don't. So I must patch the store design together myself as best I can, using whatever sources of information I can gather. I re-read the *American Booksellers Handbook*, remember stores I've liked, study my own shop building, transpose American cost figures into *escudos* and bookcase sizes into the metric system used by Portuguese carpenters. The conversions take more time than I expected, but that's true of everything I do here.

I then chart the dimensions of my bookshop to scale on graph paper and make little paper cutouts so I can play with possible layouts on the graph paper. I'm told that architects and interior designers proceed this way but it doesn't work for me at all. I move around my miniature paper furniture but I just can't visualize the space. Like learning sex from a manual, it doesn't feel like the real thing. I need to work full-size.

I take some leftover cartons from our move and cut them into life-size furniture "footprints" and move them around on the actual shop floors till they seem to fit pretty well. I also allow for the four-foot space between bookcases recommended by planners so that browsers don't bump bottoms. To prepare for meeting with several carpenters suggested by Mike Moreira, I cut out catalogue photographs of the cases I want—with wider slanted bottom shelves to allow for better viewing of books below hip level. Armed with my charts and pictures, I'm ready.

Mike and I visit three carpenters, one in Loulé, one in Faro, and one in Quarteira. They each study my shop furniture pictures and measurements while Mike translates my project into Portuguese. All three provide written estimates for the work. I settle on Senhor Feliciano da Rocha in Quarteira who seems quickest to grasp what's needed and whose shop isn't too far from our house. He says he'll deliver the finished furniture in May which means I could open the shop in time for the summer tourist season.

Senhor Feliciano's shop is behind what looks like an ordinary garage next to a small grocery store. Behind the garage door is a long downward slope toward a cavernous basement that holds a small office and several factory-like rooms containing electric saws, planing machines, lumber, sheets of plywood, and floor space for the carpentry work. One would not expect any of this when looking at the building from the street and I realize once more how many activities in Portugal go on invisibly, behind building exteriors that give no hint of what lies behind.

Senhor Feliciano is a solid, square-built man, with protruding brown eyes. He seems to be in his early fifties and, unlike most

Portuguese men I've seen, is getting bald. He speaks hardly any English, but with my diagrams, photographs and written dimensions, we are able to reach agreement. Our contract includes his price of 340,000$in *escudos* (about $2,240 in U.S. dollars) for building twenty bookcases of various sizes and a large sales desk; my down payment of fifty percent and his promise to deliver the work by *fin do Maio* (the end of May). Armed with my chart of spelled-out numbers supplied by Fernão, I write a check from our account at *Banco Espirito Santo*, hand it to the carpenter, and we shake hands to confirm the deal. It feels like a big step, the first outlay of money for outfitting the shop, aside from the building itself. Now that I've taken this plunge, I will soon order an opening inventory of books. This is the first time I've risked investing in my own business, and the first time I must worry about making a profit rather than receiving a dependable salary.

It will be The Griffin Bookshop. The name has personal meaning. When we were courting, I gave Walter a small replica of a griffin from a museum shop. With it I enclosed a note describing griffins as fierce mythological creatures with the body of a lion and the head of an eagle. Their function, according to the ancient Greeks, was to guard treasure. I wrote that I hoped the miniature griffin would guard Walter because he was a treasure to me. The gift was just a token, but Walter loved its meaning and we adopted the griffin as our symbol. Whenever we traveled, we photographed griffins on banks and museums. Now that it's time to choose a name for our bookshop, "The Griffin" is our natural choice, and what could be a more valuable treasure than books?

Because England and Portugal have reciprocal trade agreements, import duty is said to be much lower than for American books. My research has identified Hammick's Wholesale Books in London as a likely distributor. I telephone Hammick's from the phone at the post office, explain my mission and am quickly connected to a Mr. Humphrey Biggs. "Right," he says cheerily. "I'll just need to take down some details." We have a long conversation in which I supply the details he needs, including references to prove that

I'm a good credit risk. In turn, he promises to send me a ROSI (Recommended Opening Store Inventory). He is very helpful, "Be sure to ring me up with any questions." Then he cautions in his very British voice, "And do keep in mind, you must watch your carriage."

"My what?" Up to this point, we haven't discussed carriages.

"Your carriage, my dear. The costs of transport."

"Oh, you mean the shipping charges. Yes, I'll certainly have to watch those."

The rainy season is winding down at last and everywhere golfers from England and Germany stomp around on their cleated shoes. As villa owners we have begun to feel quite superior to tourists. We can buy delicious produce and fish caught the same morning from the local markets when we want to eat at home, and we also know the good cheap restaurants that serve hearty meals, whereas the visitors have to pay top dollar, mark, or pound for everything. One thing even we can't economize on, though, is gasoline which is startlingly high in price. As for telephone bills, we don't yet get them, as we've had no luck getting our shiny red phone installed. Meanwhile, we make our calls from the post office and visit the phone company once a week to plead for our own connection in Portuguese so poor that the lady in charge probably can't imagine how or why we want to call anyone.

One evening as we listen to music at the *Centro Cultural*, large abstract paintings surround us with brilliant colors that can't quite overcome the rainy winter's damp chill remaining in the walls. During the interval, I see an attractive woman enveloped in a raccoon coat, not stylish but clearly warm. Since Walter and I were so unprepared for the winter months, we still shiver in inadequate jackets and sweaters we've brought from the States. It's not easy for me to speak to a stranger, and Walter is even more reserved. But we'll need to make new friends, so I take a chance and approach the woman as she and her husband stand before a painting

"I must tell you that I am green with envy for your wonderful coat."

She gives me a bright smile. "Oh yes, I give thanks for it every day during the rainy season. Don't know what I'd do without it."

I smile in return, "I wish I'd known how cold it gets here." Soon the four of us introduce ourselves and launch a new acquaintance. We learn that they are Ben and Kitty Edwards who have now lived through three Algarvian winters.

Ben Edwards is a lanky Garry Cooper type of American with homespun appeal, short on small talk but long on know-how. His English wife, Kitty, fills his quiet spaces with cheery chatter and the brilliant smile of a former beauty. She tells us that Ben used to be an agricultural advisor for the Ford Foundation. They retired to Portugal after thirty years of postings in Africa and India where they grew accustomed to a warm climate. I remark that this climate seems not at all warm, but they assure us that spring is not far off.

During the next interval we find each other again. Our talk shifts to the other main staple of conversation among expatriates, the trials of house building. Before we return to our seats for the last part of the concert, Kitty invites us for tea at their home, an old farmhouse they are rebuilding in the hills.

On Sunday, we drive along the narrow paved road up to Loulé. From there we follow Ben's hand-drawn map through upland hills, chugging on winding sandy lanes just wide enough for a single car, till we come at last to the Edwards' house at the end of an orchard of almond and olive trees. The property has the rustic beauty of the region's traditional farms. A cobblestone courtyard serves as center for several small stucco buildings surrounded by gnarled orchard trees and bordered by low fieldstone walls. The grouping with its wide chimneys looks a hundred years old, but Ben tells us it wasn't built till the 1940s. Algarvian extremes of heavy winter rains and relentless summer sun are hard on buildings, but Ben, with the help of a Portuguese mason, is making an attractive mountain home out of what was a deserted near-ruin.

We settle down for tea in a large pleasant room with partially finished kitchen cupboards. From the window by the sitting area, we can see out over the hills that descend to the Atlantic Ocean in the distance.

Entranced by the long distances in our view, I turn to Ben, "Do you think it makes one become a better person, seeing something like this every day?"

He ponders my question, then smiles with some regret, "No, I don't think so. After a while you don't really see it."

"That's too bad," I say, "it is so beautiful I hoped it might penetrate."

Walter and I continue to admire the view while Kitty busies herself at the kitchen side of the room while randomly singing part of a song I recognize from *The Mikado*:

"My object all sublime
I shall achieve in time—
To let the punishment fit the crime
The punishment fit the crime..."

In a few minutes, she brings a tray with the teapot and scones and cream. Walter and I gain new appreciation of English teatime as we enjoy every crumb of our portions

"Can you imagine?" Kitty remarks as we sigh with contentment, "We lived here for a year before Ben got the roof on this kitchen."

"This room was where they killed the pigs," Ben explains.

Kitty continues, "This whole space was full of rubble, old straw and collapsed beams. When we closed our eyes we could hear the ghostly squeals."

We are impressed; our own building troubles seem less onerous.

"Took months to clear this out and the hardest part is done." Ben points up at the high bamboo ceiling with evident pleasure. "But there's still work to finish the cabinets."

"And the fireplace, Darling, I do so want a lovely fireplace near the dining table."

"Yes, the fireplace. And the study too, of course." Ben leads us to an archway at one side of the room. "This small room will be our study when we get it cleared out."

We look in but find it hard to assess the room's dimensions because it is crammed floor to ceiling with stacks of what appear to be flattened cardboard cartons.

"What *are* those things?" Walter asks.

"One of my less successful ventures," Ben runs his hand ruefully of along one stack. "These are car sunshades. I had five thousand made up in England. Figured with the killer sun here, they'd sell in a week." He reaches up and pulls one from the top a stack. Unfolded, the shade opens to the size of a windshield. The upper surface sports a giant pair of printed black sunglasses on blue and white striped background.

"What a great idea," I enthuse, remembering our steering wheel too hot to touch after summer parking.

"Here, take a couple," Ben offers. "You can see I've got plenty."

Walter looks up from unfolding a shade. "But why aren't you selling them?"

"Doesn't pay to sell 'em one by one. My plan was to sell 'em in bulk to the big tourist hotels, but I forgot one thing." Ben taps the printed sunglasses. "Didn't leave any space for advertising. None of the hotels wanted them if they couldn't put their name on the shades. That was that. And there they sit." Ben shrugs his shoulders. "Now we have to figure out how to get rid of these stacks so we can clear the room."

"I could sell some in my bookshop, if we ever get it open," I offer and Ben agrees to provide me with a supply when I'm ready.

Outside, with dryer weather, we have progressed from the oozing orange mud that sucked at our boots to bare and lumpy sand. We have arranged for grading and fencing, and look forward to hearing from Gillian about the promised spring planting.

It is March and as the weather grows warmer, I notice little wriggly things in the pool's stagnant black water. We tell Ben Edwards who comes to look. "Mosquito larvae," he says.

"Ugh," say I.

"It's easy to kill 'em," he advises, "just add a couple of quarts of salad oil to the water." Two days later, the oil has indeed glugged the larvae but has formed a greasy film on the water surface, making the pool look like an enormous greasy griddle. The mess is clearly beyond the expertise of our hopeful future pool man and we haven't a clue how to clean it out.

The days pass, but no planters come. We search up and down several hills and locate Gillian Field's nursery, several rustic sheds with corrugated fiberglass roofing among extensive rows of landscaping plants. In startling contrast, next to the property is a gypsy encampment of shacks and tents and next to that, a town dump.

Gillian's assistant promises to tell her of our visit, but that doesn't bring her to our doorstep. We add a weekly trip to the nursery to our routine. The assistant keeps us posted on Gillian's whereabouts.

"Dona Gillian is planting an orchard in Algoz... at the flower show in the Quinta do Lago Hotel...buying palm trees in Portimão."

A busy lady, Gillian Field, she is everywhere up and down the Algarvian coast except at our own barren patch of land. As though praying to a vanished harvest goddess, we leave written messages and verbal pleas with the assistant. Nothing happens. The Ides of March, then the end of March come and go.

A few weeks ago, I went to see the local insurance agent to get a homeowner's policy. He came to inspect our house and declared it vulnerable to theft. No policy unless we installed an alarm system. Now a man has come to install one. His work seems to consist of drilling a hundred holes in the walls so that our house resembles a wired Swiss cheese. Will it be safe? I'm not at all sure. When triggered, the alarm makes a horrible noise but whether anyone hearing it from the road would come to the rescue is hard to predict. If it were me, I wouldn't. But with an alarm installed the insurance company agrees to issue us a homeowner's policy, one more step toward modern living.

Evenings are milder now and we can stay in the dining room through dessert. Outside, the days are getting so warm that a patch of shade looks inviting and the icicles in our bloodstream gradually melt. On a clear sunny morning Walter puts on his silly golf cap, marches briskly to the car, loads his clubs and his cleated shoes, then turns to wave and blow me a kiss with, "See you later, Babe," and I know he's happy. But it does make for a long day without him, especially here where we must share one car and one of us must stay put if that one doesn't wish to join in the other's activities. In the afternoon I'm glad to hear John Henry chugging up the driveway. Walter bursts through the front door and stashes his golf bag in the hall closet. His face is ruddy from the sun, his white hair plastered down from the cap. Before heading for the shower he drinks two large glasses of water. "Played with a Brit and two Australians today. They're here from Brisbane for two weeks. Had a good game. We might go out again on Thursday."

Two years ago when we stayed with Elke at the Dona Filipa Hotel, I often saw construction workers walking down a dirt road at the end of the day. I wondered then if it was a short cut to town. Now that we live near the other end of this same road, we want to check it out during our afternoon walk. About halfway to the beach, we come upon a huge complex of crude buildings made of stacked ceramic blocks slathered with cement and topped by palm and reed roofs, like the workmen's shed on our own property. Some are small individual shacks, others are large barracks. The road leads through the middle of the complex and has chain link fencing on both sides. We see piles of building rubble all around, makeshift laundry lines between buildings, discarded plastic bottles and small trash heaps here and there. We have come upon a hastily thrown-up village hidden by shrubs and pine trees, surrounded by gleaming white villas but unmentioned and unmarked on any maps of the area. This is where the black African workers live whom we've seen crowded into trucks headed for various building sites. They stay for some months to earn money and then return home. Housed very close to us, they invisibly lead their own segregated lives. We have seen them in groups of three or four walking past our house toward Almancil on Sunday mornings but haven't known where or how they live.

Our ignorance makes me think of Doris Lessing's description of African streets of comfortable white homes backed by alleys of crowded shacks and garages that house the black servants. Lessing portrayed two kinds of life, the servants knowing everything about their white employers, but the whites only dimly aware of the life of the alleys.

Walter and I walk on without speaking till we reach the paved Vale do Lobo road.

"I don't want to go back home the same way, " I remark as we proceed toward the beach.

"I can understand that, " he agrees. "Were you scared?"

"A bit. It was all so unfamiliar." I try to untangle my jumbled feelings. "But more than anything, I felt like we were intruders gawking at their living quarters."

"So did I. You'd never know the whole thing is there, right in the middle of all this." Walter gestures toward the villas and ornamental plantings that, now that we have emerged from the compound, line either side of the road we walk on. At the little beachside plaza we pause at the open-air café to order two "*bicas*," small cups of strong espresso coffee. As we sip we are subdued, thinking about what we have seen. The workers' housing has been tucked away from Vale do Lobo's rich vacationers, but its seclusion at least affords the workers their privacy. By walking there uninvited, Walter and I both felt that we were violating that privacy and such dignity as it provides. We return home by the main road.

IX
Settling In

All in all, our move has been quite unlike the smooth relocation to a slower pace in a warm climate that we once dreamed of. The winter wasn't warm, and the pace, while definitely slower, is often disconcerting for our American get-it-done attitudes, a bit like walking with someone whose stride doesn't match your own. It's taking time to adjust.

One always hears about the Spanish and Mexican *manana,* or tomorrow. In Portugal, the corresponding phrase isn't "tomorrow" but next week, *proxima semana.* Everything is promised for next week. At first we believed the promises but gradually learned that hardly anything arrives or happens the next week. It happens when ready. Now when we hear *proxima semana*, we sigh. The truth is that people have no idea when the promised task will get done. To appease time-conscious foreigners and help them leave the premises in reasonably good spirits, *proxima semana* does the trick, at least for a while. When we first visited the telephone company office, the lady said our phone would be hooked up *proxima semana.* After more visits, she said two or three *semanas.* On our latest visit, she shrugged her shoulders in exasperation and said two or three months. We are afraid to ask again. She might tell us two or three years.

We are learning to fend for ourselves and assemble our tools—the new electric drill with a special bit to pierce bricks, a tape measure, a pencil, a picture hook, and Elke's dainty hammer from her tool kit that finally turned up. Then we unwrap the padded packing from the large painting that hung over the burled maple buffet in my mother's Zurich apartment, the same buffet that now stands in our dining area. We measure and re-measure; Walter drills the hole, taps in a molly bolt, and attaches the picture hook. Together we lift the picture, position it and step back.

"Up a little on the right."

Walter steps forward, makes the adjustment, then moves back to my side. We gaze at the soft greens and blues of the Impressionist garden scene by Herbst, a contemporary Swiss painter who was Elke's longtime friend. It's natural, I suppose, that the familiar arrangement of painting and buffet should bring memories to both of us. I think of our many visits to Elke. Ever since her death I have missed what might have been—a more loving relationship between us. Yet as I gaze at her painting, I have to admit that I do not miss *her*. If she were here, it wouldn't be any better than it ever was. I am willing, though it shames me, to say good-bye.

Walter's thoughts, however, run on a totally different track.

"This is tough," he says with a sigh.

"You mean remembering Elke?"

"No, not that. It's that nothing here is mine."

I am stunned. "But Walter, it was your money that built this house—and the shop. Without that we never could have done it, we would have just had a dry patch of land. Of course this is yours. You own this just as much as I do; we own it together."

"I know, I know. It's just a feeling." He gestures toward the furniture in the living room. "I look around and the only things I've got are my clothes and my golf clubs."

"Well, let's take the painting down, then. We can put it somewhere else."

"No, no, it looks good there."

"We could even sell the furniture."

"That wouldn't make any sense. They're valuable antiques."

Feeling helpless at his distress, I turn to put my arms around him. "Is there anything I can do to make you feel better?"

"No, Patoot, not really. I'll just have to get over it."

Subdued, I take the packing materials out to the trashcan while Walter puts the tools away. I feel as though my world has just turned upside down. In all our planning and work for this relocation, we didn't imagine that feelings we never anticipated might ambush us. I never thought I would be so disheartened by the constant penetrating cold. And neither of us expected that Walter would feel like an uncomfortable guest in his own new home. Sometimes I think we are both overwhelmed by the onrushing train of events and emotions that started years ago when we ignorantly burbled, "Let's built a villa in Portugal."

I go through alternating stretches of courage and panic. When I see Walter in doubt, I am frantic. In calmer moments, I picture this time as a kind of tunnel or interim passage from one life to another. For whatever reason people leave a familiar life for something new, because of hope or love or curiosity (or for many in these turbulent times because of fear, persecution, or poverty), we go toward the change we've determined on. All is energy and hope and we plunge ahead. For a while it's dark and confused, everything rushes by with no points of familiarity or connection. Sometimes we think of comforts we've left behind, the beloved faces, the hands to clasp for safety and affirmation, all far-off family and friends living their own lives. But Walter and I can't go back now; we've passed the chance to change our minds, only by forward movement will we emerge from the tunnel. On the other side we may find new life and warmth, some version of what the dream, so vivid but untested, was supposed to bring.

A few days later, as we have our morning coffee, Walter points to the Herbst painting, saying quite cheerfully, "We've crossed a line now."

"How do you mean?"

"We're moving from just focusing on necessities. We're decorating."

He's right. Little by little, things do improve. I am selecting bright patterned fabrics for curtains throughout the house, with vivid colors in marked contrast to the dark drapes from the Zurich apartment. We have even begun to fit out the guest room in hopes that there may actually be a guest someday. Now that it's April, the fields on either side of our property are covered with wild daisies. On the hillside at the rear of our land, yellow broom and purple heather bloom beneath pine trees and tiny wildflowers dot the ground.

While Walter is at the market, Roemer's men arrive to fix our door locks. When they finish they hand me three duplicate sets of different keys for every room in the house. I try to argue for the simplicity of a single universal key but that's not the way here. Every room has a door that locks. Every lock has its own key, and I have a key collection I could wear on a belt like an urban high school custodian.

Cleaning out the pool is proving to be a major task for Roemer Construction. As it drained, we were amazed at how much dirt and trash has been submerged in the black stagnant water: layers of sand that blew in over months, a collection of limp papers, sacks and cartons dumped there during the construction, heaps of dead insects and, as an extra fillip, the ring of scum and grease left by the salad oil we threw in to kill the mosquito larvae. It has taken two men several days of work with power cleaners and wire scrub brushes to clean it. They are supervised by one Senhor Alvares, newly assigned by Joost Roemer to oversee completion of our project. He stops by twice a day to check on progress. He is about thirty years old, with the dark hair and stocky build of many Portuguese men. Unlike Joost himself who is pleasant, bland and sly, Senhor Alvares speaks bluntly and considers himself a man of action.

"My name is João Alvares," he tells us. "That is Alvares, spelled with an 's', not a 'z.' The Jews spell it with a 'z.' I am not Jewish. Nobody in my family is Jewish. We don't cheat people and keep their money. We are Christian. You know the Jews here, you have to watch them every minute, they…"

I cut him short. "While you're watching, you'd better watch what you say, Senhor Alvares; I am half Jewish."

Senhor Alvares pauses, deflected but not daunted. He has a ready alternative subject. Of the two men here for days cleaning our pool, one is a young white Portuguese who has worked tirelessly, first hauling out the accumulated trash, then scraping the pool walls with a wire brush soaked in acid (the fumes so strong he's kept a handkerchief tied over his face). The other, a tall muscular black man with a wide-brimmed straw hat, has spent a total of maybe ninety minutes a day scratching with a shovel to level the ground around the edge of the pool. He passes the rest of his time lounging in a shady spot beneath the carob tree.

I point him out and tell Senhor Alvares, "That man doesn't work."

"The Blacks don't work," Senhor Alvares smiles and nods. Without correcting the individual worker in our yard, he is eager to share his wisdom. "I lived for twenty years in Angola. When we left there, the Blacks were supposed to run the government. They didn't work. Nothing worked. The Blacks don't work anywhere…"

I cut him short again. "Senhor Alvares, I must go inside. I have something cooking…"

Pool cleaning continues for two more days. When our now amazingly blue pool is refilling, Louis appears again. This time he gets his long-awaited contract and becomes our twice-a-week pool man.

On a Tuesday afternoon, we bask in pleasant sunshine on our terrace beside our newly inviting pool. Walter has read my letter to his daughter and son-in-law, and is adding his own paragraph, "*Bom dia, filhos* (Hi, Kids)." I'm shortening a skirt, having brought pins and a tape measure from my sewing kit in the bedroom about five minutes earlier. But I've forgotten the thread. I re-enter the house and walk through the kitchen and the hall. When I step into the bedroom, I see Walter's black leather case on the easy chair and a thermometer lying on one edge of the bed. Intent on getting my thread, I wonder idly why he has put those things there. Then I glance across to the other side of the bed. Several small items are scattered there along with an old black wallet of Walter's, open as though tossed aside. And it hits me; the sliding glass door is wide open, and he wouldn't have jumbled his things like that, would he? I rush back outside to him, my heart pounding. "I think we've just been robbed."

"What?" For a moment, he can't believe he's heard right. Then he looks at my face and starts up quickly. We both dash back into the bedroom.

Walter sees the wallet, the scattered items, the open slider. "Holy Jesus," he breathes. He picks up the empty leather case and sinks onto the easy chair. I stand stupefied, not knowing what we should do. Slowly, we look around the room and start assimilating the fact that there have indeed been burglars.

"Well, they clearly came in through there," Walter waves one arm at the slider.

"It was only about five minutes since I went outside. I came back in because I forgot my thread. They must have heard me coming."

"Or they had a lookout." Walter gets up, walks over to the slider and we both step outside. He points toward the back woods. "Someone could have been watching us from there and signaled when you went back inside, and they all got away through the woods."

We go back into the room and begin trying to assess exactly what and how much has been taken. In such a short time they got away with a lot, mostly things of mine. My purse is gone with my wallet containing cash, all my IDs, driver's license and credit cards. Also missing is my jewelry box with its contents, some pieces I've had for years and loved, especially a heavy engraved gold ring that Elke gave me, and both my wrist watches. Walter mentions that a jacket he left on a side chair has been taken. The empty leather case he still holds contained an antique pocket watch and cuff links left to him by his father.

I have a short flush of relief when I remember that I left a favorite antique gold and pearl pin not in the missing jewelry box but on my checked wool jacket in the closet. Going to the closet to make sure, I get two more jolts. That jacket, along with my beloved pin, is gone. Another leather jacket, as well as some sweaters, are also gone, as are Walter's knit polo shirts. A bit later, we realize that the top shelf of that closet no longer holds the box of thirty cassette tapes, some that Elke's friend Ursula lovingly dubbed for me from Elke's records, and some favorites I brought from the States. It takes us some time to get past the shock of so much taken in such a short time.

Not knowing how to inform the police, we lock up and drive to Vila Bonita. Odette telephones the *Guardia Nacional* (the police) in Loulé. and gives directions while Mike accompanies us back to our house. Two *Guardia* men come promptly and look into the bedroom. Even though most of the valuable missing things were mine, the two men speak only to Mike and to Walter. Mike turns to me for details of the stolen items, I describe them, and then Mike informs the men who write a careful list. When they are finished they take the list away to be typed. The next day, as instructed, Walter purchases a special government stamp at the newspaper shop. For two days more we keep finding, or rather missing, more things that are gone and each new discovery brings such a sinking feeling. Then we drive up to police headquarters in Loulé. There the *Guardia* captain on duty amends the list, affixes the stamp we purchased to make it official, and presents the ornamented list to us to take home. That, I gather, is the extent of police involvement in the matter. We are to take the list to our insurance company to claim some restitution in money. There's no thought of trying to recover any stolen items. Certainly none of the sleuthing one sees on TV, no dusting for finger prints, no studying the ground for footprints, no searching for suspects, no attempts to contact known fences or pawn brokers. Just a nicely typed list with a fancy stamp. For days, the burglary's aftermath feels like After the Fall, in what we once thought of as Eden.

Needing comfort, we share our distress with the Edwards. They too have been robbed at one time or other and remember particular items taken that they still miss.

"I had a lovely long string of pearls when I was in my twenties," Kitty tells me. "I wore them everywhere. I was young, living 'on me own' for the first time—I had a flat in London—didn't have money, only one or two frocks, but the pearls made them look elegant. The buggers broke into my flat and my pearls were gone. I wept for days."

Ben also has a story. "We were in Spain and stopped for drinks and *tapas* at a pub in Seville. When we came out, everything we'd left in the car was gone. They'd smashed a window and taken it all. Our luggage, my camera I'd had for years, and all the films I'd taken of our trip. I still miss that camera; never found one I liked as well."

I too miss my stolen things and sometimes I chide myself about that. After all, they were just things. No one was hurt; no one died. We were not stripped of everything we own and relatively few of our belongings were taken. I tell myself that we should love people, not things. And yet I did feel a kind of love for those things as if they were, or had become, extensions of myself. The heavy gold ring that my mother gave me years ago in Zurich, the leather jacket soft and pale as butter that I found among her clothes after her death, the gold and pearl pin that I've worn for twenty years. As for the other items, well, I hated the theft, but I won't miss them. But those few pieces will stay in my mind like lost friends I had hoped to have with me for many more years. And the whole event has brought a sense that some kind of human connection has been broken. I know that's foolish. I know that people have been robbed every day, and much worse, and that people in cities keep several locks on their doors and protect windows and entryways. But *we* never have. Now, after this, we join the ranks of the cautious and guarded.

Because the burglars came in while we were at home we stay pretty spooked. We rig our alarm system to cover whichever side of the house we're not occupying at the moment. That means having to remember to turn off the alarm and then unlock two doors just to go to the bathroom. And should either of us want a sweater from the bedroom, we must turn off the alarm, unlock two doors, get the hidden keys to the dresser, get the sweater, lock everything up again, and then turn the alarm back on. It feels like a state of siege.

We know we can't continue this rigmarole indefinitely, but we remain quite paranoid for some weeks while we try to add safeguards that will make us less vulnerable. At present, our house stands out of sight from any neighbors but easily visible from the road and accessible from all sides. A boundary fence will help, if the crew ever comes to build it, and we will install wrought iron grills over the windows and sliding glass doors. In addition, everyone tells us to get a dog to scare off intruders, except Sr. Alvares who owned geese in Africa and recommends them as fierce guardians. "Geese are better than dogs, much more vicious," he says.

I'm not paranoid enough for geese but Walter likes the idea of a dog. "I think it's a good time for us to get a dog," he says. "We're home most of the time now. A dog would be fun." Not my idea of fun, but I know he's wanted a dog for a long time so I agree, and Walter starts studying ads in the *Algarve News*.

From what we hear, burglaries are a common resort-area hazard. Their frequency in the Algarve has increased in recent years in tandem with increased illegal drug use, but violence is extremely rare. Thieves here don't carry arms or beat people up. They go in and out fast, taking cash, light valuables and easily sold items, just as with us. So we are not scared of violence, but tense and fearing a second "hit" because they were so successful with the first.

Walter's clothes, especially his short-sleeve polo shirts, have probably gone either to the Gypsy markets or possibly to Africa where ready-made clothing is scarce. All we can hope is that those shirts may do someone there some good.

A week after the burglary we go to the ironworker's shop in Almancil to place an order for window grills. The shop is small and dark, cluttered with sections of wrought iron. All surfaces are black with iron dust, as is the owner. We explain our need to him for grills that will deter burglars. The owner is quite willing to oblige but then asks, *"A quel desenho?"* (what design would we like). Never having given any thought to window grills before, we of course don't have a design and ask to see some examples from his shop or a catalogue. He doesn't have any. *"Nao tenho"* he says firmly and clearly sees no need for them, despite our ignorance. He gives us to understand that his job is to forge the iron; the design is up to us. Since we want nice-looking grills, not iron bars like a jail, we set out to investigate design possibilities. It turns out to be an unexpected pleasure. We drive and walk past houses with window grills and become increasingly interested to see the variations.

Whenever one begins to look intently at something one has barely glanced at before, a wealth of design details and craftsmanship emerge. We start our search at the Vale do Lobo villas nearest us and see *desenhos* that are adequate but not very interesting, then we go into Almancil which has mostly shops with roll-down shutters. Uninspired, we drive the twelve miles to Faro, where the graceful wrought iron we see on windows, doorways and gates of some older Portuguese houses displays workmanship of great charm, skill and variety. This is an art form we have not fully appreciated before. We are especially taken with one design on a door and window in the city's center, with iron shaped and curved into a large bouquet with flowers, stems, leaves and buds in intricate swirls.

"That's really beautiful," I say, "but how are we ever going to describe it?"

"I can make a sketch," Walter offers, "but I'll need some graph paper."

We find a *papelaria* (stationery store); bring back the graph paper, and Walter makes a fine sketch. Back in our villa, we count a total of twenty-three windows and two glass sliding doors, and reconsider the ornate iron bouquets. Our house would appear encrusted in an ironwork botanical garden. Back to Faro to observe more grills. On our next trip we walk on a quiet street and come to a small house of a pleasing design with a simple wrought iron gate in front. The more we look, the more we like the simplicity and grace of that gate, strong vertical bars interrupted by two scrolled iron butterflies. While Walter sketches the design, I walk around to the side of the house and see a tile plaque that reads, "*Casa de Poeta*" (the Poet's House), commemorating a poet who lived there in the 1940s. A good omen. We take Walter's sketch to the ironmonger and subsequently, when our own grills, modeled on that design, are installed and painted white, they look like lace butterflies floating on our windows.

Mike and Odette come to visit. We greet them at the door and see that Mike is carrying a small tree, its roots bundled in a canvas sack, obviously a gift for us.

"This is a lemon tree." Odette announces.

"Is tradition here in Portugal to plant a lemon tree by a new house," Mike explains.

Walter and I are delighted to receive our own traditional tree. Walter asks where it might best be planted and we all step outside to see.

"It should be near the kitchen door," Mike says. "Also tradition. That way, Marianne, whenever you want a slice of lemon for tea or for lemonade, Walter can just step outside and pick a lemon for you."

I'm not sure why the lemon tree is traditional, perhaps to symbolize the sour and sweet one can expect from life in a new home, but the gift reminds us of the kindness of friends and helps to restore our spirits after the burglary.

A day later, in order to assemble the necessary components for planting our tree, we telephone Fernão, our language teacher, to ask the word for manure. There's nothing like need to stimulate learning. We learn that, as in English, there is a polite word, *extrume*, that one can use in a plant nursery and then there's another one that would be insulting, but comes in handy in times of frustration. We get our *extrume* and plant the new tree near the kitchen door as Mike advised. It is still tiny but we feel good putting it into the ground.

On a red-letter day, the telephone company's team number three arrives to connect the phone in the shop building. We are in touch with the outside world! No more having to go to the post office or Vila Bonita to make calls. And we can also receive calls because Walter has attached a very long wire and carried the phone into the house where we can hear the ring.

As promised, our very first call goes to Fernão, who teaches us a new word, *Parabems!* (Congratulations).

We invite Fernão out to lunch to celebrate our twentieth and final language lesson and asked him to pick the place. He chooses a *tasca,* a workingmen's bistro. "Here you will see where the men spend their lunch time. Lots of good food, a bottle of *vinho* and friends."

As we enter the small building, we're greeted by friendly shouts of "*Ola Fern*ão*, com esta*" (hello, Fernão, how's it going?) and as we pass to a table toward the back, here and there a man reaches out a hand for Fernão to clasp. Most of the male customers salute him with affectionate laughter as the "Count of Vale d'Eguas." Their quips clearly raise his spirits   He smiles and nods to his audience. He likes to portray himself as a figure of some influence and has often mentioned his many friends in the area, who now include us. "This *tasca* is run by a family," he tells us. "They make their own wine and everybody in the family works here, even the children."

One family member, a boy who serves as a waiter, comes to our table and without being asked places an open bottle of red wine before Fernão who gestures to include us. The boy pours the wine into our empty water glasses and we wait for the lunch of the day. As we chat, we are surrounded by a noisy hubbub from the other tables. I notice once more that the voices of Portuguese men are louder than we're used to. Virginia Woolf, I recall, wrote about Greek drama springing from a climate of brilliant sunshine where people spent most of their time outdoors, with the result that "small incidents are debated in the street, not in the sitting room." Just so, the voices I hear throughout the *tasca* are outdoor voices.

For lunch we have lamb, carrots and green beans and French fries, an almost inescapable meal throughout the Algarve, with flan for dessert, as universal here as in Mexico. Fernão tells us its popular nickname, *trezentos e seissenta e cinquo* (three hundred and sixty five), a sign of its daily appearance. Along with his lunch, Fernão has a good quantity of the homemade wine. From his hints during the weeks of our lessons, we've gathered that he has lost several good jobs because of too much wine and brandy. Now he and Daphne scratch out a living from his lessons and her appallingly small salary as a professor at Faro University. Though they live on a desperately thin shoestring, Fernão marks our "graduation" with a gift. At the end of our lunch, he goes into the *tasca's* kitchen at the back and returns with a parcel wrapped in white paper.

"This is a traditional Portuguese Easter cake." He presents it to me with a bow. "But be careful when you bite into it. There is a surprise in the middle." Eyes sparkling and face flushed, he clearly enjoys his little ceremony and we thank him for the cake and for all he has done. We have enjoyed our twenty lessons and our conversations in Fernão's freezing kitchen, among the clutter of plants, old wine bottles, and carefully rescued cigarette butts, and we have no doubts that we'll meet again. With his guidance and the help of Berlitz tapes I can now understand much of what the workmen at our house struggle to tell me. Walter hasn't progressed as far in speaking, but he sharpens his reading skills by studying restaurant menus and deciphering Portuguese news headlines.

The next day we sample our graduation present, a round, sweet, raisin-filled pound cake with a hard-boiled egg in its shell baked into the middle. We have it plain with our brunch and again for afternoon tea with butter and strawberry jam. It is delicious.

X
New Friends

One day, our pool man Louis sees me sweeping the terrace. "You need woman to clean," he tells me. "I bring my cousin, very good, very clean. Yes?"

"No, Louis. I'm not ready yet."

Though Louis doesn't know it, he is broaching a touchy subject. For some time, I've been resisting Walter's urgings to hire a part-time maid. We know that as *estrangeiros* (foreign residents) we are expected to provide some employment for local Portuguese. But part-time domestic workers at resort homes generally work four or five half-days per week and we don't need that much cleaning. We're two middle-aged people settling into a compact three-bedroom villa, we don't give large parties, we don't spill a lot or throw things and, aside from inevitably tracking orange mud or sand into the house, we don't make much dirt. Even in our large old house in Saratoga, our cleaning lady came only one morning a week. And while grateful for her help, I wasn't raised with servants and never could relax while she was in the house. Here I expect to be even more uncomfortable with a maid who speaks a foreign language and comes so often that I have to dream up chores for her. I try to postpone the inevitable by telling Walter that we'll hire someone when we open the shop in our other building. Then I can always send the maid to clean over there.

Louis, however, who has succeeded in finding employment with us himself, is now set on sharing his good fortune with his cousin. He maintains the pool faithfully twice a week, and comes to the door every other week to collect his pay and ask if I'm ready yet for the maid. "Much work here," he smiles persuasively. "Is time for to get help. My cousin, Mafalda, very nice. Clean house very good. I bring her next week?"

"No, no maid yet. Sorry." And Louis sighs as he turns away and waits for next time.

Kitty and Ben Edwards drop in on a Sunday afternoon, she with armfuls of wild iris she has picked from the side of the road. Large white ones and tiny purple ones small as violets bloom here in May. I put them in a green glass vase on the table, a delight for the eye like a variant of Van Gogh's irises. The purple ones are all finished the next morning, rolled up like limp dead cigarettes. The white ones stay in full bloom for several days.

We have exchanged regular visits with the Edwards. Ben and Walter took to each other quickly with Walter appreciating Ben's practical skills, and Ben learning from Walter's insights as a psychologist. If it weren't for our husbands' growing friendship, Kitty and I probably would not have continued our association. Like many English women I meet here, she chatters constantly but not personally and I sometimes tire of the cascade of witty trivia and flat pronouncements about world events. Then too, at times I simply can't follow her thought due to her habit of skipping blithely over the last part of her sentences with a hasty "glub-diddle-dum" that assumes the listener can supply any missing words. Because Kitty's very British accent was at first unfamiliar to my American ear; not only did I fail to grasp those garbled endings, I often missed even the first half of her sentences. And when not baffled by what I didn't understand, I was distracted by the random snatches of song from English operettas she inserts into conversations. For no discernible reason she might break off in mid-sentence to warble:

"When a merry maiden marries,
Sorrow goes and pleasure tarries;

Every sound becomes a song,
All is right and nothing's wrong."

In turn, my evident vexation must hardly have endeared me to her. But with repeated contacts, we have grown more comfortable with each other. Recently when she dismissed feminist thinking as "ridiculous," I felt free to drop politeness and disagree with her. To my surprise she responded to my objection with genuine pleasure. "Oh, I suppose that sort of thing has its points, but they are so tiresomely serious and bad-tempered, aren't they? Such a fuss when one can manage to get one's way ever so much more cheerfully."

We have come to enjoy our verbal jousting. I seldom agree with any position she takes, but she does make me examine my own opinions, sometimes more than I do otherwise. Now that our telephone works, Kitty and I add phone calls to our contacts as a foursome. We telephone instead of visiting because I'm homebound half of each day preparing for the bookshop and in motion on various errands during the other half and, perhaps more significant, because Kitty lives on a mountain top and doesn't drive.

"Maybe you could take some lessons?" I ask.

"Didn't learn to drive in London," she states. "Couldn't possibly start here with all the mad Porgie drivers."

Her not driving accentuates the differences between our lives. I am mobile and able to decide when and where I want to go. Kitty is almost entirely dependent on Ben's driving to come down from her beautiful but isolated farm.

This afternoon we are pleased to see them and they are happy to accept our offer of coffee. Ben and Walter wander outside to inspect various sprinkler points in the irrigation system while Kitty and I do kitchen duty. When the men return we sit around the table and chat about progress and delays on our houses and about finding some outside help.

"I'm not quite ready for some of that help," I admit. "Walter wants me to hire a half-time maid, but I'm delaying. I just dread the loss of privacy."

"I can understand that," Ben says, "but I've found that privacy abroad is a rare luxury." The Edwards were posted away from home for many years. Ben tells us that when they were first assigned a house in India, they found it included five or six servants or helpers.

"They were all lined up in front of the house waiting for us as we drove up, and when we asked the government agent who those people were or why they were there, the answer was that they came with the house."

"We were quite flummoxed," Kitty laughs.

"I thought I'd get used to it," Ben says. "Then after five or six months, one day all of a sudden I felt as if I was going berserk from never having a moment to myself and I just had to flee. I bolted outside and went for a very long walk. Just to be alone and quiet."

I take Ben's story to heart. Walter and I are still getting used to having *each other* around so much of the time. If I add a maid too soon I think berserkness would happen to me in about two weeks. I still hope to hold off on any maid till the bookshop gets going.

It turns out that the Edwards' visit was not a purely social Sunday afternoon call. After we wave goodbye, Walter tells me that while they were in the garden Ben spoke of a friend's efforts to stop binge drinking, and asked Walter to see his friend as a clinician.

I am glad for Walter. His work will help him to feel more at home here. When we finish clearing the table, my mind turns to practical aspects of the new venture.

"We'll have to get your study ready. And isn't it good that we designed it with a separate entrance?"

The study has an inside door to the front hall and an outside door to the courtyard so that people can come and go in relative privacy without having to walk through the house. We haven't paid much attention to the room so far, but now work to make it more inviting. We hang some pictures and bring in Walter's papers and supplies. I'm glad that he seems quite pleased to arrange them into the massive antique desk that was formerly Elke's. I unpack some books to fill the bookcase and we buy colorful cushions for the sofa and chairs. With these touches, the room is transformed into an informal but efficient professional office.

Two weeks later, Walter leaves for Saratoga on his quarterly trip to monitor his practice. In the days that follow, his absence is so new that I haven't yet gained a rhythm for this interval on my own. Everything seems quiet and empty. Fortunately, Fernão and Daphne heard I was alone and have kindly invited me to dinner. Fernão says I can't come unless I speak Portuguese all evening. I'm a bit worried but I know Daphne talks non-stop and I hope her verbal waterfall will cover my social repertoire of five polite Portuguese phrases. Fernão says that Daphne (who is large and a bit disheveled) doesn't care about her looks, but he's wrong. Just after I arrive, she changes out of her snug red housedress into another dress just as red but looser. To my relief, after our first greetings in Portuguese, we speak English, with Fernão happily deferring to his wife's chatter with "Yes, my love" or "No, my darling" throughout the evening.

Dinner is served in their familiar kitchen, beneath the water-stained and flaking ceiling, amid pots and pans, old wine jugs, and various ancient so-called appliances. But the table is decked with a lace tablecloth, and Daphne has arranged the first course of strawberries and cheese on delicate green and gold Chinese dishes, each embellished with a fig leaf.

Fernão tells me he stems from an old titled Portuguese family and says with a wink, "My ancestors were entitled to clean the King's shoes." Perhaps there were other privileges as well, but they are clearly long gone. The only reason Fernão's family can afford even their cramped dwelling is that Portuguese law prevents a landlord from either evicting tenants or raising their rent so long as they pay it promptly on or before the due date. Fernão and Daphne have lived in this same house for twenty years and, come hell or high water, scraping or borrowing, they pay the rent on time. By way of revenge, their landlord does no repairs or upkeep whatsoever. Hence, the crumbling walls, leaking roof and precarious plumbing. Yet in the midst of this decay they have raised two children, Fernão gives his language lessons, Daphne commutes to her Faro University teaching post, and they entertain friends and acquaintances like me, and I'm impressed.

Daphne chatters and Fernão fits his words in around the edges, "A little more wine, my love?" throughout her stories of her childhood in England.

"My mother said no man would ever want to marry me because of my heavy legs and my large 'bum'." She and Fernão gaze at each other with clear satisfaction.

"After we were married," Daphne continues, "I told Fernão what my mother said, and he said that my bum was the first thing he looked at and liked a lot."

We all laugh. What do mothers know about what's attractive!

Continuing my bookshop preparations, I drive out to the airport to ask the *Alfandega* (the customs officials) about import duty on books. I'm trying to get a comparison of rates between England and America and am passed from one uniformed person to another till I reach the *Cheffe*. In response to my question about the import duty on books, the chief will only tell me from behind his impressive mustache that the rates differ. With great bureaucratic opaqueness he says I will have to submit a list of exactly what I wish to import and after they have studied my list they then will calculate the rates.

I repeat with deadpan patience, "I wish to import books."

"Ah, but books vary," he says again, his black eyes glinting as though he has snared a pigeon, and then warms to his subject. "There are educational books, reference books, novels, children's books, books with pictures, large books, small books, each type of book has a different rate."

"But can you tell me how those rates compare for books from England and America?"

He shakes his head gravely, grooms his mustache and repeats

his instructions. The Senhora must submit a specific list and then the *Alfandega* will study the items listed, and so on. I nod, we shake hands and I take my leave, sensing that freedom of information is not a guiding principle of government agencies here. I also suspect that the decision-making process for the desired specific list, book by distinctive book, might take years. I think of Fred Astaire's, "The search for what you want is like tracking something that doesn't want to be tracked." My search will have to find a way around the *Alfandega*.

Two weeks later Walter gets back and it feels very good to have him here again to hug, share meals, and discuss decisions. One task now at hand is supervising the outdoor mason, Antonio, a very thin young man who is setting in edging bricks for both shop and house driveways. Portuguese driveways tend to be very narrow and we have to keep urging Antonio to widen the access to both buildings. He does so, shaking his head at American extravagance. Now, he has made the driveway to the house with not enough turning room for a car. We don't want to have to back out onto the busy road, so Walter must stop him, pace off and demonstrate the desired dimensions, and Antonio has to do it over.

Antonio has a hard time with curves. When he works on the semi-circular driveway in front of the shop, it becomes so lopsided that we have to stop him again. Stopping him means he has to break the edging bricks he put in earlier. He maintains his courtesy but gives vent to repeated lamentations of "*muito trabalho*" (so much work). To console himself, he next sets stones skillfully and accurately along a straight line that will define a boundary wall. He guides his progress by a taut green string about a foot off the ground and fastened to stakes at intervals. I watch and understand his problem; he can't use green string to guide himself along curves.

I go to Senhor Feliciano's carpentry shop to check on his work since our agreed-upon date is a month away. He leads me down to the underground interior where he shows me six wide boards intended for the three biggest bookcases. I judge that to be minimal progress but he assures me that *proxima semana....*

Meanwhile, Walter and I still have plenty to do, in fact we don't know where the days fly to. There are always people to see, things to order for the house, applications to make to one agency or another for the shop. Sometimes I miss the logic and dependability of a regular workweek with a place to go to every day where work is separated from one's household concerns. But at other times those feelings are offset by the joy of building something of our own, quite special and different from anything we've done before, and the spice of meeting people from places we've never seen.

I leave Senhor Feliciano in peace until mid-May, two weeks before the promised delivery date at the end of the month. Then I go to see him once more. This being Portugal, I am not surprised that nothing is ready. He again promises *proxima semana*, next week. Next week, I go back. No progress. Senhor Feliciano is hard to catch. During daytime, his garage door is locked. His neighbor in the *mercado* next door tells me that he is there around eight in the morning and around six in the evening. For two weeks, I make special trips to catch him at those times without success. Then I just watch to see if the garage door is open as I pass by on other errands. When it is, I go in to plead with him in my rudimentary Portuguese and ask to see what he has finished. He is reluctant to show me, tells me to come back *a manhan* (tomorrow). *A manhan* the door is locked. When I find him again, he shows me the six boards I saw earlier, but now cut and shaped correctly for the sides of tall bookcases, wider at the bottom than the top. After two months, six boards. When he and I agreed on a contract, I gave him fifty percent of the total payment for my bookcases, intended for supplies and as evidence of good faith. Mine. His has yet to be proven. Again he assures me *proxima semana*, everything will be finished. *Tudo.* Everything. Next week. Next week comes. After coaching from Fernão and much practice at home, I tell Senhor Feliciano, *"Penso não diga-me a veridade."* (I think you are not telling me the truth). He shrugs his ample shoulders and rolls his eyes heavenward.

When we came to this foreign country, we expected that we would have to adapt to its language and customs. That has turned out to be true, but we are also learning that between us and the Portuguese lies an intervening layer of the British presence. The British have been in Portugal for six hundred years and have put their own stamp on many aspects of life for later arrivals. The biggest factor we and the British have in common is of course our more-or-less shared language, but there are other affinities as well. As *estrangeiros* (foreigners) from an Anglicized culture ourselves, we enter into activities of the English residents more comfortably than those of the Portuguese. We are more drawn to secular gatherings than to religious ceremonies; to exercise and fitness workouts than to motorcycle races; to ornamental gardening than to subsistence farming. But we don't fully fit in with the English either; we don't play darts or ride horses, and in fact are sometimes baffled by the Queen's English. Not only are we trying to learn the Portuguese language, we must also master English expressions, such as "half eight" for half past eight, or "Sunday lunch" for a multi-course midday dinner huge enough to make a horse founder.

For me there is an added layer of confusion. Many Portuguese who don't speak English speak French. My French is rusty and similarities between French and Portuguese grammar sometime muddle my thinking. Often I am tongue-tied, suspended between two unfamiliar languages. But Walter and I have both acquired vocabulary that creeps into our speech unaware. We now refer to *brita,* without mentally translating that word into "gravel," and we go to the *drogaria*, the *mercado* and the *pharmacia* instead of the hardware store, the market or the drugstore. Willy nilly we are settling in and starting to feel at home.

On a glorious day in late May I have lunch at *Joao's Barraca*, a rambling beach restaurant built on stilts over the dunes. My companions are two American women: one is Cecile, whom I met recently at a meeting of AFPOP (the Association for Foreign Property Owners of Portugal), a mostly English group formed to understand Portuguese codes and regulations. Cecile and her husband own a real estate and construction firm in Almancil. She is a tall sandy-haired Texan who was so happy to see another American at an AFPOP meeting that she arranged our lunch. She also invited Wendy Bartholomew, a psychologist whose elegant name rather misrepresents a bright Jewish girl from New York. Wendy is of average height, with brown eyes and glossy brown curls. When we meet, she is wearing jeans, a bright red shirt and bright red lipstick to match.

The day is gorgeously sunny from start to finish and we savor our grilled fish, *pommes frites*, and sangria. Mellowed by warm sunlight and rhythmic ocean waves, our conversation is very American, centering on personal facts, past history, work, feelings, hopes, disappointments. We begin with our backgrounds in the States. I was a college teacher and administrator; Cecile an art teacher and political activist (more accurately an ex-hippie) now turned realtor; and Wendy a psychoanalyst who practiced in Greenwich Village. Then we move to more personal aspects. We learn that all of us have been divorced and are now remarried. I'm the only one married to an American, they to Englishmen. Cecile has two children from her first marriage, I have three, and Wendy is childless. Despite these individual differences we share a common frame of cultural reference. We lived through the stirring civil rights movement and were horrified by the assassinations of the Kennedy brothers, Martin Luther King, and Malcolm X. During the Vietnam War and its repercussions we were either part of, or sympathetic to, the anti-war movement and counter culture of the 60s and 70s. We supported the advance of feminism and the Equal Rights Amendment and, with this shared history, we remain political liberals.

Aside from larger subjects, we also compare the intimate joys of thick fluffy American towels with the Portuguese versions which are as thin as bed sheets. We bemoan the lack of stylish affordable cotton clothing, and the scarcity of chocolate chip cookies. And we laugh. Perhaps nothing draws me to Wendy more than our wild laughter at memories of sorting through and disposing of the eccentric possessions of our deceased relatives.

"My mother had twelve pairs of silver slippers," I say.

"*My* mother saved every dress and coat she ever owned," Wendy counters and we choke with glee.

I continue my story. "We took my mother's clothing to a home for aged ladies. I still enjoy imagining twelve of them appearing in identical pairs of silver slippers."

When we calm down, Wendy says, "This has been amazing." Her talk is sprinkled with unusual emphases on syllables: am*aaaz*ing...

"I'm having a wonderful time." I say, "It's been the first relaxing 'girl-talk' I've had in quite a while."

"Yes, but you don't understand," Wendy says. "We never have talks like this here; most everyone is English and the English don't."

"And we're married to Englishmen," Cecile adds.

"They don't talk about personal things; it's not done in polite company." Wendy explains. "For instance, you mustn't ever ask 'what do you do?' when you meet someone. They think Americans are very nosy because we ask that."

"Well, what *do* they talk about?" I wonder.

"Oh, sports, the weather, horses, dogs." Wendy starts the list.

Cecile adds to it. "Cars, restaurants, rents...."

"Rents?" I'm puzzled.

"Taxes," she translates from the English and that brings us to another shared frame of reference. Now that we live in the Algarve, all three of us are spooked by our American Internal Revenue Service. Unlike British, Dutch, and Germans who live here and seem to enjoy a cordial relationship with their respective tax collectors, we Americans, though dutifully paying our taxes, endure unreasonable audits and strong IRS suspicion of expatriates.

Our talk glides from subject to subject and we extend our lunch into the afternoon, savoring the merriment and good feeling. Before we part, we agree to meet for lunch once a week and I am happy that I have made two new friends.

XI
The Dog and the Garden

A new facet of our Portuguese adventure is imminent. Walter has long wanted a dog. It didn't seem feasible in the States where we were both out of the house all day but now the dog's day has come. Walter has located a breeder and reserved a Giant Schnauzer puppy named Caesar. Everyone tells us that a guard dog should deter burglars. Walter is delighted and insists that I shall in time dote on this dog. I maintain that this would be completely out of character, but am willing to give it a try. After all, it will be more Walter's pet than mine.

On a bright morning we go to visit Caesar, one of four puppies from the same litter, now about five months old and quite large. Their names all come out of Roman history and begin with C: Caesar, Cassius, Claudia, and Cato. Their young sprightly mother frolics with them. My impression is of five large black hairy jolly clowns leaping, barking, bounding, knocking things over, and chasing each other every which way. Walter laughs at their antics and is charmed. I am, to put it kindly, less so. But at least we're getting only one puppy, not all four or two as Walter first wanted. Soon Caesar will take up residence to guard us from burglars and things that go bump in the night. In exchange, I guess we'll have to let him go bump in daytime.

We fence in a small area in the shade of pine trees behind our house for *o cão* (the dog). It is hard work unrolling heavy wire fencing and nailing it to tree trunks, but we succeed in making a satisfactory pen. Caesar is getting bigger and older by the day and we figure we'd better get him here so that we can all get to know each other and Walter can start training him. I myself want to get used to the dog before Walter's next trip back to the States in July. I know I'll be alone with him sooner or later, but that will definitely be sooner and I'm nervous. What do I know about taking care of a large bounding puppy?

Whereas I think that having one big dog is a big deal, it's flea-sized for some people. Yesterday we met a neighbor, an attractive French-Indonesian artist named Giselle with wild dark hair and flashing black eyes. Giselle takes in stray dogs as an avocation. Since Portugal teems with stray dogs, this is a daunting enterprise and she now has twenty-three dogs in residence. Kennels had to be built, and a special kitchen designed to cook the bones, scraps and rice that Giselle's husband collects each day from area restaurants. I can't even imagine the veterinarian's bill. The dogs are not for sale; Giselle has rescued them so that they can " 'ave an 'appy life." Their 'appiness crests early each morning at feeding time when their excited barking rouses us, interfering somewhat with our own 'appy life. Soon enough our own Caesar will probably join the chorus.

After weeks of standstill while a few stray daisies and poppies grew on hardening dirt heaps, things are finally moving again at our place. On Monday Gillian Field and her straw boss, a cheerful muscular young man named Afonso, pulled up in two vans. Walter and I dashed outside to greet them. "We are going to begin," Gillian announced with a cheery smile while Afonso unloaded three wheelbarrows filled with rakes and hoes. Evidently that was enough of a beginning because they then left and our hearts quieted to their accustomed waiting rhythm. But now, two days later, actual workmen have arrived and are raking up construction debris from our villa which they truck to the lot next door and bury there. (The owner lives in England and will never know, at least that seems to be the assumption hereabouts. Everyone who builds buries rubble on neighboring empty land, and so on till the very last one nearest the coast who, I suppose, throws his heap into the ocean.) A huge backhoe is lurching around and smoothing out our lumpy ground. And three masons, who disappeared weeks ago because they ran out of *calçadas* (cobblestones), have returned. They crouch along the driveways-to-be, setting in the *calçadas*, tap-tap-tapping them with small hammers and then tamping them down with wooden thumpers. We're so glad to see some action at last.

Caesar arrived this morning. We picked him up in Loulé and he had diarrhea in the car coming home, probably nerves. So we're off on the new routine of caring, feeding and cleaning up right from the start. Walter tied him to a long rope on the terrace and he's been pretty quiet out there since then. I'm glad to see that he seems sweet and not given to barking.

Right now, I'm suspended while waiting for two people to arrive. One is our landscaper who two hours ago promised to come back "in a few minutes." The other is our dog's breeder who is due to bring Caesar's pedigree papers and instructions for feeding and exercise. I keep telling myself that I shouldn't get into the bind of waiting for people here because time is so loosely understood. No one arrives for business appointments as scheduled. Sometimes people are simply late; at other times, without notice, meetings are not held at all if one of the parties has something else to do or some reason to think that a meeting would be pointless. As for contracted work like the bookcases I've ordered, people get to it when they can, which has no relation to the promised date or the client's needs. Expressed anger seems to slow progress even further; frustration has no effect at all, and pleading causes mild amusement. If there's a secret for getting things done closer to promised times I don't yet know what it is. In contrast to such contracted projects, thank goodness, stores and restaurants open more or less on time.

When Gillian arrives she promises the workers will return with more topsoil and *extrume* for the garden. We nod with respect; clearly our poor sandy soil needs large helpings of *extrume*.

"But isn't it too late to plant now?" I'm worried about the burning summer sun.

"Oh, not at all," Gillian dismisses our worries with a graceful wave of her arm. "You have a bore hole and plenty of water for irrigation. Except for winter, it doesn't matter when you plant so long as you give plenty of water during the hot months. The men will start tomorrow."

Our minds eased, we congratulate ourselves that planting has started at last and we will soon have a garden. Not surprisingly, the men do not come back "tomorrow," but they do come a week later to dump several truck loads of topsoil and a big fragrant mound of "shtroom" at the edge of our newly outlined driveway. Another team of men brings wheelbarrows, which they use to distribute the mix and then rake it into the sandy ground.

"Now we can plant," we exult when they are done.

But not yet. Several inactive days later, trucks deliver lengths of piping and hoses. Of course! We forgot about the planned irrigation system. The piping lies unattended for another week until Afonso arrives one day to take charge of irrigation design. We watch with admiration as he lays out an intricate web of pipes, hoses and sprinkler heads and hooks it all up to an automated control panel in our pump house. The next day, Afonso tests the watering patterns, and rearranges some connections. Then he sets and resets all the dials and knobs on the control panel that will govern eight garden zones through two daily watering cycles. We are awed and a bit alarmed at this complex grid just for a garden we had hoped would be "natural." A week later, workers bury the pipes and tubing, Afonso re-tests the system and determines, "*Esta bon.*"

"Now can we plant? " we are almost afraid to ask.

"*Sim,*" Afonso assures us, now at last we can plant.

Now, of course, is quite a few days later. But one morning Gillian pulls into the driveway, her green van packed tightly with pots of foliage and two bougainvillea vines trailing across the front seat. Afonso helps her unload and then we all stand by to watch as she gets to work. She moves like an artist with a huge canvas, setting out plants in pots everywhere, figuring out color shadings, heights, and growth patterns. Periodically, she pauses, squints, changes placements, stands back, looks again, arranges and rearranges the pots. Two hours later she leaves, returns with another vanload and repeats the performance. At intervals she comes to me with questions I find delightful but baffling. "Do you want the bougainvillea here or would you rather have the honeysuckle?" "Where do you want the jasmine?" "I've got a lovely Tipuana Tipu for you, would you like it right here?" I can only respond with further questions about color, whether it climbs like a vine, grows upward like a tree, or spreads out like a bush. Fortified with that information, I then generally defer to Gillian.

By early afternoon, she has finished. Her gaze sweeps over the profusion of plants in small, medium, and large plastic pots that dot our terrain and promise every shape and shading of greenery. Brushing a tendril of blond hair away from her face, she nods with satisfaction. "We'll be back early tomorrow with the gardeners."

I say nothing and Walter raises a quizzical eyebrow. Our doubts must show because Gillian hastens to add, "These plants must be put into the ground quickly or they'll dry out."

At seven the next morning we do indeed awaken to the sound of shovels and men's voices. Afonso and four teen-aged assistants are swarming across the property, knocking plants out of pots and thrusting them into the newly fertile soil. All the pots are empty by noon.

After lunch, the boys rake the lawn areas smooth, slip cloth pouches over their shoulders like slings and fill them with grass seed from a large burlap bag. Next they trudge back and forth across the land in the age-old way, dipping their hands into the pouches, waving their arms in wide sweeping arcs and letting seeds slips through their fingers. All at once these boisterous teenagers are graceful figures, their movements imbued with a timeless beauty.

By late afternoon, we have an infant garden, still looking very bare with everything small and spindly, but hopeful. With sprinklers going through their programmed waterings, automatically sequencing twice a day through eight zones at thirty-two minutes each, it is definitely a beginning. Gillian's crew will be responsible for tending the new garden throughout its first three months; all Walter and I have to do is observe and wait for all the little green things to grow.

The potential life of the little green things is complicated by the fact that we now have a big black thing—our puppy, if one can refer to an animal the size of a dinosaur tot as a puppy. Caesar is being very good so far. He hardly ever barks, is very friendly, and doesn't seem at all a nervous dog. But at six months, he's a bouncy puppy still. He tears to shreds any blanket or pad we've tried to give him for his comfort, and he hasn't yet been trained not to dig up the garden, not to jump up on people to welcome them, and not to pull my arms out of their sockets when I'm walking him on a lead. Since we don't yet have a fence around the property, Caesar spends most days either tied up on the terrace next to our living room or in the pen we built for him in the shade of the hillside trees. He must be exercised regularly and Walter is the only one strong enough to walk him. After we get the boundary fence, we can let him loose which will be good for him but perilous for the frail young plants.

Besides that, he is big and strong and unruly. When he's happy to see me, he can knock me down and that scares me. When he pulls on the lead, I can't hold him back and his speed over the rough terrain sometimes makes me trip and fall and that scares me too. Why did Walter have to get such a *big* dog?

When Caesar is on the terrace, I keep thinking how good he's being, tied up like that and I feel sorry for him. And when he looks at me with those opaque black eyes, I feel that something more or better is expected but I can't provide it. For me, his presence takes away the peace of solitude but doesn't bring the pleasure of companionship. I'm always somewhat anxious about him and

I'm extremely anxious about Walter going away next month. I'll have to walk Caesar a bit better by then but I need training as much as the dog does. We have enrolled in a dog training school up in Loulé which begins on Saturday, perhaps that will help.

Early each morning we take Caesar for a run on the beach before it gets too crowded or too hot. To get there, we walk through the Vale do Lobo golf course and since we are out before seven o'clock, we are past the fairways before the first golfers appear. On these early morning walks, Caesar races out away from us and then loops back to make sure we're still there. Though he's large and weighs about eighty-five pounds, like Tigger from *Winnie the Pooh* he doesn't yet know how to control his bounciness. On the golf course this fine morning he streaks toward us from behind and on his way past he smashes into me and knocks me flat. I'm not hurt, but I am very startled and also very soggy because the fairway sprinklers have just done their work. Walter, trying to be sympathetic, can't help laughing to see me suddenly sprawled in the wet grass. Caesar must have enjoyed it too because when we reach the beach a few minutes later, he repeats the cannon ball from behind and flattens Walter on the sand. At this point, Walter is not nearly as amused.

After we get back home, we give Caesar a hard-boiled egg for his mid-morning treat. Then we set up pool furniture and two outside tables with new blue and pink striped umbrellas. We have a swim and an outdoor brunch and gloat over our beautiful poolside.

"Doesn't this feel like a model Sunday morning?" I ask as Walter enjoys one of the region's delicious oranges. He waves an orange section in an arc that takes in the new pepper tree on the lawn, our lemon tree near the kitchen door, the *floreira* (cement flower box) filled with red ivy geraniums on the patio, and two gorgeous pink bougainvillea on the terrace waiting in pots to be planted. "The place is shaping up," he says with evident satisfaction.

Caesar doesn't resemble most Algarvian dogs. They are terra

cotta colored with sandy brown eyes, as if they had been scooped directly out of the soil and set on their four legs. Caesar is obviously a foreigner, larger, blacker, fuzzier, and more rambunctious than the native breeds. To encourage his settling down, we go to our first lesson at the dog obedience school where we are directed to a sandy exercise field. The trainer is Harold, a retired British policeman. He is tall and fit, wears a khaki shirt and shorts, carries a small leather swagger stick, and needs only pith helmet to complete the *pukka sahib* image. In a booming voice, he organizes owners and dogs into pairs. I join several other spouses at a small grandstand and watch as both Walter and Caesar do very well walking around the ring with the others. At the end of the lesson, we get Caesar a new choke collar that tightens if the dog pulls too hard, and Harold shows us how to hold it while walking with him. Maybe this will help me; I've got to have something to offset the dog's muscle power. Class over, everyone goes to a nearby pub, including the dogs who are tired from their lessons and lie under tables without any interest in each other.

Last night we had an electrical power outage, and after electricity was restored the water pump repeatedly shut down. We slept badly, hearing the pump grind off and on, and worrying about our new garden. As soon as we can decently call it morning, we get up and go to the pump house. Even though lights flash obediently on the control panel, no water comes out of any garden sprinkler heads nor, for that matter, out of any faucets in the house. It is five a.m., too early to call anyone, so Walter takes the dog for his morning beach run while I swim laps to pass the time. The sun rises while I'm swimming and I look up at our new poolside umbrellas and think that colorful beach umbrellas must be one of the most cheerful of human inventions. They signify leisure, light refreshment, fine weather, playfulness, no worry or drudgery in the picture.

But I am sharply aware that such pretty scenes can be deceiving. After my swim, no hair wash because no water. No irrigation for the plants. We ourselves will be all right in a temporary water shutdown; we can shower at Vila Bonita or at my friend Wendy's house, and we can fill buckets with pool water to flush the toilets. But for our fragile new garden, this is a potential catastrophe. At eight a.m. we rush down to Gillian's place to send for Afonso.

This time, he comes within the hour, surveys the equipment and declares, "The problem must be with the pump, and I cannot fix that. We must call the pump *enginiero*."

He leaves to do so while we stare up at the pitiless sun. Praying for rain is pointless, rain being about as likely in August in the Algarve as a palm tree on a polar ice cap. I dip a bucket into the *cisterna* several times and water by hand the pepper tree, the lemon tree and some flowers near the house, feeling myself a puny version of Isak Dinesen trying to hold on to her coffee plantation in the Ngong hills. All day I worry about the relentless broiling sunshine.

The next afternoon, a lightning quick response by Algarvian standards, Afonso, accompanied by Gillian, brings the pump engineer. They study the situation. First the engineer goes into the pump house to check the cistern and test the pump. In a few moments, he emerges shaking his head.

"*Problema* is not the surface pump."

"What then?"

"Must be the pump down in the well," Afonso ventures.

The pump down in the well? I didn't know we <u>have</u> a pump in the well.

Senhor Enginiero gathers his tools. "I must bring the truck and winch to raise the pump."

Our hearts sink. "When will that be?"

"*A manhan*, tomorrow."

"But our garden," we wail, "it's already been two days without water."

He looks sympathetic. "*A manhan*. I come tomorrow," he repeats and leaves for his next repair job, a man inured to the string of dire emergencies and woeful faces he probably confronts several times each day.

"What can we do?" we turn to Gillian who shakes her head.

"It's a very critical time," she says, bending down to touch several small shoots. "If he can fix it tomorrow I think we'll be OK. If not, I don't know."

The next day, the engineer returns with an assistant in a truck with a motorized winch. Slowly, the two men pull up length after length of twenty-foot well pipe, the same pipe we saw lowered down into that same bore hole six months ago. At last, at the very end, a ten-foot cylinder emerges from the hole, *voila*, the recalcitrant pump. The engineer and his helper dismantle a few sections and study the entrails while we look on in suspense, as though waiting for the outcome of open-heart surgery. Regrettably, this patient doesn't make it.

"*Nao e bon*. Is no good." The engineer pronounces the sad verdict. "The pump is burned out, is necessary to get another one."

"When?" Gillian and I gasp in unison.

"How much?" my husband grumbles.

"*Nada*. Is on the guarantee. The factory must pay." The engineer addresses the last question first.

"When?" we all press again.

He scratches his head. "I order today, but is Friday. Maybe Monday or Tuesday it arrive...next day I come back and install."

We all stand silent in mourning. "The garden will die," I breathe.

Blessedly, Gillian takes charge. "We'll have to get water somehow," she decides. "The cisterna pump is all right?"

"*Sim, sim*," the engineer assures her. "*Problema* is with the bore hole pump."

"Afonso will have to get water," Gillian announces. If he can arrange it quickly, we may save most of the garden." Gillian explains that local fire departments have access to reservoirs and ponds from which they transport water by truck to many households that have cisterns but no wells. "They can fill your *cisterna* and then the surface pump can work the irrigation system."

This news is like Christmas in July.

"But you'll have to pay for the water," Gillian cautions.

"How much?" Walter still wants to know.

"Of course, anything." I jump in. The tender green plants are the most important to me. I wouldn't mind losing the grass; a few bags of seed can replace the first sowing. But all those young flowers, lantana that will form a hedge at our fence, oleander by the driveway, cana flowers in front of the bookshop--and the infant fruit trees, orange, lemon, lime, fig, olive--I can't bear the thought of their shriveling up in their brand-new planting circles.

The following evening Afonso returns. Proud as Hannibal leading an elephant, he leads a huge truck with a drum like an oil van into our driveway. It chugs up to our pump house where the driver inserts a huge hose through the small window and down into the cisterna. A marvelous rush of water follows; 10,000 kilos to fill the cisterna. When the truck leaves, we adjust dials to shorten the watering cycles and turn on the water. Zone one sprinkler heads spray glorious silver droplets across the drooping heads of countless baby plants in front of the shop. Fifteen minutes later, zone two showers shrubs at the side, then zone three the new lawn on the other side, zone four the succulents at the back, and so on through the entire eight zone cycle. Afonso has saved us!

Afonso shows up at all hours when things go wrong. But he's dreadfully overworked with too many projects. *"Muito, muito trabalho,"* he says, when we praise him, much much work, with everyone demanding Afonso, Afonso, Afonso. I say we probably need ten Afonsos. He smiles and says maybe five would be enough.

The water truck has to come three more times before the new well pump is installed ten days later. The total cost is 60,000 escudos or $360, a high price for water but it has saved much of the garden. Still, we lost about a third of the new plants and about half the lawn. The landscaper guarantees what she plants *unless* water systems fail, acts of God, etc., so what we lose, we lose. At least it gives us the chance to reduce some of the elaborate garden that Gillian talked us into. We should have learned from observing native Algarvians, like Mike, who love flowers but don't plant more than they can water with a hose.

A month later, most plants have taken hold and are sending green shoots across the bare earth. An encouraging expanse of light green grass shows that Gillian was right to persuade us that a lawn would create a lovely vista beside our intensely blue pool.

With our windows now open at night in the warm weather, we hear the nightly dog chorus. Though less exotic than the lions roaring around Dinesen's African farm, we're surrounded by unseen barking dogs. Every house has at least one dog to guard against burglars (not to mention Giselle's twenty-three), and there are strays that roam in packs. All it takes is one dog yelp to set off a sympathetic barking chain across hill and dale. Now that we have Caesar we also contribute our share of the noise. Caesar is not at all fierce, but he has a basso profundo bark and, since he's only a puppy, has no idea of what he should or shouldn't bark at. He will sleep peacefully through the arrival of workmen who step right over him, but bark wildly at a gecko scuttling by. And distant dog sounds at night evidently need a roared response. Walter and I take turns getting up to soothe him, like quieting a new baby. Fortunately the sleep we lose at night can be made up during the midday siesta when Caesar, like the rest of us, is limp and logy from the heat.

We've decided while Walter is away to board Caesar at the kennel where we take the dog training lessons, a great relief to me since I can't yet control him. Caesar and I tolerate each other with mild affection and a good bit of skepticism, and I hope that in time we'll get to be friends. Caesar and Walter are another story. Caesar's dark eyes follow Walter's every move adoringly and he wants nothing more than to be at his side. We untie him whenever Walter is in the garden engaging in his new pastime of raking the planting circles around the little trees. Then Caesar stays as close to him as possible, like a foot soldier admiring a five-star general. In return, Walter already loves his dog and a few days before his trip to the States, he comes out of the house with our camera.

"Would you take some pictures of me with Caesar? I want to show the kids." He poses with Caesar next to a poolside table, an arrangement that displays the young dog's impressive height. I snap several shots so that Walter can show off in Saratoga.

It strikes me that it isn't quite true that you carry yourself along when you leave home and reproduce your accustomed life anywhere else you go. You do carry your familiar self, but conditions in another place can be quite different. I certainly have an entirely new class of things to worry about: a *cisterna*, an irrigation system, a pool, burglaries, an alarm system linked to unreliable electric power, a boundary fence that never gets finished, a carpenter who won't work, customs officials who won't reveal import regulations, a large dog, and a tropical garden in a sand pit. We drive five miles to get our mail and the newspaper, I dry clothes on a rack, we have no TV and understand only fragments of the language. We gave no thought to any of these things in our Saratoga lives, but *viva a diferença*!

XII
Keeping On

We have now lived in the Algarve for six months. Landscaping is proceeding, our villa is partially furnished, electric power has been connected to the house, the hot water heater installed, and we've even acquired a washing machine. Though a familiar brand, its instruction booklet is printed only in Portuguese and Arabic. I've deciphered the Portuguese but don't yet understand why I can't open the machine's door until it has washed everything for two hours.

With some remaining qualms, I agree to Walter's urging that we hire a maid. When Louis next inquires, I tell him I have only enough work for two half-days a week. He nods thoughtfully and when he returns for the regular pool cleaning, he says that his cousin Mafalda would be glad to work two afternoons a week. I try one last delaying tactic and tell Louis that she must provide her own transportation. "I will have a bookshop, *uma livraria,* in the other building," I explain, "and I won't be able to leave."

Louis trumps me with a satisfied smile. "My cousin Mafalda is buying a *bicyclette.* She will have it next month."

A week later he brings Mafalda to meet us. A plain sweet-faced young woman, she emerges from Louis's dusty blue car, smoothes her dress and approaches us shyly. We exchange simple greetings and, in my minimal Portuguese, I explain our requirements.

Mafalda and Louis confer and together tell us that within a month or two she will get a *bicyclette*, (what we would call a moped). They further assure us that she lives near by, and until the bicyclette arrives, she'll find walking to and from our house *não problema*. Our terms have been met. Mafalda seems pleasant and eager to work at a reasonable wage. I have no more excuses. We agree that she will clean for us on Tuesday and Friday afternoons for a trial period of three months. Having settled the matter, we shake hands all around with much smiling and nodding to show good will.

Mafalda is twenty-six years old, the daughter of a poor Algarvian farmer, with the stocky figure of many women in the region. Promptly the following Tuesday, she trudges up our rutted driveway carrying a black leather purse and a plastic bag containing her apron and clogs. As soon she enters the house, she exchanges her sling-back street shoes for the clogs and puts on the blue and white checked apron that has armholes and fastens over her street clothes like a housedress. Before starting to clean, she opens her purse, takes a photograph from her wallet and hands it to me.

"*Meu bebe,* my baby."

I see a tiny brown speck of a baby's face within a froth of lacy white bonnet and gown, surrounded by white cushions and flowers. A formal christening portrait I imagine and having few Portuguese words, I smile and make admiring sounds.

"*E morte,*" Mafalda explains. The baby is dead.

In shock, I realize that I am looking at a picture of the infant's funeral bier. I search for an appropriate response, but even beyond the language barrier, I don't know what to say. The photograph is a stark reminder that we are in a foreign country. No American woman would, without preamble or warning, put such a picture into my hands. I have seen photographs of children who subsequently died, but those were taken earlier while the child was still alive. One could remark on charming features, bright eyes, sweet smile, any of the attributes of living children. But never, outside of nineteenth century history books, have I seen an image of a treasured child in death. My murmurs change to sounds of pity.

"How did the baby die?" I ask at last.

Mafalda sadly shakes her head. "Morte..." she searches for English words. "Baby die when born. Doctor not come for long time."

"Where was that?" I ask, thinking that as a rural woman she might have had her baby at home.

"Faro Hospital."

The biggest, the only hospital in the Algarve. Her story distresses me not only because of its personal sadness but also for what it signals about health care in the region.

We look at each other in silence for a few moments. Then Mafalda carefully restores the baby's picture to her wallet, closes her purse and briskly sets to dusting the furniture. The photograph was her way of introducing herself more fully. She will be working in our home and wanted me to know who she is and what matters most deeply to her.

July has come and with it Walter's next trip to the States. At 8:00 a.m. I kiss him good-bye at Faro airport and then drive to the dog training school for my first lesson alone with Caesar. He ignores all my commands and interferes with other dogs and owners. Two or three times I feel on the verge of tears. At the lesson's close, I take Caesar to his pen and leave him.

For days I continue upset by the bad lesson, thinking that there's just no basic affinity between me and the dog. Yet I also feel guilty for leaving him at the kennel. I'm like the woman in Doris Lessing's *The Fifth Child* who takes back her dreadful son from the asylum, not because she wants him or loves him, but because she cannot live with the thought of what is being done to him. That's how I feel when I think of Caesar in the kennel. But I try to enjoy my vacation away from him by reminding myself that he is not being mistreated there.

Several days pass and I again drive up to the kennel for dog training. I think Caesar has grown if that's possible and he's stronger than ever. He pulls me so strongly on the way out that I stumble and fall down. But more or less we manage the lesson of the day which is not the usual one that focuses on basic (hah!)

commands like heel, sit, down, stay, etc. Today's lesson takes place in a field high in the hills above Loulé and is an exercise in "tracking and seeking" actually intended for more advanced dog-students. Caesar and I go along though it's a bit like taking a kindergartner to FBI intelligence training.

The dogs are expected to find articles belonging to their owners that have been scattered across the field, supposedly dropped by a robber on the run. They should then discover and apprehend the robber (actually Harold, the trainer) who lurks in the bushes. Caesar performs well for a puppy though he does miss the main points of the exercise. He finds my pink socks under a tree, but certainly doesn't bring them back to me, nor does he pay the slightest attention to the lurking robber, even when the villain throws pebbles at him to gain his attention. But I am pleased that he comes back to me when I call and we are not a total disgrace like last week. I've decided to bring him home on Saturday. That way we can practice the commands before next Wednesday's lesson.

I take Caesar down to a remote stretch of beach that is usually empty in the mornings. Today, however, a solitary gentleman appears in the distance. Caesar gets set to hurl himself at the approaching man. I grab and tether him. The man who is elderly says, "thank you very much" with evident relief and I say the usual stuff, "he's only a puppy," "he wouldn't hurt you," etc.,etc., that people always said to me when their monster dogs leapt about. It never reassured me a bit. Now I'm on the other side and try to think of some calming words. "He doesn't bite"? He doesn't, but he might well knock you down in his enthusiasm and that's no comfort to an older person. "He's a puppy and still learning his manners"? Pleasant, but vapid since so far he clearly hasn't learned them. The only convincing action is putting him on the lead and that means he's got to come when called.

I guess I'm glad I took the dog home. A new and difficult thing is on its way to being mastered, and it can't be as terrifying as learning to drive a stick-shift car here last summer. By now I am proficient at driving and, with pertinent language tips from Fernão,

I can even mutter *"Filho da Puta"* (son of a -----) when another driver cuts me off. Winning out over difficulty does wonderfully increase confidence, but at my age I should be at the stage when accumulated knowledge and experience are meshing smoothly. That doesn't seem to be my lot; something new always appears and finds me unprepared. While I don't seem to become wiser, at least I don't grow hemmed in and stale. I guess that's all to the good.

Anyway, Caesar now looks to me for his sustenance, physical and dog-emotional. He watches me, alert for any move I make and eager for attention. Dogs watch as if all good things in the universe come to them, or can be withheld, through the person nearest them. It's a heavy responsibility. I'm trying to resist the seemingly bottomless desire for attention by thinking that I'm giving Caesar the best I can. Two good runs each day, piss walks at regular intervals, food, and as much stroking as I can manage without his flattening me. With that, I can relax.

Yesterday at dog training school Caesar and I were magnificent! Progress over last time about 100%. We even got applause, once when he slithered over a jump obstacle at my command, and once when he was in the "sit" position and let me walk away for five paces and then came to me when I called. We were mighty proud. At the café afterwards, Caesar was so tired he just flopped down; I had to drag him across the terrace to make room for the other dogs who lay all about as their owners had coffee or brandies.

Harold told me, "Good show today!" as he tossed down his brandy. I was pleased and reached down to give Caesar a pat. Harold approved and said, "You know, dogs will do almost anything for praise from their master, even stupid things they have no interest in like jumping through hoops or walking on their hind legs."

Caesar does seem to want a few things besides praise, like getting food, chasing birds, and burying big bones, but praise is clearly important too. I'm not so different. I also wanted praise at the dog class, and when I got it from Harold and the other owners,

I felt wonderful.

All in all, during Walter's absence, the dog and I have made great progress. He doesn't knock me down any more since I followed the trainer's advice and sobbed bitterly the last time Caesar flattened me on the beach. He now comes when I call and he enjoys my grooming him. His weak area is still "heel" which he can't seem to include in his repertoire. Either he pulls so hard on the lead that he nearly strangles himself with the choke collar, or he keeps his head wedged into my knee. Neither maneuver makes for a graceful owner-dog walking duo. Caesar also lacks understanding of his guard dog duties, but because he is so large, with no action on his part he does inspire fear in those who see him for the first time. As for the rest, we'll keep on with the training.

Walter gets back from the States in good spirits, suitcases packed with treasures.

"First of all, I've got birthday presents from the girls for the *mater familias*," he hands me three soft packages wrapped in purple tissue paper. I tear them open and find pink and flowered summer skirts and knit shirts made of cotton. These are most welcome. Since cotton isn't grown in Portugal, cotton clothing here is hard to find and very expensive.

"And look what I've got for Caesar," Walter proudly unpacks packets of Heartguard pills and various grooming combs and brushes for the dog. Then he hands me back issues of New *York Times Book Reviews*, bank statements and accumulated mail and finally, best of all, two packages of Famous Amos chocolate chip cookies.

I take my booty to the living room and look through the mail while Walter, tired from the long flight and the drive from Lisbon, sleeps for a couple of hours. To celebrate his return we go out to dinner at *A Floresta*, a local restaurant we've come to like. Except for a stark neon-lit display case at one side (seemingly obligatory for the region's eating places), the lighting is soft throughout the rooms, the furniture is wooden and rustic, and the waiters are friendly both to the few *estrangeiros* like us and to the resident

Portuguese clientele that surrounds us. Tonight we savor the grilled
sea bream, caught by Quarteira fishermen this same morning, its
snowy flesh a subtly sweet contrast to its rock-salt crusted skin.
Walter and I are happy to be together again and we talk and talk
sharing our news.

The midday sun burns at white heat and we try to get our
errands done before eleven. Early Saturday morning, we drive
to the market at Loulé and buy a small grill to satisfy Walter's
new passion for grilled sardines. This way, we can both be happy.
He can grill outdoors just as Mike does, and I, like Odette, won't
have to cope with the pungent odor of sardines throughout the
house. We also buy a straw basket to carry our groceries since
few *mercados* here give out shopping bags, and we complete
our purchases with some strawberries from a sidewalk stall. The
strawberry season is coming to an end and the berries, though still
delicious, are getting a bit mushy. Women vendors are eager to
move them out and shovel them from bins into plastic bags, their
arms red with juice up to the elbows.
We rattle back down the long hill and are home by half past
ten. An hour later the heat is too intense beside the pool for me
to write in my journal and I have to move to the shady terrace.
It seems only a week or so since we sought warmth from every
sliver of sunlight. Now early morning and late afternoon are the
pleasant hours. How quickly it all has changed.

Senhor Feliciano begins to figure in my weekly lunch
conversations with my new American friends Wendy and Cecile. I
learn that he owns the building where Cecile's real estate office is on
the second floor. Evidently Senhor Feliciano remains unperturbed
by her pleas for attention. "We beg and even threaten to move out
but he just stares at us and nothing happens."
"Same with me," I say.
"I tell you what," Cecile offers. "I'll lend you my secretary.
Rosa can talk to him in Portuguese about your problem with the
bookcases."

Before my next visit to the carpentry shop, I stop at Cecile's office and explain my problem to Rosa who speaks excellent English. With Cecile's agreement, I take Rosa with me and drive to see Sr. Feliciano. She tells him in rapid and voluminous Portuguese that if the job isn't finished by next week as promised, I'll want my money back. *"Proxima semana,"* he again promises. In our tug of war, who will give in first? I take Rosa back with thanks for her help and wait for next week.

When I again visit Senhor Feliciano, I am cheered to see that he has now produced three bookcases, exactly in accord with the designs and measurements I gave him.

"Muito bem" (very good), I offer in acknowledgement of his efforts, and he deigns to accept my praise with a slight nod of his head. With this progress, I begin to believe he is actually working on my order. Maybe my work has now reached the head of his queue and he will complete it this month.

Hope revived, I telephone Hammick's, the English wholesaler, and assure Humphrey Biggs that I'm near to placing an order for books. Humphrey, like a wise uncle, is patiently steering me toward the practice of bookselling. When I ask his advice about stocking rental books, he encourages me to do so, with a caution. "You must have a deposit. If a book sells for five pounds, your deposit should be five pounds. Then tourists can rent it for twenty-five pence, and if they carry it off in their plane, they can have the pleasure of knowing they bought it for twenty-five pence more than it costs."

I'm grateful for his guidance and, since he does want my opening book order, the benefits aren't all one way.

The beach where Wendy, Cecile and I had our first lunch is lovely, but too far from town for three working women. We now meet each week in Almancil at the bistro, run by a cute young Irish lass, Megan Grenville. She has straight brown hair, blue eyes and plentiful freckles. Her bistro serves appetizing sandwiches, which appeal to us more than the typical Portuguese midday dinner of lamb, potatoes and green beans and carrots.

"I wish you'd hurry up with that bookstore," Cecile says as the three of us cluster around a small café table. "I'm tired of having to order books by mail."

"So am I," echoes Wendy, "and you can't browse by mail."

"You'll have to advertise, of course." Cecile points her swizzle stick at me. "When you're ready to open, I'll put it in the AFPOP newsletter. That'll get the expats."

"There's the *Algarve News* for them, too," Wendy says. "You could buy an ad there, or maybe I could do a feature."

Wendy, a trained psychologist, has few patients here. Since she and her husband Nigel like to dine out, she has persuaded the editor of the *Algarve News* to pay her for writing restaurant reviews. "The pay is peanuts," she says, "but it covers our dinner costs and gives me something to do."

I am learning that such versatility is in line with the Algarve's frontier spirit. As in any frontier not every advance idea works out as planned. Plucky people like Wendy turn their talents to what's at hand.

Wendy and Cecile's enthusiasm at the prospective bookshop is matched by that of Kitty Edwards when I next see her. "It will be heaven," Kitty says, "to tootle down to your shop when I want a good read, and not have to wait for the post to bring us books from the U.K."

Year-round foreign residents like my new friends represent a potential market that I hadn't figured on and I'm exhilarated. But I bump back to earth when I stop in once more to check on Senhor Feliciano's progress. He has not continued beyond the three bookcases he showed me last week. I can only convey my frustration by glaring and sighing, maneuvers that have as much effect on Senhor Feliciano as a flea hopping around on a buffalo's back. I decide I need to acquire some compelling Portuguese phrases with which to confront him, and go upstairs to Cecile's real estate office to consult with Rosa who gives me a new phrase which I write down. I go back downstairs, but the garage door to the carpentry shop is now closed.

After a few days, when I can again gain access I ask, "*Porque o Senhor não abaca meu trabalho?*" (Why don't you finish my work?)

Unperturbed. Senhor Feliciano points to the same three bookcases. Then I bring out my rehearsed reply, "*Não brinca comigo*" (don't play games with me). He shakes his head at my lack of faith and says he isn't playing games, has *muitas problemas*. Be that as it may, he is certainly making *muitas problemas* for me.

Frustrated, I decide to ask for my money back but by this time my Portuguese has evaporated. In confusion I can only stammer my ultimatum in poor French, "*Alors, donnez moi mon argent*" (give me my money).

Senhor Feliciano refuses. "*Não, não esta possivel.*" On and on we go with me limping along from phrase to phrase, until at last I leave deeply discouraged, knowing I'll have to go back again in a few days.

At home I complain to Walter who is sympathetic but no more astute than I about how to goad Senhor Feliciano into activity. A man of good questions, though, Walter keeps thinking. "It seems a shame to let everything depend on this one carpenter," he says a bit later. "Isn't there any other way you can open the shop?" I note that for him this has become *my* problem and my shop.

I don't have an immediate answer to Walter's question but as the day wears on, it stimulates a new resolve. I decide to order books as soon as I can, even if I have to open the shop with books displayed on planks over wooden saw-horses. Walter is right; I can't let one carpenter determine my whole future. Things move forward, I conclude with restored energy, when one starts working on alternatives.

I begin the next day with a long conversation with Humphrey Biggs. I start by saying "I'd be willing to send some money to you up front if you could just get the ROSI opening inventory list to me quickly." He says, "Hold on a moment, I'll just consult a bit with my superiors." After a few minutes he gets back on the line. "We suggest that you post ten thousand pounds sterling as a down payment and we'll be pleased to send you the ROSI straight away." That seems like a whopping sum to me but I don't say no.

I counter by suggesting I might send five thousand, and *he* doesn't say no. We leave the exact figure up in the air.

We consider timing. "I plan to open the shop in September and then close it in early December when we go home for the holidays."

Humphrey is appalled. "But my dear, you'll miss the Christmas season. That's when you make sixty percent of your income for the year."

"Actually, Humphrey, I'm not sure there *is* a Christmas selling season for English books in the Algarve. Anyway I can't possibly miss our Christmas at home in the States. That's where our family is, our children, and our first grandchild."

Humphrey accepts this with a regretful, "Oh. Quite."

We work on. Since we'll be in Saratoga for Christmas, Humphrey advises me to delay book delivery till January or February for a spring opening at the start of next year's tourist season. I fret at having to wait so long, but I can't see an alternative. We close our conversation by exchanging promises: Humphrey will send the ROSI and I'll send $5,000 (dollars, not pounds) which will serve as a deposit on my initial book order. It's progress of a sort. I hang up the phone thinking that the shop's opening keeps receding like the end of a rainbow when one heads toward it. All I can do is keep on so that all will be ready when spring comes.

Today is my birthday, marked by early phone calls from my daughters which cheer my morning hours. Then Gunnar Nielsen telephones and asks me to stop by to pick up the new identity card he ordered for me to replace the one taken by the burglars. I park John Henry like a little red tugboat behind the huge silver Cadillac in front of his office. Gunnar greets me with a boisterous, "*Bom dia*, Marianne," waves me to a chair in front of his desk, and disappears into the back office's dark interior. In a few moments, he and his daughter Ingrid come back smiling. Then Mrs. Nielsen, whom I hardly ever see, also appears. She is a stocky dark-haired woman, unremarkable except for her startling green eye shadow. As his wife and daughter beam, Gunnar presents me with a bottle of wine tied with a red ribbon and the whole family wishes me a happy birthday.

I am touched and surprised. "How did you know?"

Gunnar hands me the identity card and points to my birth date on its front. "Not so difficult," he booms, and we smile and shake hands.

I drive home with my gift and when I get there I see that this is a milestone day for another reason. Walter greets me with a big smile and leads me to the shop building. While I was in Almancil, at long last and probably to placate me, Senhor Feliciano has delivered the three bookcases he has finished! They look fine in the shop and I am encouraged. Maybe he will now get to work on the other seventeen items.

Thus energized I ask Wendy if she knows of any graphic designers who might work on designing letterhead and a logo for the shop. Wendy guides me to Cynthia Green, a young woman with a small design shop on the edge of Almancil. Cynthia is in her thirties, attractive with fair skin and dark hair, and the chirpy high-pitched voice I've come to associate with many English women here. I explain my wish for a distinctive design for the shop's letterhead and signage and Cynthia pleases me by suggesting bookmarks as well. We agree on a terra cotta colored paper. I then explain the bookshop's name and bring out photographs and drawings of statues of griffins that I've assembled.

"The ancient griffins guarded treasure and looked fierce and scary," I say, "but I want my shop's griffin to look friendly, not frightening to children. Maybe it should be a funny griffin. Do you think that's possible?"

Cynthia, her brow a bit wrinkled, studies the pictures, then looks up with a brave smile.

"I've not done this type of logo before, but it shouldn't be a problem. I'll get started straight away," she promises.

A few days later, she brings a very nice design with lettering in dark red ink, which looks fine against the terra cotta paper. The words "The Griffin Bookshop" form a circle around the central logo. I like the circle, but the seated griffin at the center is a droopy animal that looks less like the mythical blend of a lion and an eagle than that of a dog crossed with a chicken. This dispirited beast isn't what I want, but I don't quite know what to say.

Cynthia sighs. "I'm really not an artist you know. It isn't my forte."

"I like the graphics a lot," I tell her. "I'll have to think about the griffin sketch."

"Right." She agrees cheerfully, leaving me to start the thinking. I could keep Cynthia's lettering and layout but I guess I do need an artist. Where to find one? A bit later I remember seeing art exhibits at the *Centro Cultural*. It's worth a try. I drive there, locate the German owner in the gallery shop, and explain my mission. The owner is chilly but consents to speak to a Belgian artist who lives nearby. I'm given no name, no address, no telephone. The artist will call *me* if he's interested. Maybe.

Today is Sunday when stores and offices are closed. I can't go shopping or keep prodding for the bookshop, and the summer sun is too hot for Walter to play golf, so it feels like a very long day for both of us. Late in the afternoon, we decide to drive down to the beach. It is high tourist season and we avoid the resort complexes and head for the open stretch of coastline where local people go. Even here, it is more crowded than we remember. Ninety percent of the people are Portuguese. Very few topless girls. Young men playing *futebol*, and couples playing paddleball along the water's edge where the sand is packed down. Children of all skin shades, some playing, some clinging to their parents in awe at the huge water. Three slim Africans sit in a row apart from other people, the sun so bright and they so black that they look like cutout silhouettes against the white sands. Some older Portuguese men their faces and hands brown and grizzled from outdoor work, bodies pale and unused to the sun. Pretty girls with long hair, chunky grandmothers. Nearly all the people look like members of the same enormous family. A busy happy beach on a summer's day. We're glad we came.

XIII
Discoveries

On a Monday, mostly to nudge the bookshop along, I drop in at the moving company that transported our furniture and books from Zurich. Nelia is the beautiful young woman who managed the move, and it occurs to me that she might know something about import duties on books. It turns out she does. Nelia provides the answers that the customs officer kept concealed behind his mustache.

"There is no duty on books from European Community countries," she tells me. Then she consults a ledger and adds, "and there is a 7.3% duty on books from non E.C. countries."

This information confirms my hunch that I'm limited to importing books from England. I've been hoping to bring in American books as well, but added customs duties would make those too expensive.

Meanwhile, to improve my social and business skills, I have resumed Portuguese language lessons to which I am far more suited than to fieldwork with the dog. I've gone beyond the introductory Portuguese taught by Fernão, who has become our friend. My new teacher, Philipa Milbrook, is a Portuguese woman married to a Canadian. She's more organized than Fernão who has his distinctive seedy charm but no curriculum beyond the basics. Philipa can help me to learn grammar and improve my conversation.

Walter has decided not to join me in further lessons. Like many Americans, he's had little training and no need for speaking other languages. I've noticed in our lessons with Fernão, when Walter practices pronouncing a difficult word, instead of improving with each attempt, he gets worse.

"Say Fernão Magalhãens" (the Portuguese name for explorer Ferdinand Magellan)

"Fernão Magalanes, Magalens, Mogalines…."

By now Walter does quite well with written Portuguese and can decipher much of the newspaper because of his years of Latin. He can also pronounce the names of his favorite dishes in restaurants. The dictionary is available for other words he needs and that's enough for him. He will be hampered in communicating with local people but I sympathize and understand. Without an aptitude, learning a new subject can be onerous. Whenever I try to learn the intricacies of the stock market which Walter seems to understand with ease, I am similarly nonplused.

Somehow, through the expatriate grapevine, word has spread that Walter has opened a practice. In addition to Ben's friend, he has two new patients, both English and both extremely nervous about coming to see him. One is a girl on the edge of anorexia who is brought by her parents. The other is a middle-aged man who is glad there is no sign in front of our house to identify the practice. "Wouldn't want people to think I'm a nutter," he told Walter.

It is a light professional schedule so far, but I can tell that Walter is glad to be working. While he encourages me in the bookshop project, it's increasingly clear that it will be mine rather than his. To be fair, he did signal that right from the beginning. I hoped that he would become as charmed with the enterprise as I, but I have to admit that so far it's been short on charm.   And I'm ever more aware that helping people and feeling needed as a therapist is as important to Walter as breathing. A change of location hasn't changed his vocation. Without it, I'm coming to think, he wouldn't quite know who he is. If he can find English-speaking patients here, or if they find him, we'll be all right. But a sunny perpetual golf retirement could never be enough to keep him happy here or anywhere.

Since Nelia was so helpful I visit her again, hoping to learn something about pricing. Nelia informs me that Portugal has laws about book prices—one can't just add the costs of shipping on top. I take a deep breath as I absorb this information which really sets me back. Since most English-language books come from outside of Portugal, I wonder how any shop can afford to import them. I remember Humphrey Biggs' caution that I must watch my "carriage." The more I learn the more ignorant I feel. The fancy business plan I designed two years ago in my "Small Business Management" course now seems ludicrous. If I can't find a way around the price ceiling, I would be running a charity service, not a business.

As I thank Nelia for her help, I can't help thinking that my bookshop quest has come to seem like trying to start an enormous intricate machine where one has to keep rushing to turn a crank here, check the spin there, add oil or water in another spot, change gauges somewhere else and still the damn thing won't run, though the humming indicates that start-up is getting closer all the time.

Though perplexed about the future, I still pay regular visits to Senhor Feliciano who remains content with his achievement in delivering three bookcases to my shop. He reminds me of it when I ask him about the rest of the order and doesn't seem to plan on completing any more now or in the foreseeable future. Has he perhaps grown bored with making bookcases? I direct his attention to the drawings for my sales desk. He just looks doubtful. With my new questions about pricing, I myself grow doubtful. I start to wonder about alternative uses for our shop building. Could we rent it out? But it's too soon to cry uncle.

Despite my resolve, my spirits are flagging. How could I have planned so much in advance and not researched book pricing laws? Instead of an angel bringing a bookshop to a deprived region, I seem to be a rushing fool. I share my discouragement with Wendy and Cecile at our lunch. Usually we laugh as much as we talk, but today my distress has momentarily stilled our laughter.

Cecile responds like an experienced businesswoman. "You mean you've gotten this far and you haven't even researched how to get books into your shop?"

Her question is clearly reasonable but makes me feel even worse. I have no answer. We sip our Cokes in silence and ponder the situation.

Then Wendy takes pity on me. "You might get some advice from Martha Stimpson. She owns a book and art supplies shop in the town of Porches, about an hour's drive from here."

Gratefully I take down directions to the shop in Porches and that afternoon I telephone. The owner seems friendly and agrees to meet me. A few days later I find her in her shop on the upper level of a small strip mall on the EN-125. Martha Stimpson is a sandy-haired blue-eyed woman of about forty, wearing an artist's apron. I introduce myself and she greets me politely, then gets right to business with a little speech she must have rehearsed since our telephone talk.

"I must tell you, I don't mind you opening a bookshop, but if you were to carry art supplies as well, I should feel very hostile as I plan to open an art studio."

"I don't know the first thing about art supplies; I just want to sell books," I assure her.

Clearly relieved, she then shows me proudly around her shop, pointing out book titles that sell well and a bright array of paint tubes, brushes, and art instruction books. She is setting up a back room as a studio where she hopes to offer art lessons. I admire everything and we exchange brief summaries about who we were before the Algarve. Martha is a young Canadian woman with two little girls who came to the Algarve with her husband who now teaches at an English primary school here. Martha taught at Athabasca University in Canada, a counterpart to the college for adult learning where I spent six years, and we explore this enjoyable parallel for a few minutes.

After this pleasant beginning I ask my questions about importing books. The information she gives strikes me as immensely important. "I buy most of my books from two large distributors in Lisbon." she says. "They do the importing and deal with the customs."

That still leaves me with the question of pricing. "How do you know what to charge for the books?"

"Oh, the distributors set prices. They let me have the books on consignment." My evident surprise leads her to explain. "It's really quite simple: I take what they send me, and I keep thirty percent of the proceeds from what I sell and send them seventy percent. And I can also send back any books I don't sell in a reasonable time."

She makes it sound as easy as ordering a take-out meal, but I'm still wondering how it works. "Can you choose the titles?"

"No, that's the only disadvantage. It might be a problem for what you want to do, but my main interest is in art supplies; books are a side business for me. If I want particular titles, especially art books, I do have to import those directly from England. But it's not a lot of trouble. A friend of mine drives there pretty regularly and he carries them back."

"And how do you know how much to charge for those books that you bring in yourself?"

Martha laughs. "Oh, I charge whatever I think people will pay."

She is unaware of any government regulations, which I take as an encouraging sign. Evidently, no one is looking over her shoulder. It all sounds blessedly easy. The one drawback is the lack of choice. To have a well-rounded collection, I'll still need to buy the shop's opening inventory from England. But after that, I could fill in with available books from Lisbon.

My conversation with Martha restores my belief that I might actually have a shop. She kindly gives me names and addresses of her two Lisbon distributors and also mentions that her main customers are year-round foreign residents during winter, not summer tourists. I have yet to see whether that would be true in my location so close to the resorts of Vale do Lobo and Quinta do Lago, but I come away grateful and encouraged.

I have lunch with Wendy, this time without Cecile who has another appointment. With just the two of us, our talk becomes more personal. Wendy wears strong reds, blues and greens that look good in the brilliant Algarvian sunshine. She has thick curly brown hair and large brown eyes and is not beautiful but her animation and warm interest in people make her attractive. These qualities and her colorful wardrobe probably attracted her husband. Wendy tells me that when she turned forty and had been divorced for some years, she was beginning to think she would never meet a suitable man. She decided to treat herself to a birthday vacation on a Greek Island. There she met Nigel, an English engineer who had chosen the same island for his holiday. Nigel lived and worked in Arabia. Also divorced, he had two teen-age children who lived in England with their mother. Away from their accustomed lives and habits, at leisure in a beautiful place, Wendy and Nigel fell in love. Some months later he followed her to New York and proposed. They married and then there they were, the Anglican oil industry engineer from Arabia who loved desert heat and isolation and the Jewish psychoanalyst from Greenwich Village who loved big cities, fashion shows and nightlife.

"We had to decide where to live," Wendy says. "Nigel couldn't face a cold climate so I, like a fool, agreed to try Saudi Arabia. I was in love and I didn't think it could be as bad as the media said. It wasn't," she gives a dramatic sigh. "It was worse!"

"Because you're Jewish?"

"Partly, but mostly because I'm a woman. For women it was *much* worse. I should have known the minute I landed. They went through my luggage and confiscated my Jane Fonda exercise book and tapes. It had pictures of her in a leotard. Obscene. Not allowed."

"What happened then?"

"I stayed for three months, couldn't drive a car, couldn't even leave the house alone. Finally I told Nigel, 'I love you but I can't live here.'"

They struggled with their problem and finally compromised on the Algarve. "We've been here for three years now," Wendy tells me. "It's not perfect but Nigel has work with all the building going on and I'm free to move about. I find things to do, like being the restaurant critic for the *Algarve News*. I do miss my own profession, though."

I understand and think of Walter's pleasure at the start of a practice here. "You really should meet my husband; you two are in the same line of work. Maybe you and he could explore some possibilities," I suggest. "Why don't we all plan a dinner together?"

She is enthusiastic. "And we should ask Cecile and her husband too. I know just the place, a perfectly chaaawming French restaurant in Loulé. I'll book a table for the six of us."

On the agreed upon evening, we gather at *Aux Bons Enfants,* a cozy French restaurant ideal for conversation. I sit across from Wendy's husband Nigel, a dapper Englishman with a stream of small talk about their two horses, two Great Danes and two cats. Lest Nigel's chatter tempt me into stereotyping the English, I note that Cecile's English husband Charles is pleasant but taciturn, contenting himself with smiling into his wine as conversation swirls around him.

Wendy and Walter hit it off. "The trouble with being a psychologist here," she says, "Is that the English don't go to psychologists. They see it as a real stigma."

"I gathered that," says Walter, "One of my patients told me if the word got out that he'd come to see me, he'd be labeled as a nutter."

"Oh yes, as indeed he would be," Nigel agrees. "We don't run to you every time we hit a bad patch, you see. It isn't like America where it's taken for granted. After all, over there everybody's either a psychiatrist or a patient."

We all laugh. "It's true," I point to Walter. "He's a psychologist;

I'm a patient."

The owner of the restaurant, a handsome young Frenchman, approaches to ask if the meal was to our satisfaction.

"It was wooonderful," Wendy croons and we all agree. As a reward, we are each given a small glass of brandy as a *digestif*. As usual Walter pretends to take a sip and leaves the rest. When the others have finished, I exchange a silent marital leave-taking signal with Walter's eyebrows. "Well, this has been very nice," I say to begin the farewells. No one moves.

"Very nice indeed. Calls for another brandy," Nigel says. Walter and I cover our glasses to indicate that we have had enough while another round is poured. Then a full bottle of red wine is ordered. The talk grows louder; the room grows smokier. Walter and I are clearly out of step with local custom. The evening appears to have no end. What had been enjoyable spirals downward into an ordeal of waved cigarettes and drunken ramblings.

Finally I plead a headache; not a complete lie because my nostrils are stinging from the smoke. Walter and I emerge onto the street to breathe freely at last. On the ride home I try to sort out my thoughts. The dinner that I had expected to be a pleasant expansion of lunches with my new American friends has been worse than disappointing. All in all, the evening's tide of alcohol has alarmed me, having brought back painful years of similar debacles with my children's father.

"I'm sorry," I tell Walter. "I had no idea they all drink so much."

"Not your fault, honey. We're just not used to it."

"Well, I don't think I can get used to it. I've got too many bad memories. And you, not drinking at all. How could you stand it?"

"I'm pretty familiar with drunks, you know, I see a lot of them." Much calmer than I am, he pats my knee. "Mostly when they're in their cups they're just boring."

"What worries me is if that's the social life around here, we can't be part of it."

"We don't know that yet; tonight was just one evening."

As our little car hurtles through the dark countryside and down the long hill from Loulé, I am silent and dejected.

"Easy does it, babe," says Walter, practicing what he preaches.

If the shelving and the book ordering had gone as planned, we would be gearing up for the shop's grand opening. But that's delayed for six months. I feel as though I am living the life of old age, retirement in a sunny clime, long before I'm ready to do so. But I don't know a cure right now, so I try to enjoy it and there's still work to be done around our house.

Our garden plan includes a little palm tree near our front door centered in the courtyard formed by the shop and house buildings. We want to surround the tree by a circular design of small *calçadas* in one of the beautiful black and white paving designs so famous in Portugal and Brazil. As we did for our window grills, we drive through Faro streets and squares to search for a model. Just like the ironmonger, masons can follow a template but have no designs in their heads. I find that odd. They have been skilled for years at the practical aspects of stone-setting, but don't see it as an art, or imagine themselves as potential artists. And yet both these features, intricately shaped iron grills and pavements with decorative cobblestone swirls, are distinctive national art forms just as are the beautiful blue and white *azulêjo* tiles.

In a park at the Faro harbor, we find a tree surrounded by *calçadas* shaped like large flower petals. Perfect! Walter reproduces it on graph paper and we bring the sketch to Afonso who makes a template to appropriate scale. Then the masons set in the stones. Three days later, the little palm is planted and everyone admires the result. In a few years when the tree has grown taller, we'll have a picture-postcard holiday house, evoking images of lazy days and romantic nights. We'll try to hold on to that idea even though our days are often hectic and our nights devoted to quieting Caesar.

One Sunday afternoon, I'm reading on a poolside chaise and glance up from my book to enjoy the view of our garden. Idly

I observe a few tiny black worms inching from the grass across the terrace that rims the pool. I wonder without urgency what they might be and turn back to my reading. Next day as I walk across the terrace to water a rose bush, I see more of them. Are they larger? I can't be sure. By the third day, there are hundreds, definitely larger and fatter. Memory's light flashes on: caterpillars! But the caterpillars I knew in the U.S. ate leaves from trees. Here we have only pines and several new fruit trees. I get Walter and we walk around checking the trees and are relieved that they seem untouched. Yet when we look at the lawn, we see that brownish patches now dapple its former green. I dash for the telephone. "Senhora Gillian, please," I plead with her greenhouse assistant.

"Senhora Gillian *não esta*. Not there. *Vai au* Portimao." Gone to attend a landscapers' conference in Portimao, a coastal city an hour's drive from us.

"Oh no! She has to come. Or Afonso has to come. We have caterpillars eating the grass. It's all turning brown."

"*Diga?*" What?

I've looked up the translation for caterpillars, "*Lagartas*."

"*Ah, sim, sim. Lagartas na relva*. Caterpillars in the grass. *Vou falar Senhora Gillian*. I will tell Senhora Gillian."

All afternoon Walter and I keep walking out to check the lawn. By evening we can hear crackling and crunching. The caterpillars are everywhere. The green of the lawn is disappearing into their now fat bodies. An infestation full-blown in only three days. The speed of the attack has been amazing, its results alarming.

Gillian doesn't come, but after another day of grass gorging, her foreman Afonso arrives, pulls out several handfuls of dead dry grass and confirms the verdict.

"This is bad. They eat the roots," he explains. "We will have to spray tomorrow."

We have grown accustomed to Portuguese custom; once the report is delivered, the messenger disappears. But this time things move more quickly than usual. The next afternoon, Afonso returns, accompanied by two teen-aged boys wearing bathing trunks and sneakers. They take two cylinders with plastic hoses like scuba gear from the truck, strap them across their bare backs and start fumigating the grass. They walk back and forth, leaning forward as they wield the hoses, bending directly into clouds of the pesticide they are spraying. Walter and I are appalled. Half-naked, bareheaded, ungloved, eyes-nose-mouth uncovered, these boys are oblivious to the deadly fumes that envelop them as they walk. To us, the threat to their young lives seems far more serious than a lawn's chewed root system.

"Afonso, that's very bad," Walter warns. "They should wear masks and some protective clothing."

Afonso shrugs his shoulders and smiles.

"That's poison," I insist. "They breathe it in. It can cause cancer."

"It kills the *Lagartas,*" Afonso assures us.

"But you should protect the boys."

"They are used to it. All the *jardinieros*, the gardeners, are. It must be done or you won't have any gardens." He moves away from us, not wanting to hear more. The boys criss-cross the lawn and finish. They pack up their gear and climb back into Afonso's truck. "I will come back in two days to see if all the worms are dead," Afonso calls cheerfully and drives off.

True to his word, he does come back but the caterpillars are not all dead. A second spraying is needed.

"In the States, people wear masks to protect themselves from the fumes, " we try again, hoping to encourage some basic protective measures.

"Yes, is a good thing," Afonso agrees to placate us but the second spraying repeats the first, with his team of barely clad young boys circling around with their cylinders as if on a snorkeling holiday.

It has been a severe infestation. The lawn is brown and dry. Any place one pulls, grass comes out in handfuls with dead scraggly roots attached. Small comfort to know that the culprit worms were interred as part of the devastation. Some days later, Afonso's troop of gardeners return, this time with rakes, hoes, wheelbarrows, bags of grass seed and pellets of fertilizer. The dead lawn is raked up and carted to our property's edge where the boys throw it over the side fence into the neighboring untended field. They spread fertilizer and sow new seed by hand. Then the high-tech automatic irrigation system is set for two daily thirty-two minute cycles. In a week, the new lawn is a green tinge; in a month grass is in; in two months it will need weekly mowing. Meanwhile, the bushes and shrubs are taking hold. Bougainvillea is spiraling up around the pillars by our front door. Here and there a flower blooms brilliant fuchsia. The three months of our landscaping contract with Gillian Field are done; we are on our own.

The garden is much larger and more complex than we wanted or know how to manage. Flowers beside the buildings depend on hand watering. Ornamental plantings and grass further off are watered automatically by irrigation sprinklers, but their performance is erratic. Then there's the new lawn that will need regular mowing.

Louis when tending the pool, surveys our new greenery. "You need gardener now. I take care many pools *and* gardens."

"How can you do all that?" I ask.

"I have helpers," he assures me. "Two boys, good with flowers."

We haven't known anything about his gardening business, but have been pleased with Louis. He comes to work on schedule and keeps the pool water in good balance even through frequent power outages that disrupt the filtration. He has brought us Mafalda who is a great asset. We decide to expand his contract on a trial basis to include the garden.

"But we would expect you to supervise, Louis. Not just two boys."

"*Sim,* I come also," Louis promises.

XIV
Another August

A year ago I stayed at Vila Bonita and watched over construction of our villa. Again this August the heat slows everything down. Some things stop altogether. The banks, for instance, went on strike this week. In Portugal both start and end dates of strikes are announced in advance, making them more protest gestures than complete work stoppages. The bank workers' complaints appear in newspapers and the strike's timing allows both management and labor to spend some time at the beach with their families.

I learn of a one-man work stoppage when I meet Philipa, my new language teacher, at the post office. She must pick up her mail because her neighborhood has had no deliveries for three weeks. The regular mailman is off on vacation. His replacement tried to walk the route for one day but returned with most mail undelivered. He said it was too hot for so much walking, and quit. That evidently was that. The mail will wait till the regular mailman returns. I can't picture a similar situation in the States where we've been raised to believe that neither rain, snow, nor sleet will stop the mail. Such efficiency isn't valued so highly here. And maybe snow and sleet are more energizing; in the cauldron heat of Algarvian summer who can care all that much? Letters won't melt or rot and they lie quite obediently where they are put.

We visit Mike to ask his advice about Senhor Feliciano who does no work and just smirks at me when I ask about progress with my bookcases. When appealed to, Mike narrows his eyes, takes a deep drag on his cigarette and asks, "Do you want a soft or a hard intervention?" A bit fearful, I ask what he'd recommend, and he advises "hard," but doesn't define his meaning. Walter smiles and the two men nod, seeming to have reached an understanding. I am reluctant to ask more, lest the details be incriminating.

As we drive home I ask Walter, "What do you think Mike will actually do?"

"I don't know, but it will be interesting. He's got a lot of friends." Walter envisions the prospect of Mike summoning some sort of Algarvian Mafia to strong-arm the carpenter.

Two weeks later I return to Senhor Feliciano and am met once more with his blank stare and shrugged shoulders. From there I drive to Vila Bonita to tell Mike it's time for the "hard" action he recommended. His response is disappointing. Walter hoped that Mike's posse would ride over to spur the carpenter into action. But when it comes down to it, all we get from Mike is, "I think is time to get a lawyer and you should threaten to sue."

Walter swallows his disappointment at the vanished posse, and I'm not really surprised. It's easy to talk tough when you're far from the battlefield, but most people hate an actual confrontation. Mike is no different. And since no one is going to come to my rescue, I'll go on badgering Feliciano till I at least get half of my stuff. Then I will have gotten the fifty percent I paid for. If I can't get that soon, *then* I will try a lawyer.

We have one cloudless summer day after another. Wendy invites us to attend a horse show at the *Centro Hippico,* once a large country inn, now converted to a riding club with a multinational membership. We drive there on a sunny morning, curious about what awaits us. Riding is a popular sport in Portugal and Wendy and Nigel own two horses. Nigel, like most English people we meet, shares his nation's devotion to both horses and dogs. Wendy, who formerly shared a Greenwich Village apartment with one cat, now lives on a remote hilltop with Nigel, two horses and two Great

Danes. She has been taking riding lessons and recently began to enter competitions. She and Nigel helped to set up the course of moveable fences and potted trees arranged as obstacles for today's event. Each competitor must ride through the series of obstacles and jump over the fences within a time limit of ninety seconds, with points to be deducted for each mistake or seconds of delay.

One by one, the riders take their turns. Wendy is still new enough to riding to appear a bit awkward as she approaches the first jump. But with her customary grit she has practiced diligently, and we cheer as she completes the course on time without a fault. Nigel, trim and wiry, seems the ideal English squire on horseback, his back straight, his carriage perfect. Unfortunately, perhaps because he sampled a bit too much brandy before the ride, his horse shies three times refusing a jump, and Nigel is disqualified. He takes his disappointment with good humor and joins us in the stands. Other riders complete the course with varying success. Handsome Robert Middleton, an actor with London's Old Vic before he settled in Portugal, particularly impresses us. He and his black mare clear every obstacle with grace and win the day's first-prize trophy.

I admire the courage needed for such competitions. Some days you do well, other days you don't, but you just keep trying and go out again another time. Not having had that kind of training when I was young, I never thought about practicing and repeating a performance often enough so that you don't slink away in mortification if you don't do well at any particular occasion. For me it was private, with only the end results open for public judgment, like an exam, a term paper, or a poem

Afterwards, while the riders tend to their horses, Walter relaxes in the spacious lounge and I decide to explore a country road. I pass an ancient stone aqueduct whose arches frame a field where several farm people are gathering beans. The vista looks centuries old, except that the pickers put their beans into sacks made of neon-blue plastic, the material of our time, ugly but lightweight and practical. I walk on through rolling hillsides of daisies tossing and shimmering white against the sapphire sky and I'm aware of the brilliant light that surrounds me. Painters talk about the difference in the light in southern Europe. I am not visually gifted, yet I'm aware that the colors I choose here are different from those I liked in Saratoga. There, clothing or furnishings in soft woodsy tones or pastels seemed ideal. Brilliant colors that were overpowering in that pale northern light are well suited to this dazzling sunshine, like the plumage of tropical birds. Only the new artificial colors, like those plastic bags the pickers use, remain harsh.

When I return from my walk, we congratulate Wendy on her fine performance, commiserate with Nigel for his disqualification, and then we all move to the verandah for a bountiful lunch followed by three kinds of stunningly sweet cake, all tasting exactly the same. We come home in a benign stupor that sends us to chaises beside our pool. Walter works his crossword puzzle and I record this lovely day in my journal.

At the *Centro Hippico* I noticed again that when people first meet here, they give brief summaries of their lives before they came to the Algarve, and then drop the subject. In this place we are all so involved with day-to-day activities that, except for our different accents, the past has little relevance. I, for one, seem to have lost interest in mine. Unlike my first summer here at Vila Bonita when I spent my days writing about my girlhood in Woodstock, I now am too taken up with daily life to care about those distant events. That long ago girl, young wife and mother, returning student, seems like someone else and I am cut off from feeling much about her, good or bad. Even later disappointment about my career has faded away. Who could care, especially if I myself don't? As for my youth, I can't even see it as ancient history; it feels more like paleontology. Will it all come back again when I grow really old? Old people seem in closer touch with their very young selves. We'll see. For now, I grow older in a different way-- interested in the present and the future, a bit bored with the years that went before.

I wonder how being here feels to Walter. His Portugal is a sunny golf course, the morning newspaper and crossword, going to the *mercado* in Almancil and the fish market in Quarteira for sardines or *lulas* (the baby squid), clearing underbrush in our hillside woods in afternoon shade, enjoying dinner at a local restaurant or preparing our meal at home. Sometimes he takes a midday nap. I see him reading through articles and statistics on alcohol consumption and addiction, in between he writes letters to his colleagues or our children. Two or three times a week he sees his few patients.

He doesn't seem to mind this routine, so different from his busy schedule in Saratoga. Still, I feel that he lacks a real purpose here. He doesn't seem to want it over; somehow Portugal has been a dream for him, too. He could easily have backed out after his 1987 illness, but didn't want to, perhaps because he longed to do something adventurous. This Portugal sojourn is, I think, the biggest risk he has ever taken—except for marrying me, that is. He has relied on me to translate our idle musings into an actual adventure for both of us. He wouldn't have done it without me. The odd thing is that I couldn't do it without him either. I need those warm eyes on me, his faith that I can do anything so long as I don't get discouraged. And he is the one person who can assure that I won't get discouraged.

I am discouraged about the dog though. Since Walter's return from his latest stateside trip, Caesar's responses to me are quite different, especially when the three of us are together. I think he's trying to knock me out of the picture. He has again banged into me two or three times at the beach and he won't come when I call nearly as well as he did. Yesterday morning, he jumped up on a young man repeatedly despite our calling and shouting "no." The young man was furious and I didn't blame him. I've decided not to go along on those walks for a while. Let Walter handle the dog till he learns a bit more obedience. They will have a better time together and I'll enjoy more peaceful beginnings of my days.

At the training lessons we keep working on commands for things we want Caesar to do. Unfortunately, the lessons don't address the host of things we want him *not* to do, like not jump on people in enthusiastic greeting, not bark at innocent passers-by along the road, not tear new plants out of the garden. Sometimes it seems like a neck-and-neck race between our efforts to grow and cultivate, and Caesar's instincts to chew, tear, and uproot. I suppose another year of puppyhood will tame those instincts, but a year seems like a long time to protect a garden.

After dog training sessions, social hours at the café often wind up in a shambles because people criticize each other's performance on the training field. This easily leads to criticisms of character and ancestry of both dogs and owners. The dogs share the same tendency. They can be lying peacefully under the tables and in a second turn into a snarling yelping dog mixmaster. Next week there's a dog-owners *meeting*, heaven forefend! We just want a well-trained dog that is reasonably enjoyable to live with, but in order to get the training, we've had to join the *"Canicultura Clube"* (dog-training club). Now we are caught up in paying dues, attending gymkhanas and meetings at which people wrangle with each other, all with heavy lacings of alcohol. It is all far more intense than we bargained for and we still only want to train our dog.

The bright side of this odd affiliation is that we have met William and Sonia, a couple who also wish to train their dog without making it an ever-expanding obligation. William is a rough-hewn man with dark hair, large features, and a pleasant expression. He tells us he's a "Geordie" and speaks like an American movie caricature of English stable grooms or farmers. Quiet at first, he talks quite a bit when he gets started, often with a sense of injury. As one of the disadvantaged working class in England, he is offended by the government's financial assistance to immigrants while giving no help to its own people. For some reason he also feels that Maggie Thatcher is "for the people" because she is against welfare and other "handouts."

In one of our chats, William told us that he was raised in orphanages. Because of that, he has probably felt somewhat excluded all of his life. Mostly he seems a simple proud man who picked up and left when he couldn't get ahead. He is a master carpenter, so he should do all right here in time. I was surprised at his interest in my bookshop.

"I'll be hoping you can bring in some American books on carpentry, they're better than the ones we've got in the U.K.," he says and I'm pleased though ignorant of his subject.

His wife Sonia is pretty with soft blond-white hair, blue eyes and a young face. She's very slim and flat-chested, with delicate, almost spinsterish movements. Her voice is soft, musical, a little nasal. The accent is quite unlike William's, more general middle-class. William tells us she worked in fashion, but it's not clear at what; she does not look fashionable. She is artistic, though, and says she paints though her paints are still packed away, even after she and William have been here a year.

The four of us are different in so many ways, nationally and individually; we probably would never have met had we stayed in our own countries. That's one of the interesting aspects of living in a new environment.

The boundary fence and gate are now complete and Caesar is loose. When he is bored, he tears up the new plants, especially at night while all is quiet. Last night he destroyed a bougainvillea just planted yesterday by the terrace. Uprooted, dismembered, parts strewn all around; it was a brutal murder.

I hate it, dread going out each morning to find another beautiful plant ruined. We'll resume tying him up more of the time but that nullifies his guard dog function. Walter says we just have to watch him more. I don't want to watch him more; I want to enjoy my garden. I feel as though I've been given a baby at the wrong time of life and it isn't even my child. In truth, I resent Walter for inflicting this on me. I should be generous and glad that he finally has the dog he wanted for so long, but I can only manage those good feelings for about three minutes each day. The rest of the time, given the choice, I'd give Caesar back in a flash. Because we spend so much time talking about the dog, Walter says that he thinks Caesar has brought us closer together. I keep remembering the peace and beauty of pre-Caesar days. If he has brought us closer together, it's like a cyclone might have. How differently we see things sometimes.

For example, when Afonso comes to make some repairs to our irrigation system he starts to discuss the work with Walter. Walter passes him along to me, saying, "My wife knows more about the details." That seems to be the division of labor we have evolved. I have essential charge of the details of daily life. I wonder why. Sometimes I resent it, but it must be self-chosen. Abstract thinking often leaves me feeling inadequate, but I can master the practical details that get us from one day to the next. I resent them but cling to them, would have no sense of forward motion without them.

It's the same with the dog. Walter can hold on to his picture of "dogginess" and describe Caesar fondly as "that crazy mutt," while beaming as I feed, play with, and groom the dog, check his paws for burrs, his coat for ticks, wipe his sandy feet when he comes inside, take him to the vet for shots, and try to rescue the plants he has trampled or torn apart. Throughout all this it is Walter who, as he says, "enjoys the dog's presence," whereas I increasingly rail against it. So it seems he has made the better choice about what part of dogginess to take on. A puzzlement.

I had an odd dream last night of walking down the street with my three daughters as children. They all have shaggy dog legs. I say to Sheila, the smallest, that she's just one of the young dogs now. Helen's legs have blonde fur to match her blonde hair. Seems perfectly normal for the little girls to have dog legs like Caesar's beneath the dark blue winter coats they actually wore years ago.

How nutty! The dog legs of course are Caesar's. At the dog school I object when people call Walter and me Caesar's "Dad" and "Mum," yet I do take care of him like a child. Yesterday, I shampooed him and was pleased to see his coat glisten in the sunshine. So because some of the functions are similar, my dream unconscious must be starting to confuse him with my real children of long ago.

Mirabile dictu, Senhor Feliciano has delivered nine more bookcases! It's the end of August and I've lost the summer tourist season but still, hurrah! We have now passed the halfway mark with work done for my fifty percent down payment, made in February. I'm curious to see the carpenter's pace from here on. He might do better now that he's eager for the rest of his money. No lawyer is needed. I gloat. The cards, finally, are in my hands!

I have only a short while to savor my new sense of power. Within days, Senhor Feliciano completes the second half of my order and delivers all the remaining furniture. The pace of this whole contract has been clearly dependent on whose wallet holds the money. With my deposit, Senhor Feliciano was in no hurry to convert cash into bookshop furniture. But once halfway, he knew he would see no more money until he finished the promised work. And now he and a helper unload the truck and place the sales desk and remaining bookcases in spots I indicate in the shop's two rooms.

As he pockets my final check, Senhor Feliciano looks around at his handiwork and asks when I plan to open for business. I say in careful Portuguese that I'm not sure when because his delays have cost me the summer selling season.

With his customary shrug of the shoulders he signals that it's all very regrettable but has nothing to do with him. Then as he leaves—after six months in which I have struggled, huffed and puffed to make myself understood in his language; sent Rosa the Portuguese secretary to convey my frustration; deputized Mike to threaten him; and visited his carpentry shop each week to plead awkwardly for completion of my bookcases—Senhor Feliciano winks at me and remarks in perfect English, "Well, winter is a better time for reading anyway."

I am so astonished that I am struck dumb. *Nao brinca comigo*, don't play games with me...I remember having rehearsed that phrase for one such visit during this long delay. Well, Senhor Feliciano has played one big game I never suspected: all this while he has been quite comfortable in English!

While I am still speechless, we shake hands to signal the conclusion of our contract and he saunters out the door, climbs into his truck and drives off.

A bit later I calm down to savor the moment. I get Walter from the house and we marvel at the newly furnished shop. Now I can turn to next steps. I'll need a cash register, paper supplies, a stool to perch on behind the grand new sales desk, some tables and chairs for future customers who wish to browse and, oh yes, most important of all—books.

XV
Autumn at Vila Gilfinn and Beyond

Our maid Mafalda seems very sweet. Her name intrigues me and in our two-volume English-Portuguese dictionary I discover that the original Mafalda was a twelfth-century Portuguese princess. After a brief marriage was annulled, the princess entered the convent of Arouca in northern Portugal where she did many good works. She was later beatified and is venerated as the patron of young girls. Our own Mafalda tells us that hers is still a popular name in Portugal.

Mafalda's English is minimal, but we understand each other. At one point, when I say "good," she corrects me with *"bom,"* giving a little toss of her head and a shy smile. She promises to teach *Madame* to speak Portuguese. She responds with bright fluttery smiles to Walter's jovial *"Bom dia, Mafalda, com esta?"* when she comes into the house. She calls him *Senhor Walter* and has quickly grown fond of him, sometimes bringing him figs she has roasted and stuffed with almonds. But she never speaks to Walter about her dead baby as she often does with me. Every month she goes to visit the baby's grave. It was the great loss of her young life, and more than anything, she and her husband want to have another child. Despite these confidences, she addresses me formally as *"Madame,"* because I am the lady of the house and the one who supervises her work.

Mafalda has a strong sense of propriety. When I once referred to her as our *governante,* the Portuguese word for housekeeper, she corrected me. *"Não, Madame.* I am your maid, *criada.* A *governante* work in a big house with many maids, many *criadas.* Is much more big, *importante."*

"Well, you are important to us, Mafalda."

"Sim," she agreed, confident of her own value.

She is not interested in higher status but does expect a personal connection with us. The fact that we are American, not English as are most foreign residents in the area, interests her greatly and she is always eager for news of our family. She has learned the names of our children and their families from photographs I pinned onto a bulletin board in the kitchen, and when new photographs appear, Mafalda can identify most of our relatives with little help from me. Her own life centers around family occasions and relationships. Every month when her hopes of getting pregnant are again disappointed, she tells me sadly, "no baby this time."

Whenever Mafalda arrives, before setting to work she finds me for a brief time of speaking together as women. Our "speaking" is pretty rudimentary and filled with pauses as we grope for words in each other's language. Mafalda has learned fragments of English from her work in other households and wants to learn more, but we both still cling to nouns—the names of food, flowers, common household objects and cleaning tools, along with proper names of people and family titles like father, mother, sister, and so on. As I continue my once-a-week language lessons in Loulé I gradually gain more Portuguese words and phrases, and Mafalda gently corrects my mistakes. Our efforts at conversation take some time at the start of her afternoons, but once she begins her cleaning tasks, she speaks little and leaves me free for my own activities.

At my lessons I am now reading a children's book, *O Arvore* (The Tree). To do so requires a dictionary and much stammering but I enjoy it. My teacher, Philipa, is the first person I've ever met who is truly enamored of grammar. She gets excited about conjugations and tenses and tells me I'm the first American *she* has ever met who uses the subjunctive (an attribute I wasn't aware of).

With her help, I study verbs and struggle for control of Portuguese pronouns which are particularly unruly.

At the close of one lesson, I ask Philipa about the daily *telenovelas*, the Brazilian soap operas that seem to captivate Portuguese television viewers.

"Oh, I love them," she says, "The language is so colorful and imaginative because Brazilians are not afraid to experiment. Language, clothing, food, everything is more creative than here. The Portuguese are much more traditional; they are slow to try new things."

"That must be why all restaurants serve the same five dishes."

"*Exactamente!* This country has the same fruits and vegetables as France, even more when you add the olives and almonds, yet French cooking is famous while here they don't get past stewed *cabrito* (goat)."

"But the fish is good," I respond, moved to defend my new home.

"Yes," Philipa smiles. "*O Pesce esta bon.*" (The fish is good.)

Mafalda's three-month trial period has passed successfully and Louis was right about her excellent work. Her twice-weekly cleaning routine verges on ritual. First she wipes all surfaces, then she uses ammonia to scrub any mold forming on the white stucco walls, then shakes out the area rugs, and mops with water and liquid wax all the tile floors throughout the house, whether they need it or not. In damp weather the floors take hours to dry and Walter and I must hop from dry spot to dry spot, or seek refuge in the shop building. On Tuesdays, Mafalda washes clothes in our new washer and hangs them outside to dry. On Fridays, she irons. She ends her routine by sweeping the terraces. When she finally takes off her apron, retrieves her purse, and walks back down the driveway onto the road heading toward her home, we exhale in relief. But we have no doubt that we have been thoroughly cleaned.

Some weeks later, I notice that Mafalda now concludes her afternoons by weeding the flowers close to the house and shop.

Evidently, she is not satisfied with Louis's gardening and is pitching in. Seeing her do so confirms my own increasing worries about Louis. He has never brought the helpers he claimed to have and though he described his business as a pool and garden service, he clearly prefers the pool part. He still comes regularly to adjust chemicals and vacuum the pool, but when we point him to the garden, he rakes dispiritedly around a tree for a short while and disappears as soon as Walter and I go inside.

These disappearances, signaled by Louis's old car roaring off down the driveway, become an issue between him and Mafalda. One day when I am writing letters inside, I hear Portuguese voices I don't recognize in dispute outside my window. I look out and am astonished to see Louis and Mafalda facing off on either side of a flower box. Louis clutches the long pool-skimming pole; Mafalda in her blue and white checked apron waves her dust rag, and they are shouting at each other in a torrent of Portuguese. Clearly, Mafalda's soft-spoken shyness, and Louis's halting phrases are limited to English. They are both so suddenly and vigorously verbal, with eyes flashing and arms waving, that they seem like two people I don't know. I'm not able to grasp most of their rapid exchange but I gather that much of it concerns *os flores*, the flowers, and that Mafalda is not happy about them.

We are not happy about them either. Our garden is fragile but instead of giving us more time as the plants grow, Louis is giving us less. He used to show up promptly two times a week to tend to the pool, now he comes less often and at odd hours, either early in the morning or during our dinner hour, seemingly so that we can't corner him to complain. Mafalda and I continue to water the flowers near the house and shop, Walter has begun to mow the grass, but elsewhere weeds and thatch stimulated by the automatic watering system threaten to overcome the young plantings.

One day Mafalda comes to me, clearly distressed. "*Muitos jardims*—many gardens Louis has—*todos flores mortes*—all the flowers dead."

I am shocked and worried. This is even worse than I've thought. Louis is not just neglecting our own garden but many others as well. Perhaps he has taken on more work than he can handle and doesn't know what to do. We don't know what to do either. Gardening in a desert climate like this is a precarious enterprise at best. Without steady maintenance, everything can be lost in a few weeks, especially in the searingly hot dry summers. We keep hoping that Louis will mend his ways.

Then one day, we notice that the pool water, formerly a dazzling blue, is turning greenish and cloudy. Louis's avoidance of garden maintenance has evidently spread to neglect of the pool. Thinking back, we realize that we haven't seen him for two weeks. He has no telephone; we have had to depend on his showing up regularly for any necessary communication. Now when he doesn't appear, we have no direct way of contacting him.

Reluctantly, I again turn to Mafalda. "Is Louis sick?"

"*Nao*, I see his car in town."

"He doesn't come," I say. "The pool is dirty. We will have to get someone else if he doesn't come. Will you tell him?"

She agrees without protest. I am somewhat concerned that Mafalda, who came to us through Louis, might be upset if we dismiss him, but she allies herself with our worries without hesitation. "Louis, big *problema*," she says, shaking her head.

Louis does not come back, not even to collect his final paycheck. We put word out among friends and after a few weeks of struggling with pool and garden ourselves, we find a young man to be Louis's replacement. Because Louis has stayed away, we couldn't ask him why he stopped working for us. Perhaps he likes pools and discovered that he doesn't like gardens. He couldn't bring himself to tell his customers so he simply stopped doing gardens, ours and others as well. His vanishing has made the situation more difficult for us than a spoken notice would have been, but we have learned that is not unusual here. Most Portuguese people we have met avoid telling us anything that might not be pleasing. To them, stating a negative or disappointing fact seems a breach of courtesy. Better to promise or agree, and then evade. Non-appearance for an appointment or task gradually brings understanding; it does not have to be explained in advance. We are often frustrated by this custom, but eventually we get the intended message. The filthy pool left by Louis was his "I quit."

Several times we catch glimpses of Louis in his blue Fiat around town. Unlike when we first met him, he looks unshaven and unkempt. We wonder if his neglect of his business signals deeper problems, but we never get close enough to find out.

Fortunately, unlike her sponsor Louis, Mafalda likes working for us. She spends mornings cleaning a large villa in Vale do Lobo. The *outre Senhora*, her other *Madame,* works her very hard and she is not allowed to leave until she has made up the bedrooms of the teen-aged children and many late-sleeping guests. From there, on Tuesdays and Fridays she walks to our house where she is supposed to work from one o'clock till five, but the late-risers often prevent her arrival before two or two-thirty. This means a very long workday for her and, now that the autumn days are shorter also means that she has to walk home in the dark. The promised *bicyclette* has never appeared. We now realize that Mafalda's family cannot afford a new moped for her, but we have grown too attached to her to make it an issue. In late September we sometimes notice her husband José's car waiting for Mafalda. "José come when he can finish work early," Mafalda tells us, admitting that their house, which she had assured us was close by, is in fact three miles away. Now, when José doesn't come, Walter drives her home.

In return, Mafalda seems genuinely fond of us. Our flowers are sparse now and she often arrives with bouquets of roses or carnations for our table, or sometimes even for planting. I haven't inquired too closely about the source of these flowers, but she comes directly to us from her morning job and has told me that her *outre Senhora* has a very large garden.

Almost two years have passed since my mother's death. While looking through some old papers from her desk, I happen on a brochure for a small hotel on the Italian Riviera, and notice a blonde hair caught on one edge by a scrap of scotch tape. Automatically, my hand moves to pull it off when I realized it must be Elke's hair. Such an uncanny feeling. She herself has been in the ground in Zurich for all this time, but far away in Portugal I find a strand of her hair and suddenly see her before me. I cannot remove the hair, just fold the brochure and put it back with the other papers.

Since telephoning is far too expensive except for birthdays or emergencies, letters back and forth help us to stay connected to the family and friends we have left in the States. This mode of communication feels a bit like the nineteenth century, but has become a pleasant routine. Each week I write to one of our five children and Walter adds his own closing paragraph. I also keep up a more sporadic correspondence with friends and it feels good to maintain those ties of love and affection that nothing can replace.

It's fun and interesting, though, to meet new people from all over the world. About a third of our new acquaintances are Portuguese; the rest are English, Americans, or Europeans who have settled here. Since we are all far from home, we tend to make friends more quickly than we would in our own countries; in fact we are gaining quite an active social life. A ramshackle barbecue with Fernão and Daphne on their small patio; another barbecue with Wendy and Nigel at their gorgeous mountain-top villa; tea with Ben and Kitty or William and Sonia; an Asian dinner with our Indonesian-Dutch neighbors, Dola and Kurt Van Riin. And we also invite our friends for lunch or dinner. I used to feel superior to expatriates who clung together, but now I see how barriers of language and culture become formidable during any stay longer than a few weeks of vacation. So we, too, gravitate to people who speak English because we can relax. I'm not proud of that but it's true.

Word of Walter's new practice seems to have spread and he receives occasional telephone calls from people with alcohol or emotional problems who seek his help. Most are English, and after one session, Walter emerges wide-eyed, rubs his beard and mutters, "different breed of cat."

"Are your patients here different from those in the States?" I ask him.

"I'd say so, especially the English. They wait so long to come for help that they're usually sicker. It's that fear of being seen as 'nutters.' And they don't understand the concept of therapy at all. They've given in and made the big decision to come, and then expect me to give them some kind of miracle cure. And fast. Maybe after two sessions at most. No long-term effort, and certainly no changes in their living patterns."

"Must be frustrating."

"Frustrating, sure, but funny sometimes, sometimes sad. That part—not wanting to change anything--isn't really different. Wanting to keep on doing the same things as always, and yet have a different end result, that's true of alcoholics everywhere. But here they can go for longer without facing the consequences. There's not a lot of help available."

"It's good you're here now, at least for some of them." I say.

"I guess so," Walter answers. "But I can't deliver the instant voodoo they'd like." Shaking his head, he goes back inside to write his treatment notes.

At an elegant dinner at Ron and Cecile's house with fine china, crystal, silver and lace, three dogs are in residence, as well as several cats. After dinner we move to the living room and the whole menagerie troops in quietly and settles cozily among us, like the coming of the peaceable kingdom. Though I see that it's possible, I can't even imagine us being able to duplicate such an idyllic tableau with Caesar who continues to rampage through our days.

We begin to speak a bit about giving him away. If Walter doted on Caesar, living with the dog might be easier, but in fact I'm with him more than Walter is. Aside from the group dog training lessons, Walter keeps his distance from both training and play. One day I watch him take the dog by his collar, lead him out of the house and close the door behind him.

"Sometimes I think you don't even like Caesar," I remark.

"I like him all right, I just don't feel like dealing with him right now." Walter goes back to his newspaper.

"Maybe having to deal him is more trouble than you thought?"

Walter puts down the paper and sighs. "Maybe. I thought having a dog around would be enjoyable, but I guess I pictured a calmer dog."

"An older one, maybe."

"An easier one, anyway."

I wonder aloud, "Do you think your dog fantasy was like my bookshop fantasy? About how nice life would be if we just added these things?"

Walter chuckles. "Could be. And they've both turned out to be a lot harder than we expected."

"Amen to that."

Walter is taking advantage of the cooler weather to play golf two or three days each week. Meanwhile, I feel at loose ends. When Wendy drops by for an afternoon coffee, I confide my frustration at the bookshop's delay. "I'm always busy around this place, but it's stupid stuff. You know, getting groceries, decorating, keeping after repairs. Without the bookshop, I feel like I'm just marking time and my brain is rotting away."

"Why don't you try doing a little writing for *Algarve Magazine*," Wendy suggests as we sip our coffee in the living room. "Marvin Wilson, the editor, is always looking for people who can produce an occasional article for tourists. I could mention your name."

"What would I write *about*?"

"Oh, he'll assign you to whatever comes up." She is wearing a bright yellow shirt, red shorts, red and green sandals, and looks like a bird of paradise. Her plumage brings me courage and I agree to try.

The thought of an assignment beyond our property is definitely cheering. I search out several past issues of *Algarve Magazine* and study them with new interest. It is a slick full-color publication aimed at tourists and prospective real estate buyers, with a few travel features and lots of ads for hotels, restaurants, villa builders, and home decorators. The same publisher also puts out a bi-weekly tabloid newspaper, *Algarve News*, which carries news features of interest to expatriates. The *Magazine* touts the idyllic setting; the *News* describes travails such as bureaucratic delays, building problems and roving dog packs. The two publications might be termed *Algarve Hype* and *Algarve Gripe*. Since coming here to live, my interest has shifted from one to the other depending on our current involvements.

Wendy is as good as her word. She gives my name to Marvin Wilson who telephones several days later and asks me to write an article about Salir, a little town in the mountains beyond Loulé. I will be working on trial. If my article is accepted, Marvin will take me on as a freelance correspondent. The pay is not even peanuts, as Wendy describes, since even peanuts cost something. Beach pebbles might be a better description. But one can say yes or no to assignments, come and go as one pleases, and for me it will be fun to be out and about. I'm excited, re-read the *Magazine's* travel pieces. With some trepidation, I decide that my first clear task is to *find* Salir.

Walter is glad to join me and we take Caesar along as well. I hold the area map on my lap while Walter drives us inland. The ride through the hills is beautiful and at one point, we leave the car to give Caesar a run. We climb a mountain path and discover a magnificent view of a long ridge where Moors fended off Christians, or vice versa (even the Portuguese are vague about such shifts). Our way back down takes us past a hillside farm where Caesar bolts ahead. Before we can catch up he has deprived one prize hen of all her tail feathers. While she keeps squawking, the culprit and his mortified owners scuttle out of sight into the underbrush and back to the car as quickly as possible. We continue on our way and begin to see country families in traditional Algarvian garb crowded into donkey carts, as well as individual farmers leading donkeys that bear cloth sacks of carob beans or heaps of straw flouncing over their spindly legs like Hawaiian hula skirts. As we reach the top of our climb, we pass a few houses and shops, a picturesque old church, and a ruined tower to which the neighbors have hooked their laundry lines.

We keep driving until I say, "I think that was Salir."

Walter turns the car around and this time we park at the church.

"One could drive right through this town without even noticing it," he says.

"I know. We just did."

We leave the car and try the church doors. Everything is locked. We buy a Coke at the dim local café, which looks like every other small town café. Then we stroll over to look at the tower, which seems to be part of a larger crumbling wall. There is not much to see. I picture baffled future tourists who might be directed here by my article. To generate historical interest for this outwardly unimpressive village, more research is called for.

I turn to Daphne who is even more helpful than I could have expected. She invites me to Faro University where she introduces me to fellow faculty members who specialize in the region's history and archaeology. One of these, a young woman who has written her master's thesis on Salir, accompanies me as interpreter to visit the director of the regional museum in Loulé. Both of them gladly give me information about the town's history as the site of repeated struggles between Christians and Moors, its castle complete with a legend of a ghostly princess fatally caught between the warring forces. I learn that Salir was a medieval tariff station and granary, a crossing point for travelers between the ocean and the interior of the country, and that it is still a farming center mainly for carob oil. After my interviews, I revisit Salir. This time I take time to view the various sites and respond to the charm of the locality. I am then able to write an appreciative article which is accepted for the magazine.

Marvin invites me to propose some topics I might write about for the *Algarve News*. Walter and I discuss possibilities. My ideas are for features about language lessons for new residents, or about Portuguese television. Walter suggests an article on alcohol use in the region. Marvin chooses the alcohol story.

"Well, now we're in for it," I tell Walter, a bit chagrined that Len prefers his idea to mine. "I don't know much about alcohol or alcoholism."

"You didn't know *anything* about Salir," Walter points out.

"Right. But this is really your subject, not mine."

"I know something about alcohol use in general, but not much about the local scene. And I'm not a good writer but you are. Maybe we can put that together."

He's right. He has broad knowledge of the field; I have the better writing skills. We'll use some of the contacts he has made to research the local aspects. I begin to savor the thought that we can collaborate in this writing, a new prospect for both of us.

We decide to put off starting our collaboration to take a week's vacation. It's time for a little breathing space and since we have never seen northern Portugal we decide to do so before the winter rains set in. We leave Caesar at the kennel, put Mafalda in charge of our house, drive the familiar route to Lisbon and from there continue north to Coimbra and Oporto. Both cities are busy with people rushing among streets crowded with hundreds of small shops. Many buildings are crumbling and blackened with grime, and we see litter everywhere. I can't blame it all on Portugal; parts of New York City are the same. But national character, too, plays a part. In contrast to Switzerland, where everything is well tended even in the most remote Alpine hut, here the trash heap often sits right beside the home and litter blows freely between the two.

From Oporto we drive along the Douro River on heights that are green and mountainous, quite different from our beachfront Algarve. Every available scrap of land is terraced to grow grapes for wines. The narrow road snakes back and forth in perilous hairpin turns amid spectacular scenery. I search for possible ways to describe the route: hair-raising, breath-taking, gut-wrenching, words seem tame against the reality. The entire trip is filled with our gasps and exclamations, "Look over there," "Watch out," "Good God, how far down does that hillside go?"

Small Portuguese villages are strung thinly long the steep

slopes. Every now and then we pass through larger towns, some lovely and well maintained, others crumbling into decay, each with an ancient castle and stories of early Christian or Moorish kings. We've heard that Portugal is a poor country, and see it both in the cities and in the many beautiful buildings left to molder in small villages. Too much history and too many castles for people to support their upkeep, except in a few sites.

We stay overnight wherever we find space: in a beautifully restored convent that is now a Pousada, a drab motel, a comfortable hotel, and in the extravagant palace at Buçaco. On our homeward drive, we again go through Oporto and admire the graceful steel bridge, designed by Eiffel, creator of the famed tower in Paris. We wander down steps at Lamego where statues of Biblical kings look like giant chess pieces. Continuing south, we return to Coimbra and visit the golden university library, stopping for the night in a new hotel across the river.

At breakfast next morning in the dining room we hear people at the next table talk about an earthquake in San Francisco. We rush to the hotel's lounge and stare intently at the television to learn more. My daughter Julia now lives there and we are frantic to know if she is all right. The TV shows horrifying pictures of a motorcyclist riding on a collapsing bridge but the only verbal information given is that no Portuguese residents were hurt in the quake. Still in distraught ignorance, I telephone, regardless of whatever time it might be in San Francisco. To my immense relief, Julia herself answers the phone, sleepy but unharmed. We return to our breakfast and slowly calm down.

After packing our bags, we resume our trip back to the Algarve and home. During this week's journey through our adopted country, we have been tourists again with everything new to us. We found the countryside remarkably beautiful and are glad to have seen it.

XVI
The Algarve News

After our week in northern Portugal, we return to our villa. We pick up Caesar from the kennel and our accumulated mail from the *Correio* (post office), and re-stock our *frigorífico* (refrigerator). For now I'm quite happy to plan our next writing assignments, especially since the bookshop is delayed until spring. Sometimes I wonder if I'm going ahead with it mainly because of the story in my head, the goal set for this venture that I write about in my journal and in letters home. Not opening the shop would spoil that story. And without the bookshop, what else would we do with the building and all those long struggled-for bookshelves? I see no solution for this odd predicament and put it aside for the moment.

One morning after our marketing, Walter and I stop at the bistro and take our *bicas* outside to enjoy the mild warmth of the late October sun. We see a little girl walking along the street, carrying a net shopping bag that holds a bottle of wine. The bottle looks large and heavy when carried by so small a child and I'm surprised that she's allowed to do so, "She can't be more than seven years old,"

Walter lifts his small cup to take a last sip of strong coffee while watching her. "She's probably been sent to buy the wine for her family's lunch."

I consider this for a moment. "I remember being sent by my parents to buy cigarettes for them when they ran out. I suppose kids can't do that today."

Walter nods, "No minimum age limit here for buying wine, I guess. Portugal is a wine producing country."

It's true. We've noticed that wine and spirits are sold everywhere, including in small grocery stores and big supermarkets. Even gas stations sell brandy. As I think of that, I venture a question about our promised feature article about alcohol use in the region.

"So, how are we doing to do this? You're the one who knows about alcohol."

Walter searches in his pockets for the coins to pay for our coffee. "And you're the writer."

"O.K." I take out my wallet in case more coins are needed. "How about, we interview people together, you ask the right questions, and I'll take notes?"

"Sounds good," Walter agrees.

"But you'll have to tell me what's important." I'm still cautious. " I'll do the rough drafts, then you'll have to edit."

"I love to edit." He flashes me a wicked grin. He has gathered the right change and goes inside to pay. And so we're set to begin our joint assignment as journalists.

Since the *Algarve News* is aimed primarily at English-speaking residents, we interview several physicians whose practice draws from expats as well as Portuguese. They are perceptive about drinking problems they see among expatriate patients. "Heavy drinking is the root cause of most of the medical problems I see here," says one doctor. "Alcohol is cheap here," says another and adds, "Some people may come away from their home countries just so that they *can* drink freely."

From our own doctor, a Portuguese physician in Almancil recommended to us by Gunnar Nielsen, we learn that drinking is a big problem for his Portuguese patients as well.

"Most are poor," he tells us. "Sometimes they don't have enough to eat. The men especially are heavy drinkers. The families, too. The houses are cold in winter, some people drink simply to keep warm. And there is much depression. Especially in the hills where there is so much poverty. The young people come down to work in beach hotels and restaurants, and then they do not return to the villages. The old people stay behind and they see no way out."

This portrait of rural hardship is so different from that of the aging idle foreigners in beach villas. Yet so many people among both segments of the population, whether living in poverty or in relative comfort, seem to have serious problems with alcohol.

When we return home I transcribe my notes and, after reading them Walter says, "We've got to find some way to bring in the automobile fatalities. Drinking drivers are a major factor everywhere, and that's got to be true here too. I'd like to see some statistics."

"There's a small library in Lagoa, near the *Algarve News* offices," I suggest. "Maybe they have some records."

"Worth a try. We'll drive over and see if they have anything."

The library is a pretty little building near a park. In its single room we see a modest supply of books and magazines but no customers at the moment. Three women employees are on duty. One is behind the circulation desk, another is shelving books, and the third is the cleaning lady, in apron, who is washing the tile floor with mop and pail. In my best Portuguese, I ask the woman at the desk if the library has any information on automobile accident rates. All book work and cleaning stops as the three women gather around us to discuss my request. The library itself has nothing specific they tell us, but all three, including the cleaning lady, come up with ideas of where we might find what we want: the county offices at Loulé, the police in Faro, or the Lisbon newspapers. We thank the women and leave without statistics but heartened by their warmth and interest in helping us.

Taking the library ladies' advice, we see the chief of police in Faro, hoping that he can provide some statistics about automobile accidents. Conceição, a most helpful young woman who works for the *Algarve News* accompanies us as interpreter and translator.

As Conceição translates, the chief sighs and admits that no one likes to keep accurate records of automobile fatality and injury rates here.

"Drinking is a big problem here with the drivers, Senhora. Our police are busy all the time with the accidents, taking people to hospital, or to the morgue." He pauses and shifts in his chair. "Unfortunately, we don't see everything that happens, especially at night."

"Isn't that when most accidents happen?" Walter asks.

"We are not sure of that. Our policemen are not on the roads at night."

Walter and I exchange shocked glances. "What time do they quit?" he asks.

"Six-thirty in the evening."

"But what happens if people are hurt?" I ask.

"The hospital sends an ambulance."

No wonder statistics are hard to come by. During the hours when accidents are most likely to occur, no one is on hand to record information. Thus, no one keeps tabs on the degree to which alcohol use has impaired drivers. Thanking the police chief for his frankness, we are still incredulous that the highway police do not work during nighttime hours. Such laxity must be more than carelessness. Production and sales of wine provide the Portuguese government with substantial income from taxes. Too much negative publicity could hurt tourism and harm both Portugal's image and its economy.

For the next few days, I pass typed pages to Walter who covers them with circles, arrows, and hand-written corrections. He adds some comparative statistics on automobile fatalities he has obtained from the International Council on Alcoholism and Addictions. Those rates for Portugal are comparatively even graver than we had feared. There are 27 fatalities per 100,000 driven miles in England; in Portugal the rate is 108 per 100,000. I incorporate Walter's changes and type a clean draft which we edit once more. Then I telephone Marvin to describe our findings and ask if he would consider two articles instead of one. He asks to see them and we promise to deliver in a week—*proxima semana.*

Marvin approves both articles and though we are aware that we have barely skimmed the surface, Marvin asks us to move on to problems of drug abuse and drug traffic.

"There's even greater interest in that whole subject," he assures us. "People are getting concerned, what with burglaries and car thefts on the rise, that sort of thing. I'd like to see the *News* do something on that, and you're the ones who can do it."

We are heartened by his confidence but Walter points out that this new assignment means moving from a medical and health problem to one with legal and criminal ramifications. He feels less qualified in the area of drug trafficking, and we have no personal connections to any potential interview subjects. Marvin, however, makes some phone calls and arranges a meeting for us with a friend's son trying to recover from heroin addiction.

The three of us meet at an outdoor café in Albufeira. There the young man nervously agrees to share his story in hopes of helping other young people avoid his downward spin of boredom in school, idle adolescent companions, alcohol-laced parties leading to experimental marijuana use and from there on to heroin. His story is harrowing but not new; we've heard similar ones in the United States. We hear of them again days later when we interview the teen-aged daughter of Philipa, my language teacher. She describes the prevalence of drugs among her schoolmates and the stress of seeing several friends move ever closer to addiction.

In addition to personal stories, we learn some of the legal aspects of drug use and traffic from the senior inspector of the national *Policia Judiciàra.* He tells us that Portugal has seen a steep rise of criminal activity of all types in recent years, including bribery of public officials, and money laundering. Burglaries and thefts alone have increased by thirty percent in one year. The Algarve in particular, with its one hundred miles of open coastline and many secluded harbors, provides ideal entry points for drugs, part intended for international traffic into Europe and part for local consumption. Drugs are available in every Algarvian town.

When Walter asks if there are any treatment or prevention programs, he hits on one of the inspector's major frustrations.

"There is no useful education," he tells us. "The younger teen-agers all use tobacco and alcohol, and go on to hashish. The schools give talks for the parents," he adds with some bitterness, "but for the children? Nothing! *Nada!* No education for them at all about drugs."

Our final interview is in Lagos with two parents, the mother of one drug addict and the father of another. We cluster together on some upholstered display sofas at the back of a furniture store owned by the father. Our two hosts are very impressive, active not only in the support group they formed for families of addicts, but also in treatment centers and halfway houses. Despite their dedication, neither is optimistic about the overall chances for recovery among the young people they see. They tell us of their own children's lives, each story similar in its general outline to that of the young man we interviewed earlier. In this conversation, we witness not only the fear and remorse of an addicted person, but the desperation and sadness of parents mourning for their lost children. Our hearts go out to them. Our leave-taking is warm; the usual parting handshakes are replaced by hugs and kisses on both cheeks. The couple press their group's meeting schedule into our hands and urge us to return.

On the drive home Walter and I are quiet. My notebook is full of stories we have gleaned from our encounters. We can produce the assigned articles, yet I feel uncomfortable at the transience of these contacts. Recently I read that a journalist experiences the world shallowly, always moving from assignment to assignment, never staying to probe deeply. This season has been my first time as a reporter and the trust and self-revelation of those we have met both pleases and troubles me. The people who have spoken with us so movingly about themselves, all seem to want some further connection. I can well understand that; in ordinary life the giving of one's life story to another person is an intimate act that carries with it expectations of further association and caring. That is the normal path of a developing human relationship. But Walter and I have had to move on to other interviews, other stories, and that seems somehow unnatural. It was probably our discomfort as novice journalists that made Walter agree to attend one of the parents' support group meetings after we return from the States next February.

"Will you really go back for one of their meetings?" I ask him.

"I'm not sure. Maybe."

Perhaps he will; for my part, I don't expect to. I lived for ten years with my children's alcoholic father while his increasing deterioration destroyed our home and ruined his life. The stories I've heard here bring back too many painful memories and I can no longer cope with this whole huge subject of addiction and its overwhelming sadness. Walter is better than I am in facing it. He is a healer by nature and by profession, whereas I am just fortunate to have escaped. For this project I have been simply the writer but now I am overwhelmed and want to escape again.

We have learned that the Algarve has many of the same problems seen elsewhere in the world. Here it seems that the government and private sectors are just beginning to find strategies to cope with increasing use of both legal and illegal drugs. Clearly there is much work to do and Walter has been energized by our experience.

One afternoon we take Caesar for a walk along the beach, which is nearly deserted now. The day is cloudy, the tide is out, and we walk quite easily on the packed sand as we talk about our recent collaboration.

"I'd like to do more research and compare alcohol consumption in various countries in Europe," he says, "that might make a good article."

"Yes, it might," I agree, but I have to tell him what I've been thinking. "Walter, it's been great working with you, but I'm going to have to stop. It isn't really my subject, you know. And I want to get back to getting ready for the bookshop."

Walter turns to look at me, his white hair ruffled by a soft wind. "I know," he says. "These interviews have been upsetting for you, I can understand that." We walk on for a few moments as he thinks, and then decides, "But I'd like to go ahead on my own. And if I do write something, you'd still help me edit, right?"

"Of course. I like to edit too, you know."

Caesar comes bounding back through the froth at the edge of the surf and we both duck out of his way, getting sprinkled with a few drops as he rushes past.

"I think I could give some help here, maybe at the Faro Hospital alcohol treatment clinic," Walter says. "I could bring them a lot of stuff from the States, programs that have a good success rate, treatment options, better AA outreach. If we can get past the language barrier, that is."

"Dr. Cruz speaks good English. You could call him. I bet he'd be glad to hear from you."

Whereas I feel relief at having finished with my work on this large and painful subject, Walter may just be getting started. I'm heartened to think that now we each have a mission here.

As November draws near, nights grow colder. I have taken out the electric blanket and again wear socks to bed. But the days are still mild. On November 1ˢᵗ, his son's birthday, Walter makes a large cardboard sign that reads "Happy Birthday Terry," strips down, and wades into the pool. Holding the sign to cover his own birthday suit, he directs me to take his photo for a mailed greeting.

The damp cold is slowly creeping into the house as the season advances. Because of the high cost of electricity, we have no clothes dryer. The outdoor drying, finished in two hours in the hot summer, takes two days and nights in rainy weather when we must bring the damp clothes indoors. Despite the deepening cold, I'm not keen to leave this place where we have made friends and created so absorbing a life for ourselves. But as we say our good-byes and pack our bags for six weeks in Saratoga, I grow increasingly eager to see our children and the friends awaiting us there.

I ask Wendy what we should do for Mafalda's Christmas, and Wendy tells me that a bonus of one month's pay is customary. I give Mafalda that amount during one of her afternoons with us, and in response, she and her husband José, who speaks no English, pay us a formal and stiff visit for tea on a Sunday. Both the bonus and the visit are aspects of traditional Portuguese employer-employee relations.

William and Sonia, our friends from the dog school have agreed to house-and-dog sit for us while we are away. It fits with their own needs, because they can stay at Vila Gilfinn in relative comfort while William repairs the roof on their own small house in the hills. To keep Caesar company, they will also bring their own little dog Seixta, who is tan, no more than eighteen inches high, and catapults straight up and down on all four paws as if he were on springs. I wonder how big burly Caesar will get on with this tiny bouncy companion while we are away.

William drives us to Faro airport and as we lift off I think that we've accomplished a lot since our arrival last January. Our two buildings, the house and the shop, as well as the landscaping are in good condition. We have a circle of friends and our writing assignments have also brought contacts among the Portuguese. During this time Walter and I have learned to live together in retirement. We're together in or around the house most of the time, and often together as we drive to do chores or attend events. At first so much togetherness felt strange and a bit uncomfortable. By now we've learned to leave each other some space, and enjoy coming close to chat, eat, watch TV, read in bed and cuddle there at night or early morning. All in all, this first year here has been a gentle loving time for us.

Even so, I never imagined that we would be here for so long and still not have the bookshop open. Ruefully, I must admit that the delay fits with what we noticed years ago about the pace of work here: everything takes twice as long as you expect. But I'm still determined to see it through. I promise myself that after we get back here I'll resume work toward bringing the Griffin to life as soon as possible.

XVII
Stormy Weather

Weak February sunlight glints on the windshield of the rented car we are driving from Lisbon back to the Algarve. At the close of our winter weeks in Saratoga with our family and friends, we found it hard to say goodbye. Whichever place I'm in—Saratoga or the Algarve—I grow attached and am reluctant to leave. But now we're full of plans and glad to be back in our adopted country. Walter has a briefcase crammed with alcoholism publications he hopes to share with professionals in the region. As for me, while in the United States I selected titles for an initial inventory, took a deep breath, and sent a deposit check for five thousand (dollars not pounds) to Humphrey Biggs at Hammick's Book Distributors in London. These books represent the standard "mid-list" readings that form the backbone of a solid bookshop. I will expand this inventory with flashier best sellers which, thanks to Martha Stimpson's advice, I plan to get from Lisbon distributors. The Hammick's shipment is due this month.

The car's back seat holds a large poster tube containing drawings of my longed-for griffin. I was unable to find a willing Algarvian artist, but succeeded in locating one in Saratoga who created a funny, plump and irresistible griffin that makes all who see him smile. I am eager to bring the drawings to Cynthia Green so she can complete the design for the shop's logo.

Despite his crammed briefcase and the studies he hopes to pursue here, Walter is still interested in the shop's progress. "I'm second banana," he assures me, " but I'm still *your* banana," he adds with a mock leer. Now that we've had our stateside vacation, we both agree that it's time for the shop to shift into high gear. Our heads full of ideas, our luggage full of documents, we are newly energized to go forward.

But we haven't counted on the Algarvian winter.

As we leave the north-south highway and travel east along the EN 125, the sky becomes overcast and we notice that many villas seem to have lost their stark whiteness. Gardens appear disheveled; many flowers lie beaten to the ground.

"Must have rained hard here," Walter remarks.

"Mmm," I'm growing a bit anxious to see how our place looks.

The answer awaits us as we turn into our Vila Gilfinn's driveway and it is worse than I could have imagined. The winter rains have turned both buildings and even the boundary walls from white to dingy green. The shop's driveway and turning circle are impassable; in some spots *calçadas* have erupted into random heaps, in others there are large cave-ins. What was a fresh new garden is now etched by deep gullies from flooding waters.

"Oh my God," I breathe. Walter is silent, his jaw set; both of us shocked at the wrecked landscape. As he pulls up to the front door, I can hardly bring myself to step out into whatever else lies in wait. Almost at once we are stopped by the sight of the terraced walk between the house and shop. It now has a wide trench through the middle with broken paving stones heaped on either side.

The front door opens and William and Sonia come out to join us as we stand in front of the trench. "Had to chop through to give the water a channel," he explains, "Or it would have come right into the house."

We nod, too stunned to speak, and follow them indoors, hardly able to focus on the torrent of apologies and explanations. I'm relieved to see that inside everything is spic, span and polished. Clearly William and Sonia have struggled to take care of the place through a dreadful season. Sonia leads me through clean neat rooms. In the master bedroom our bed is resplendent with a frilly bright blue spread that has replaced our plain beige one. "Mafalda bought that for you with her own money. She put it on just this morning." Sonia tells me. I am touched by Mafalda's generous welcoming gesture and aware that I'll have to live with frilly blue for a long time.

After our tour of the house we all sit down to Sonia's painstakingly prepared lunch of cold cuts and cheeses. We hear about the terrible winter and its one bright note: the two dogs got along fine. "They were even swimming together out in back," William says, "And I mean through the flooded lawn, not the pool. You should've seen 'em." Afterwards, though sick at heart, we do our best to express our thanks for all their care as William, Sonia, and little Seixta take their leave and return to their own house in the hills.

Walter and I put on rubber boots and walk glumly around our property. Outside, despite William's best efforts, winter storms and rains have done extensive damage. The ornamental trees have survived, but most flowers are gone. Aside from continual wetness that has mildewed all building and boundary walls, the biggest problems were clearly caused by faulty drainage. Rushing floodwaters carved deep gullies in the soil and undermined the paved areas. The shop's circular driveway is not passable by car due to multiple cave-ins from misplaced drainage pipes. The long-ago river has reclaimed its right of way.

"We'll have to call Roemer," Walter says. "They'll have to get crews in to re-lay the pipes and repair the paving.

"That'll take weeks," I mutter, "and how do we know they'll do it right next time." We walk around to enter the shop by its back door. The chandeliers and bookcases still look fine, but some ceramic floor tiles have risen and become stained.

I am quite frantic. My opening stock of books from London is due to arrive here and now there is no driving access to the shop. And the inside floor tiles will have to be re-set. "I can't cope with this," I wail several times. "I just can't cope with all this."

"We've had a long night and day." As always when I'm frantic, Walter tries to keep us on an even keel. "Let's just get some sleep first and then we'll think about what to do."

The next day we contact Joost Roemer and start discussions about the pipes but I continue agitated because of the impending book shipment. I had hoped to open the shop in March, but now there's no place to receive the delivery, no way to process books or put them on shelves. After two sleepless nights, I finally call Hammick's in London and cancel the order. It will cost me half of my deposit, but that's less expensive than investing even more to return thousands of books or store them elsewhere. Right now I am too discouraged to even think about how or when to open the shop.

Walter tries to comfort me with "One day at a time, Patoot. You can do it, just give yourself time."

When Mafalda shows up for her scheduled afternoon, she acquaints us with the Algarvian custom of first scrubbing all outdoor walls with water and bleach and then painting them with whitewash. She works cheerfully right along with us as we start scrubbing all around the property. So we prepare to jog along for the coming weeks getting the damage under control.

Every morning after our coffee, Walter and I put on our boots and old clothes, gather scrubbing brushes and rubber gloves, fill pails with water and Clorox and then head outside to attack the green mildew. Kerchiefs around our necks can be pulled up to cover our noses from the sharp smell of the Clorox brew. We give the task four hours each day, two in the morning and two in the afternoon. On her afternoons, Mafalda joins in, concentrating on boundary walls. In a week, we have almost worked our way around the house and are starting on the shop. When the scrubbing is done, we'll start the whitewash.

Sometimes, after a meal at the nearby Pituxia restaurant we stop and look at the deserted blackened house across the road. "At least our place was just green," I sigh. "It would be black like that if we didn't clean it."

As a pleasant respite from our daily scrubbing hours, we've had lovely welcomes back from our friends here, and have been out to dinner and lunch almost every day. Our articles on alcohol and drugs have also brought us a new affiliation. Dr. Jose Pestana Cruz from Faro Hospital has invited us to join the Lions Club of Faro. We'd like more contacts with the Portuguese community and are glad to attend an introductory dinner meeting held in Estoi. I've thought of Estoi only as the site of a large farmers market and the birthplace of Mike Moreira who described his family's rural poverty. But Walter and I walk along pleasant streets and find that the restaurant itself is elegant. Our Lions Club hosts tell us that Estoi even has an historic palace, now sadly neglected as are too many of Portugal's architectural treasures.

The gathering consists of fifteen people; most are Portuguese but there are also an Iranian, a Frenchman and us. We are greeted warmly and do our best to follow at least a trickle from the waves of Portuguese small talk that surround us during the cocktail hour. As dinner is served, I am seated on Dr. Cruz's right, the place of honor since he is the Faro Lions Club president. Walter sits across from me and beside the chief psychiatrist of Faro Hospital who speaks to him in careful English. I overhear their plans to meet again to discuss working together to develop a better alcoholism treatment program for the hospital, and I think things are looking up for Walter here. Not just pulling weeds and planting cactuses after all. In view of the stalled bookshop, I'm a little envious. But I cheer myself by thinking of yesterday's phone call from Marvin Wilson describing our *Algarve News* articles as "super."

Dinner is excellent with several courses. It is also long. We are pleased and honored by having been included but our language skills are strained. As the meal wears on, the guests speak animated rapid Portuguese to each other, laugh at humorous remarks, and occasionally turn kindly to translate into painstaking English for us. We smile and nod and try to keep our thoughts from drifting. I keep waiting for some curtain of incomprehension to lift, but it doesn't. I feel again the erasure of humor, quickness, and personality that comes with being unable to speak. When we take our leave at the evening's end we both feel in need of silence and a night's sleep.

On another evening, we meet Wendy and Nigel at a spacious movie theater in one of the plazas of Vilamoura, a nearby coastal resort. The theater's interior has tiers of wide reclining seats covered in butterscotch leather. As in most European movie houses, the film is interrupted at mid-point by an intermission. Many people head for the snack bar for sweets or the ubiquitous brandy while Wendy and I repair to the ladies room.

We're at the mirror, washing our hands, checking our make-up, and talking about the movie which is *Born on the Fourth of July,* the story of Ron Kovic, a paralyzed Vietnam veteran who organizes anti-war protests. "It really brings it all back, doesn't it?" Wendy remarks as she renews her fire-engine red lipstick.

A woman emerges from one of the stalls, "You're Americans, aren't you? I'm from Texas and it's just so good to hear American voices." We smile and she goes on. "I've gotten used to hearing mostly English, the Queen's English I mean."

"How long have you been here," Wendy asks the universal question of expats meeting each other for the first time.

"Five years. But it's almost over, we're going home next month," the woman giggles with excitement, "and I'm just counting the days."

"You haven't liked living here?"

"Oh, it's been all right, I guess," she ponders the question while washing her hands. "My husband was sent here on business. He hasn't minded, but I don't know…" her voice trails off, then resumes. "We could stay but we've decided to go back home." She looks up at us in the mirror. "We miss the comforts."

The overhead lights flicker on and off to signal the end of the intermission. I wish her good luck as we file out of the room.

"I know what she means about missing the comforts," Wendy murmurs. After days of scrubbing mildew, so do I.

Because I can never reach Gillian Field, who is going through marital troubles, I asked another landscaper, Jessica, to walk about the garden with me and quote a price for spring clean-up after the stormy winter. This morning we trudge around the property. She keeps saying what a large garden it is, and points out flood-damaged trees or plants best removed. Many others are just fine, thank goodness. Jessica advises truckloads of manure to be rotated into the sandy soil. This garden has cost so much money and still demands more and more. I blame Gillian since she got us when we didn't know what to do with the moonscape the builders had left. And now Gillian is unreachable.

While I am walking around with Jessica, Caesar streaks past us, having just pulled down a flowering vine. Jessica looks sadly down at the remaining stubble and then at the dog bounding up the hill, trailing several vine tendrils. She sighs, "I guess living things are more important." And I, holding another severed vine in my hand, wonder wasn't this a living thing too? Another form of life to be sure, but perhaps one which at my age becomes ever more important to me because of its peace and its beauty.

Since canceling my book order from Hammick's I have felt quite disoriented. We are now painting our way around our outside walls—house, boundary and privacy walls. The weather is pleasant, and the work is not unpleasant, just slow. But thoughts of the bookshop seem to recede with each meter of wall and each tale of the recession in Europe and resulting dwindling numbers of tourists and new settlers in the Algarve. Villa and condominium sales are flat, builders are shutting down, realtors are going out of business. At the time of the crash of 1987 that we first heard of on the plane from Lisbon, the stock market fell twenty-three percent. Its after-effects are now reverberating far beyond New York; markets seem stalled everywhere.

During our weeks in Saratoga we learned that no one is buying property there. It's the same here and, from what we're told, in London. Mortgage rates in England have risen sharply, and people are rioting about a proposed poll tax. Now twenty percent fewer English are coming to the Algarve. Their numbers are in part compensated for by more Germans, Scandinavians and Dutch, but that isn't reassuring for my planned English language bookshop. I wonder, will people still rent villas at Vale do Lobo, stay at the stately Dona Filipa, or the big new Quinta do Lago Hotel? Those are the resorts that would affect my book sales.

I keep painting. I'm not exactly unhappy but feel confused. Partly I'm ashamed that I didn't just keep pushing on with the shop; partly I'm enormously relieved not to face thousands of books in all our mess. My mental limbo feels a bit like when I gave up on my original diffuse dissertation topic and hadn't yet started the one I actually wrote. A bookshop in Portugal, the goal I've worked toward for years, again seems in doubt and that floats everything up into the air. I paint on, meter after meter, with the question "What now?" looming over my head like a huge cartoon-balloon.

March arrives and yellow broom is in bloom on the back slope, along with some purple heather and tiny blue flowers like miniature stars. We are gradually restoring whiteness to our dream villa. The garden is being dosed with generous heaps of extrume. All in all, the place is shaping up. As our surroundings brighten, my spirits rise and my thoughts go back to circle around the Griffin.

Paintbrush in hand, I walk over to Walter who is refilling a bucket with more white paint. I'm wearing one of his old shirts over my sweater to protect it. He's wearing one of his old shirts too, one he likes but I don't. It's got baggy red sleeves, a gray flannel torso too tight for his bulky frame, and is now getting daubed with white paint. I decide not to caution Walter, more streaks might hasten the shirt's demise.

"Maybe I shouldn't order books from England at all," I say.

He puts the paint can down and waits for me to say more. "Maybe if I start small with a modest investment, I could give myself time to see how it flies."

"That makes sense, " he picks up his brush and resumes painting.

"Lots of shops around here are tiny." I continue. "The one I saw in Vilamoura was the size of a closet. Maybe I could use just one of the shop's two rooms to start."

"And we could easily drive up to Lisbon and get your books there," Walter looks up at me and nods. "We could rent a van."

I feel a flutter of excitement. Through the next days we hold periodic mini-conferences as we paint. If I use just part of the shop in the beginning, we might even consider renting out the other part to a compatible business. Thinking along lines that would at least get the business started makes me feel more energetic and hopeful.

We talk about getting books on consignment from distributors in Lisbon and Faro. Then we can simply begin when we are ready rather than taking a big plunge with a prepaid opening inventory from England. That may even be better than trying to duplicate a big urban bookstore. Who knows if one would even be appealing here? I remember what I used to like about exploring foreign places was that the shops were <u>different</u> from those I saw at home. When we visited Zurich, or Berlin, or even the Caribbean, I used to love finding the old orange-backed Penguin books, and other titles I never saw in New York City or in my own neighborhood. Maybe some distinctive holdings here would actually work better. At the end of a week, it's decided; we shall stock a small bookshop in May and open in June.

Rain in torrents for three days. Fortunately it clears by Saturday afternoon when we're invited to a celebration of Fernão and Daphne's twenty-fifth wedding anniversary. For days Fernão has been as excited as a small boy. He keeps referring to Daphne with all her bulk as "my fiancée," while she beams at him. Just in time, the sun comes out and the wedding feast takes place in the drenched garden behind their house with its peeling stuccoed exterior. The dozen or so guests have all brought flowers and food to make a festive party. Fernão and Daphne arrive after their private ceremony at the church in Vale D'Eguas. Their teen-aged son gives an awkward wedding toast and we all stand around, sipping champagne and nibbling appetizers. Fernão's sparse hair is slicked down and he wears a new blue foulard; Daphne is an ample vision in purple satin. Fernão gazes adoringly, takes her hand, and salutes her as "my bride." Daphne smiles and blushes. Lovely.

The day after more heavy rains, Caesar trots into the kitchen with muddy feet. I try to wipe them off with an old towel. He tries to wrestle me for it. I yell at him to stop. He seizes it and rushes outside again eager for play and mischief. And I erupt into a wild tirade, slam about the kitchen screaming, and bang the door shut in a fury. Wild, raging, and quite unexpected. Poor dog. My sudden fit reminds me of myself at similar hysterical moments during the years I was raising three small children. I'd think I was OK through their squabbles, and the next moment my nerves would snap and I'd be a roaring maniac. But even in such moments, I never wanted to get rid of my children. When I tell her, Wendy is sympathetic and says we should be able to give Caesar away quite easily because people here are eager for large guard dogs, especially those with pedigrees. The thought calms me.

I have spent several hours today restringing little plastic tubes like lozenges for the beaded curtain I hung last week at the kitchen door to the outside. Curtains such as this allow people to keep their doors open to let fresh air in and keep insects out. The blue and white one I bought seemed all right from the picture on the package, but seen from across the pool it looked like we'd hung a huge blue and white argyle sock in the doorway. To complete this unattractive picture, Caesar got into it the first night and mangled several strands. Rather than simply repairing those strands, I decide to un-plaid the design by restringing the whole thing into a white curtain with two simple broad blue stripes at the bottom. Big mistake.

I return to the hardware store in Loulé where I bought the curtain and ask for more tubelets. They send me to a small factory housed in a garage about five miles out of town. There I find five women surrounded by large canvas sacks, some filled with tubelets in bright colors and others with the metal connecting loops. The women are stringing these things together into curtains. I buy the supplies I need and come home to start my project. Seventy strands, each with thirty-five macaroni-sized tubelets strung together with metal loops and hooked on to a wooden cross bar at the top. I find I can do about four or five strands an hour, alternating the white tubelets with two broad bands of blue ones at the bottom. I must count carefully. If I string too few or too many of each color onto a strand, it won't match the others, and re-doing takes more time. I wonder, why do I get into these things?

As I sit here doing repetitive manual work with my fingertips getting abraded, I remember my oh-so-long-ago very first job at a radio factory where I sat hour after hour hunched over a square black cardboard applying black glue and tiny black felt pads to some small black iron brackets. After two weeks I was promoted to operate a punch press, and then to an air- driven screwdriver on an assembly line. They were all repetitive motions requiring manual dexterity and mind-numbing patience for the most minimal accomplishments. That job taught me a lot about the working life of millions of people. I saw that again with those women sitting there stringing plastic curtains day after day for low pay and meager satisfaction. Thank God I could eventually gain an education to escape such drudgery.

Walter has shared materials about corporate and government employee assistance programs, particularly those with alcohol and substance abuse components, with the physicians and psychiatrists at Faro Hospital. They have been asked by the Portuguese military for help with these problems, with the result that Walter is invited to speak at a conference held by the military in Sintra. A limousine picks him up and drives him there. Two days later, I watch as the sleek long car pulls back into our courtyard to return him to our doorstep. The driver, a young sailor, jumps out, opens the rear door, snaps to attention as Walter steps out, and salutes. Walter, former World War II navy cadet, returns the salute smartly. He smiles as he marches toward me and, while we are both amused by the incongruous setting, I can see that he relishes this bit of pomp and circumstance. When he unpacks his overnight bag, he hands me a flat red leather box with a flourish and says, "They presented this to me as a token of their appreciation."

I open the box to find a medal the size of a saucer. "Boy, they must have *really* appreciated your speech. But how did they understand you?" I wonder, knowing that he spoke in English.

"Oh, they'd translated the written speech and handed out copies. I guess most followed along with that when I talked. But a lot of them knew English, and I had a good number of questions afterwards. It was fun and who knows, maybe something more will come out of it."

This week I've been in the shop pricing Elke's German books. We've brought those we want to keep into the house, and I'll display the others in the shop for sale second-hand. I price by impulse, noting the price on a post-it slip inside each book. So far, I've done eighteen out of the twenty-seven boxes of her books I had sent here. The work is quiet and enjoyable; the books themselves are interesting and in them I find unexpected things she placed between the pages—newspaper clippings and book reviews (out of thousands more that Julia and I threw away in Zurich), postcards, shopping lists, letters, bills, reading notes—all left by Elke over many years. I feel closer to her in this task than in others since her death. Many had to be done in a great hurry; this is leisurely and calm. Among her books I find the great German classics: Goethe, Holderlin, Rilke, Heine, and others whose names I've heard. The ten volumes of Goethe have obviously been read and re-read over years. Many volumes by great Russian poets contain a letter or inscription from the young poet, her friend and fellow translator who spoke at her funeral. I get a sense of Elke at her best, as she wanted to be thought of: a person with an eager questing mind interested in art and culture, with absorbing work of her own, surrounded by bright artistic friends who admired her beauty and talents. That was the life she always wanted and at last achieved. I think of her gracious apartment with its fine antique furniture, vivid paintings, lovely china, crystal and silver, and this intriguing library of books in three languages. One could truly love this woman if one knew her only through the things she chose, lived with, and left behind. In them, one doesn't find the rages, the grandiosity, the need for adulation, the drive for control, or the lack of empathy that unhappily comprised too much of her complex nature. At least for me. When I was young, I had to resist her to survive; she was too dazzling and dominant for me to be anything at all unless I could fight clear of her efforts to mold me into a replica of herself. But she is gone and I like my solitary hours with her books now, as I did my solitary play during childhood. Through her books I can admire her without confronting her. There is sadness, too, for all the missed opportunities, all the love that couldn't be realized. But it is some comfort to have it now as a kind of memorial.

XVIII
Trial by Fire

We drive to Faro airport for Walter's quarterly trip to the States. "I hate to leave you, Babe," he says as we kiss goodbye. I believe him but I also know that he looks forward to these two-week intervals where he can supervise his staff, see his long-time patients and do clinical evaluations of new ones, all in his native language.

On the way back from the airport I drive to Loulé to look for chairs for future bookshop customers. The pricing might be termed "fluid." At my first stop, the chairs cost 4,500 *escudos*. Next door, the same chairs are 4,000. I return to the first place and they are now 3,600. (If I had continued going back and forth, could I have done better?) I buy eight straight-backed wooden chairs with cane seats for 3,600 *escudos* each (about $21 U.S.). The warehouse men, with jolly ingenuity, wedge all eight chairs into my car and tie the trunk shut. Fine, but I can't see out of the rearview mirror. The idea that I should want to amazes the men, but they remain good-natured when I ask them to take out four of the chairs. I drive off with the first four without giving them any money. They are quite content to trust me till I return for the second set.

While Walter is away Wendy and I decide to have a ladies evening out. As I leave home to meet her at a nearby restaurant,

I keep lights on in the living room and bedroom to deter potential burglars. Wendy and I linger over an elegant meal. Our talk is partly filled with laughter about the vagaries of life here and then turns serious as Wendy confides that after five years she is very tired of those vagaries. I sympathize but am still new enough to feel resilient.

I get home by ten o'clock. As I approach the front door I smell something odd. Lights are still on inside and I can't quite figure out what is different. I brace myself, fearing I'm about to surprise another burglary in progress. My fingers tremble as I fumble with the door key. Then as I enter the front hall, I know what I smelled. Flames are shooting out of the main electrical box that holds all house circuit breakers. These circuit breakers should have shut off power in case of trouble. Instead, the whole box is on fire.

In shock, I stand in front of the flaming wall and try to think. I remember that water is not a good idea for an electrical fire. Salt might work, but my box of kitchen salt would be ludicrously small. I have no idea how to summon a Portuguese fire department. In desperation, hands shaking, I telephone Mike who says he'll be here in five minutes. I think that maybe I should try to save something, in case the fire spreads, but I can't think of anything portable to save. Except my passport, which is locked in the bedroom. Like a sleep-walker I go through the living room to get the key from the kitchen drawer, edge past the flames, unlock the bedroom door, retrieve the passport and carry it and my pocketbook out to the car. As I stand there, not knowing what to do next, Mike--may his name be praised by the Heavenly Host—arrives with his fire extinguisher. We go inside and he aims it at the flames. Nothing comes out. He tries again—nothing. We stare at each other in panic. Then, he snatches up the hallway rug and holds it against the wall. We both beat the rug with our hands till the fire is smothered. To make sure, we stand there for a long while staring at the wall, which is now black and smelly but no longer in flames. Giddy with relief, we both laugh, then give each other a strong hug. I keep saying, "Oh Mike, thank you, thank you," and he laughs, "I love you, Lady, I love you." He is so happy to have been able to come to my rescue, and I am so grateful that he has done so. Dirty and messy as everything is, we share a moment of sheer joy.

Only when we have calmed down does Mike think to telephone the *Bombeiros* (fire department) in Quarteira. He is told that our house isn't in their jurisdiction and he should call Loulé. How frantic I would have been if this had happened while the fire was still burning. Now Mike grimaces at me but calls Loulé. To their credit, two *bombeiros* respond quickly in a white mini-van which they park out by the road. Nattily dressed with no fire-fighting equipment, the two men walk up the driveway and join us in the house. They look at the blackened electrical box and, speaking in Portuguese, tell Mike that they can't do anything because electrical fires are the jurisdiction of EDP, the electrical power company. During their explanations we hear some crackling from the wall behind the box.

"Are they going to let the house burn down while they're disputing jurisdiction?" I ask Mike in English.

"I'm not going to let them leave," he mutters to me, also in English, "The EDP would come and say a fire in the wall <u>behind</u> the box is not <u>their</u> jurisdiction."

Turning to the two firemen and resuming Portuguese, Mike insists that they inspect the wall behind the box. They put their heads together and confer for a few moments, then reluctantly agree. Since they have no tools they must borrow mine, the puny screwdriver and dainty hammer out of Elke's lady-like tool kit. With these, they gingerly loosen the charred box and pry it from the wall. By this time the fire has truly gone out, the brick wall having given it nothing more to burn. After carefully wiping their hands on a towel supplied by me, they leave.

All of this has certainly been different from my impression of American fire fighters rushing about in huge trucks with sirens, men in great boots and slickers bursting in with hatchets and mighty hoses, smashing great holes in walls and drowning furniture with heavy floods. I worried about that kind of zeal but this Portuguese brand of understatement is alarming in its own way.

After the two spiffy fire consultants have gone I give Mike a brandy and then he leaves too. I carry candles, kept handy during power outages, to the bedroom. Still stunned I retreat to bed, but sleep eludes me. The acrid smell of smoke and soot stings my nostrils all night long.

In the morning I inspect the damage. By daylight I can see that everything throughout the entire house is black and gritty. Since the electrical box has been destroyed, I have no electricity and no running water without the electric pump. Blessedly, the two gas burners on our range still work. I go out to the pump house and dip a pail into the *cisterna* for water to wash. While it's heating, I contemplate the mess and try to think. I can't begin to fathom how many people, phone calls, agencies, inspections and approvals will be needed before electrical service is restored. Of course all inside walls will have to be washed and repainted. I test the phone and, by some miracle, hear the sweet music of a humming dial tone. At least I'm not cut off from the rest of the world. Later on I'll phone Walter. Right now I'm still a bit numb. I chide myself for not having thought to throw the rug on the fire right away while it was still small. From now on I'll know that we need a fire extinguisher (one that works) and that fires can be smothered. Those are good things but it seems that I only learn the correct response to the last crisis; I'm never on top of the current one. And who knows what will come next?

When I'm moderately clean, I sip my coffee and try to counter my shock. At least the house didn't burn down, its contents are dirty but not damaged, and no one was hurt. Now I'll have to start wiping, dusting, sweeping, washing. In an odd way, it's a repeat of our clean-up operation after the winter flooding. Only this time the mess is inside and from the opposite cause, fire rather than water. It occurs to me that today is Thursday, Mafalda's afternoon to clean. I picture her shocked face when she will come through the door and I almost laugh. Boy, will she be surprised at how dirty the house has become since her last cleaning!

In the middle of the second night after the fire, the burglar alarm starts buzzing as its battery dies and buzzes continually for twelve hours. No emergency repairman from the alarm company comes. I lie awake with a pillow over my head and try to keep from reaching conclusions out of discouragement. But the feeling grows that life here is turning out to be just too hard. Daily necessities take too much time and effort to permit any higher functioning; contending with them is not at all what we had in mind when we thought of settling in the sunny Algarve. Our friends here, Wendy, Nigel, Kitty and Ben, distract themselves with dinner parties but the conversations seldom stray from tales of struggles with houses, gardens, horses, cars, rainstorms, burglaries, recalcitrant builders, or the rising rate of inflation (now at thirteen percent). Sleepless through the night, I remember the American woman at the movie who was going home because she and her husband missed the comforts. Tossing and turning on my gritty bed, I think miserably, "me too."

When morning comes at last, I shelve night-thoughts and larger questions. Time enough later on for ultimate decisions about our sojourn in Portugal. I decide to wait till Walter comes back and see what he thinks.

Seven-thirty a.m. days later. I'm having morning coffee and an apple. The apple because I can't keep orange juice cold—no refrigerator, no ice. It's been a dreadful time. At first there was relief that Mike had put out the fire and gratitude that no one was hurt. But now I'm in the aftermath, a long slow difficult period when normal life has ceased. All my energies are centered on bringing back that normality.

First there was the dirt. Couldn't touch anything without getting blackened. I still don't wear light colors; what's the use? I look at my hands and wonder if I'll ever have clean fingernails again. Then the repeated phone calls and trips to agencies. People arriving here at all hours to inspect the damage, and my reporting of facts over and over, talking, contending, slowly finding out what can be done, when, who can do it, how much it will cost, who will pay.

On Tuesday, Joost Roemer and his electrician came, along with men from the electric company, everyone circling about to pin responsibility, everyone wriggling out from under. Who was at fault? The builder? The electrician? EDP? Who knows? No one ever has seen anything like it, no known similar instances, etc. etc.

Yesterday the insurance assessor came, inspected the soot covered rooms, photographed the charred electrical box still dangling from the wall, made diagrams, wrote notes for his report. Then the painter came, shook his head at the blackened walls, gave his estimate.

Without electric power, I grow concerned for garden watering. I telephone Joost again to say that we must get some temporary hook-up to power. He has a good idea and rigs up an electric cable from the empty rental house on the hill behind our property to the sprinkler controls in our pump house. At least the garden will now get water.

Partly to get away from the mess, I decide to look for new fire extinguishers, one for us and one to replace Mike's. I finally find them at an auto supply store in Loulé.

From there I drive to my weekly Portuguese lesson with Philipa where I sit in a trance of exhaustion after too many sleepless nights. Fortunately I now share these lessons with Fiona, a beautiful young Irish woman who helps relocated executive families to settle here and become familiar with the region. Today Fiona gamely carries the student participation load. We are now trying to master personal pronouns, a dense underbrush of variations and exceptions to rules.

When at last I am home again, I find Mafalda who has spent many extra hours scrubbing and washing floors, cleaning soot from furniture, dishes and books. Today, she is working in the bedroom, where she is replacing the newly washed and ironed frilly blue bedspread. "For Senhor Walter, he come back soon," she explains.

I tell her, "Mafalda, you are a godsend."

"*Diga?*" (What?) she pauses from plumping a pillow.

"*Presente de Deus,*" I attempt to translate.

Mafalda smiles modestly as she carries her pail of water to

the living room where she wrings out a cloth, and continues her cleaning. A while later, she sadly brings me what was a tabletop sculpture of a woman dancer created by a Chinese artist who was a friend of my mother's. The figure's traditional Chinese garments, made of intricately folded paper of bright colors, are now covered with soot. Mafalda has tried to blow off as much of the soot as possible, but it still coats the fragile paper garments. The little figure has become dingy and cannot be restored to its former beauty. Even so, throwing it away seems like a betrayal. With a sigh, I point to a high shelf of a bookcase and Mafalda reaches up to place the statue there.

Walter just phoned from Lisbon and is driving home. Glory be! Just three hours and he'll be back. When I see his rented car pull into the driveway, I rush out to meet him and hug him as soon as he steps out of the car. I am so glad and relieved that he is here. Knowing that he's tired from the eighteen hours of flying and driving, I've resolved to hold off any litany of woes till he's rested. But I can't shield him from seeing the remains of the fire. As he steps into the blackened hall, the first thing he sees is the crippled dangling electric box.

"Holy Jesus," he says as he puts down his suitcase and then we walk through the rooms. The furniture has been wiped clean. Mafalda vacuumed the rugs two days ago and we carried them outside where she beat them. Then we rolled them up and stored them in the garage. The floors are bare and Mafalda has washed and polished every inch of them. The house is as clean as we could make it but there's no hiding the blackened walls and soot-dimmed windows. Walter looks at everything and shakes his head, muttering, "Worse than I thought."

"The painters are due to come. It'll be better then," I keep a firm latch on further speech.

I sit with him at the table while he eats a sandwich and riffles through some accumulated mail. Then on the way to the bedroom for his much-needed nap, we pause before the electric box which compels our attention like a demon's shrine.

"Oh Honey, and you had to go through this alone." He pulls me into a long hug.

For dinner, we drive to *A Floresta* and order their special grilled prawns, *pommes frites* and salad. With my first sip of *vinho verde* I relax and prepare to express my discouragement. Just as I take a breath to begin, Walter reaches across the table, takes my hand and says what I've been ashamed of thinking. "Why are we doing this? It just doesn't make sense any longer; it's too hard. And for what? "

"I don't know anymore," I admit. "I've been thinking the same thing this whole week. The fire, the mess, and we'd just finished cleaning up after the winter." I find myself close to tears. "It's just one thing after another. Nothing works right, and everything that goes wrong costs a lot of money. And now we've got no showers, no refrigerator, no lights. I keep working at it but it just doesn't get better."

"I know, and I hate having to leave you here alone to deal with this kind of thing.

"So, should we quit?"

Walter pauses for a long moment before answering, "I think so. I've thought that in Saratoga ever since I got your phone call about the fire, and seeing the place now just confirms it. Coming to Portugal was a nice idea but it just hasn't turned out the way we expected. And you know what? We don't have to prove anything."

I murmur the refrain from the gambler's song, "Know when to hold 'em, know when to fold 'em…"

"Right. And know when to run."

The waiter brings our meal and we eat in silence, peeling the garlicky prawns with our fingers. Each of us is quietly testing the impact of our decision. Right now I'm simply glad I'm not alone in wanting an end to the string of minor disasters that have consumed most of my time for months. I feel almost giddy as I imagine effortless days ahead. No more power failures, no more five-mile drives for the newspaper and mail or every quart of milk we might need, no more unreliable phone connections and exorbitant bills, no more floods, fires, infestations, no more freezing inside the house, no more dampness and mold, no more orange mud, no more unruly dog. I savor my list and push aside the one that brings a pang—no more bookshop?

The relief holds as we drive home until we glide to a stop in our courtyard and face our front door. The house still exists, as do the shop building, the pool, the garden, the woods on the back hillside, and the dog who is loping over to the car to greet us. The whole property hasn't evaporated into the starry Algarvian night just because we've decided to leave it. It's still here and has to be dealt with.

When we are reading side by side in bed, I turn from my book to look at Walter. It's so good to have him there, big, cozy in his plaid flannel nightshirt, his white hair rumpled. I'm in my flannel nightgown with socks on my feet. This is marriage, I muse, accustomed, comforting.

"So we've decided to leave," I say, partly to confirm our decision, partly to hear myself say it.

"Yes, I think we have to."

"OK." I am reassured for the moment. Yet the solid reality of what we have set up here is intruding on my relief. "But <u>how</u> are we going to leave? We can't just close the door and walk away."

"No. It's tempting but we don't have to do that. We'll sell the place."

"The market is down. No one's buying."

"Walter lets his book sink to his chest. "Maybe. We'll advertise, maybe in England, Germany, Holland…It might take a little time but someone will want it. Look, it's a good location and when it's cleaned up it will look nice again."

When it's cleaned up. I think of all the steps that lie before us. "Do you think that the people who owned the black moldy house near *Pituxia* just got tired of all the hassles, closed the door and left?"

Walter chuckles. " Probably more to it than that, legal troubles, death, who knows."

"Probably. But now I feel I understand that house better. I could understand just walking away."

"No you couldn't, Boops. It's not like you. We'll sell it; it may take a while but it will sell. It's a nice place, you know that. A house with a separate building for a business. The right buyer will snap it up."

"A nice retired couple from the States..."

Walter laughs again, then turns out his light and folds himself around me. "Let's get some sleep. We can't do anything right now." I turn off my light too and in a short while I hear his breathing in the steady rhythm of sleep. I try to lie still but ideas are squirreling through my brain. Ideas for ways to get out beyond the attractive one of abandoning the whole kit and caboodle. Put the house up for sale; slowly sell off Elke's books, antiques and paintings from the bookshop, or crate up and send them to America; put the house in the hands of a villa management company for rent as a vacation property; replace the antiques with cheap but sturdy rental furniture. Rent the shop building out for a café or boutique. The ideas circle without resolution, grow fragmentary, and I finally drift off to sleep.

In the morning, we accept the stubborn fact that we are still here for now. Even if we eventually decide to return to the States, for the time being we have to continue what we've started. And this morning we must focus, not on distant plans for escape but on immediate needs. The garden gets water through the rigged-up cable, but we need a place where we can shower. Vila Bonita will do for a few days. We have no working refrigerator and there's no place to buy ice so we can't keep any food. Clearly the first order of business is to get electric power restored, and we start out on the series of phone calls and visits to bring that about.

A few days later, a crew of workmen arrives with pails, mops and liquid bleach to scrub the blackened walls. A few more days and Roemer's electricians come to repair the circuit box and restore the electric current. That starts the heaters and pumps, giving us hot and cold water. If we're lucky we'll soon get painters to restore whiteness. Meanwhile, the weather has turned sunny and pleasant. Wildflowers are in bloom everywhere. Our patch of woods is full of small blue iris we can pick by the armful. In another month or so, all this blooming will dry out in the summer heat, but right now it is beautiful. Walter and I go for lunch at one of the seasonal beach bars built on stilts that has just re-opened. We sit on a high veranda overlooking the ocean. As we relax in the sunshine, the series of mishaps seems to fade like old photographs. We eat grilled sea bream freshly caught this morning, and feel tension waft away on the salt breeze.

"It's like a roller coaster, living here," I say, "so hard at times, and then so beautiful like this." I wave my arm to encompass the view.

Walter nods, "And right now we're coasting along at the top of the ride." he points toward a sprinkling of sails in the distance floating on the waves like white almond blossoms. Unhurried and mellowed by sunshine, we linger through the afternoon.

The newly mild spring weather encourages excursions. We meet Wendy and Nigel in Faro for a shellfish dinner at the harbor and then stroll through the lighted streets to a chamber concert at the historic *Theatro Lethes*. The theater is a little jewel box, its interior shaped in an elongated U with four tiers of boxes. We sit in the top tier far above the musicians but acoustics are so good that we hear every note. On stage, the pianist and violinist wear black tie and tails; their page-turner wears a neon green T-shirt and purple sweat pants. Obviously, a loose dress code. They play Stravinsky, Cesar Franck and a Schubert sonata, which seems at home in the lovely eighteenth-century space.

The lighting of the *Theatro* is a bit haphazard with half the bulbs burned out. In the soft glow, the panorama of boxes across from us on all four levels of the narrow U looks like a doll's house with live figures. They are so close to us that we can see a whole array of responses to music. Among those seated at the front we can observe rapt attention, shifting positions, murmured remarks to companions and a bit of dozing here and there as the evening wears on. Those seated further back in the boxes fade in and out of the shadows, uncertain presences revealed only by an occasional glint of eyeglasses, a movement of hands, or a program fanning the close air. I wish for a photographer's skill to record the concert's chiaroscuro progress.

Afterwards, as Walter and I drive back from Faro, the evening's glow stays with me. Spring is here; our house is white once again and there is now nothing to stop us from putting it on the market. Yet we haven't done it.

"I know we've agreed to leave here," I say, glancing over at Walter as he drives. A passing car's headlights silver his hair. I hesitate for a moment and then plunge ahead. "But I'm thinking that I might still go ahead with the bookshop. At least get it started? To make the shop building look active. What do you think?"

"Oh, no question," Walter hasn't a moment's indecision. "You've got to do it now. Even if we do sell, it will make the property more attractive. A going business will add to the value, show off the good location."

"Right. And anyway, I can't seem to just drop the idea."

"And you shouldn't. You're almost there now. And then later on, when we're ready," he looks over to smile at me, "maybe that nice couple from the States will want to run a bookshop…"

And so, while we seem to have agreed that we'll return to the States someday, we postpone plans for leaving Portugal until an undefined far-off future.

As weeks pass Walter gains several more patients. He now sees three or four regulars in addition to those that try therapy for a quick fix, as they would try a new place in hopes of leaving the old self behind. When two or three sessions don't eliminate their problems, they generally fade from Walter's schedule. A few, however, are serious about wanting to change their lives and following the Alcoholics Anonymous dictum they "keep coming back." Walter gives me brief summaries of their situations but I know them mainly by their cars when they park in our courtyard near the side door that leads to Walter's office.

232 MARIANNE GILBERT FINNEGAN

There's the dark blue Peugeot with a faded convertible top, the kind of car my old Nancy Drew mysteries described as a flivver. That belongs to a freckled sandy-haired buxom young woman who lives on an offshore island. She has retreated there to get away from her former life as a stripper in Parisian nightclubs, and to wean herself from dependence on drugs and alcohol which led her into that life.

Most noticeable is a long dark green Jaguar that arrives twice a week. It belongs to a German émigré who made millions by developing Algarve real estate. Successful and shrewd in business, he is bewildered by his personal life, and wavers between helplessness and rage as he tries to placate two women, his bejeweled middle-aged wife, and his young, acquisitive Portuguese mistress. His rage seized him so fiercely one day that he threw rocks at his beloved automobile, inflicting several dents on its gleaming surface. That's when he knew he needed help and came to Walter. Even when the Jaguar is no longer in our courtyard, I can always tell that the millionaire has had his hour because the house reeks with the pungent scent of his after-shave. I don't know if his ladies enjoy it; to me it smells like pine-scented detergent.

Marianne and Walter 1983

Elke in Zurich, before our first trip to Portugal

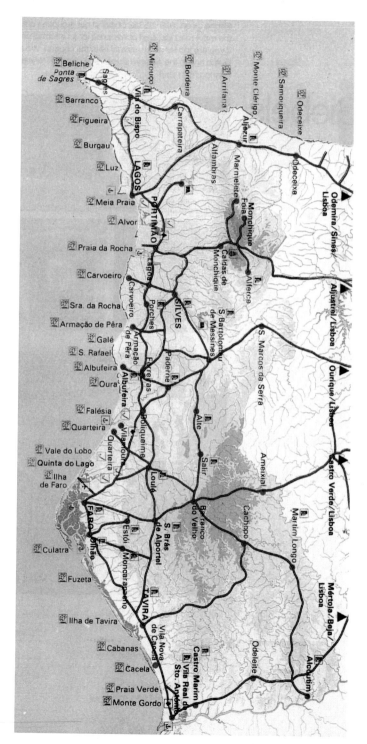

Algarve Map

**Dreaming
Of
Portugal**

Elke in the Algarve

Our Property

The start of building

Vila Gilfinn — Waiting for our garden

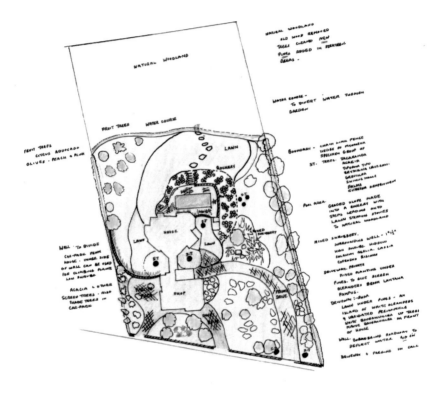

NATURAL WOODLAND

NATURAL WOODLAND
OLD WOOD REMOVED
TREES CLEANED NEW
PINES ADDED IN STRATEGIC
AREAS.

WATER SOURCE -
TO DIVERT WATER THROUGH
GARDEN

FRUIT TREES   WATER SOURCE

FRUIT TREES
CITRUS AVOCADO
OLIVES - PEACH & PLUM

LAWN

ROCKERY

BOUNDARY - CHAIN LINK FENCE
HEDGE OF MYOPORUM
SPECIMEN GROUP OF
ST. TREES: JACARANDA
ACACIA
TIPUANA TIPU
BAUHINIA (VARIEGA)
GREVILLEA
SALIGNA MALE
PALMS
CUPRESSA SEMPERVIRENS

POOL AREA: GRADED SLOPE MADE
INTO A ROCKERY WITH
STEPS LEADING ONTO
LAWN STEPPING STONES
TO NATURAL WOODLAND

RAISED
FLOWER BED

MIXED SHRUBBERY.
SURROUNDING WELL - 1½ ½.
HIGH SHRUBS. HIBISCUS
SOLANUM ABRILA. CASSIA
COPROSMA BISINISA

DRIVEWAY: PRIVATE
RAISED PLANTING UNDER
PINES. TO GIVE SCREEN
OLEANDERS BROOM LANTANA
PAMPAS.

WALL TO DIVIDE
CAR-PARK FROM
HOUSE · INNER SIDE
OF WALL CAN BE USED
FOR CLIMBING PLANTS
LOW SHRUBS

ACACIA & OTHER
SCREEN TREES · ALSO
SHADE TREES IN
CAR-PARK

DRIVEWAY:-AREA
LAWN UNDER PINES - AN
ISLAND OF WHITE OLEANDERS
& VARIEGATED PERIWINKLE
WHITE BOUGAINVILLEA UP TREES
MAUVE BOUGAINVILLEA IN FRONT
OF HOUSE

WALL SURROUNDING BOUNDARY TO
DEFLECT WATER 40 CM

DRIVEWAY & PARKING IN CELL

HOUSE

LAWN

HOUSE

LAWN

ST

ST

SHOP

PRIVATE
DRIVE

ST

The Plan for our garden

Walter
and
Caesar

Caesar's
sparring
partner

Views of the Vila Gilfinn

Our Griffin

The Griffin Bookshop

Julia, Marianne, Helen

The Griffin's Grand Opening Celebration

XIX

The Griffin Book Hop

This is the day we've waited for. Walter has washed our car, filled it with "petrol," put our bags in the "boot," and we set off for Lisbon to buy books. We will spend the next two days visiting D'Internal and Distri-Cultural, the two largest distributor of English language books. I am so excited I can hardly breathe and Walter and I exchange grins every few miles. Wendy rides in the back seat and shares our enthusiasm. "This is woonnnderful," she says several times and smiles as our eyes meet when I glance back at her. Because she has lived here for three years and her Portuguese is much better than mine, I asked her to come with us. Gunnar Nielsen has set up accounts by mail for me at both distributors, but through repeated telephone attempts I've found no one who speaks English at D'Internal. Wendy is happy to join us and hopes to find a repair shop in Lisbon for their American stereo system.

The three-hour drive is by now familiar and passes smoothly. After we have checked into a small *pensão* on a side street (no more luxury hotels now that we expect to make these trips regularly), Walter settles in for some quiet time with his *Herald Tribune*. Wendy and I find D'Internal on another narrow street within easy walking distance. Two men are unloading crates from a huge truck parked in front. I clutch Wendy's arm and burble, "Look! Books, books, books!" We enter through an iron door into a small reception area where we meet Senhor Manuel Pereira, a slender young man who runs the warehouse. Behind him I can see a cavernous room with metal shelves crammed with books of all colors and sizes. I can hardly wait to get closer to see the titles, but control my impulse. After an initial greeting, I proudly display my account number for the Griffin Bookshop. Wendy explains my mission and Senhor Manuel responds with a friendly smile and gathers catalogues and publishers' brochures which he puts into my hands. I signal that I will return *a manhan*, tomorrow.

"Ask him if I can select the books then," I whisper to Wendy who conveys my request.

"*Sim, sim, certo*" (yes, of course), he assures me and we all shake hands. Later back in the hotel room Walter, Wendy and I pore through the materials and I jot down questions such as: Do they carry all the books English publishers list in their catalogues? Do they have books in English about Portugal? Children's books? Gardening books?

The next morning, I go back with Walter, muster my courage, and stumble through my prepared questions. Senhor Manuel, like so many courteous and warm-hearted people here, appreciates my attempts to speak his language and answers my questions as best he can. They have books in English on many subjects, fiction and non-fiction. I will be able to buy most books on consignment and return any I do not sell. For those I do sell, seventy percent of the sales price will go to D'Internal. I also learn that we won't be able to carry the books away—computerized inventory must be reconciled. My order will be shipped directly to The Griffin Bookshop.

Senhor Manuel then welcomes both of us back into the stacks to explore the inventory. We scuttle through narrow aisles between bookshelves reaching to fifteen-foot-high ceilings, and clamber around more books stacked on the floor space between aisles. After months of titles on lists, I am thrilled to be among actual books I can see and handle.

"Look, here's Charles Dickens, practically every novel."

"And not just books from England; I've got *Huckleberry Finn* and there's Hemingway. I can have a mid-list after all." I wander on, exhilarated at the riches around me. Walter finds a stool to perch on and gets absorbed in a volume of Ibsen's plays. "*Hedda Gabler*, I haven't seen this since college," he mutters. Books everywhere and I want all of them. Senhor Manuel shows us an alcove where we can stack those we pick.

When we later rendezvous with Wendy, she has succeeded in finding a repair shop and we share a quiet dinner at a small nearby restaurant. Afterwards, I'm too excited to sleep. Lying on the twin bed in our *pensão*, I buzz with plans. As I try to settle down from my first day of actual book-buying, I think it's great to be an entrepreneur!

The next morning we drop Wendy at the huge *Amoreiras* shopping mall, and drive to Distri-Cultural at the edge of the city. In their huge warehouse, I get wonderful help from Bernt, a young German who speaks excellent English and Portuguese. Bernt looks like a pirate gone to seed, with wild hair, rumpled white shirt and pants, and a red bandana around his neck—everything baggy and dusty from books and packing papers. But he knows his job and gives me good advice. He walks me through miles of aisles with great energy and good humor, telling me I need this or that title for my shop, and loading up a trolley with books as we walk. I learn that large glossy coffee-table books are an exception to the consignment system; I must pay for those in advance. I decide that their bright colors and handsome photographs will lure customers looking for gifts, and add several to my trolley.

Both warehouses promise to deliver next week (*proxima semana* rides again). I must wait in suspense, but after all this time, it looks like the shop is imminent. Walter and I invite Wendy for dinner on the rooftop restaurant of the Hotel Tivoli where we stayed during our first trip to Portugal almost seven years ago. The three of us watch the sun set over the Tagus River, glad to have completed our missions.

A week later, on May 29th, both orders of books arrive. Nine boxes in all.

"There should be about five-hundred books here," I tell Walter who is carefully slitting open the boxes. "But they don't look like much," I fret as I start to stack them on the two tables.

"Let's see how they look once they're on the shelves," Walter says, "If these look too skimpy then, we can always go up to Lisbon again to get more."

"Right, especially since they're mostly free. I love this consignment arrangement."

We've decided that, if all goes according to plan, we will open quietly and unofficially two weeks hence for six hours a day: 10:00 to 1:00 and 3:00 to 6:00.

"I kind of like this toe-in-the-water opening," I say as I randomly place books on shelves to see how they look.

"Yes, it'll give us time to test our systems," Walter grins and points to the metal cash box to hold proceeds from sales.

"And then we'll have a big splash grand opening later on."

The first shipment of books that I spent hours picking out, turns out to total only 470 books! I decide to return to Lisbon to pick up another batch. Walter has appointments with two patients here so I'll go by bus. The touring buses are very comfortable and I'm eager to gather more booty. Meanwhile, as I catalogue books I puzzle about inventory control. For books on consignment I have till September to pay for what I've sold and to send back the rest. Or keep longer? I'm not sure. There's a fluidity about dates quite unlike my American training. And the shipping lists show only price and general category, such as *Livros de Bolso* (paperbacks), four at 1540$, six at 2330$, like buying a dozen eggs or a gross of oranges. They don't mention specific titles. I wonder, do the distributors' own records have more details and do I need more for mine? Without clear answers, I'm noting on an index card for each book the ten items I was trained to record for an American bookshop: ISBN number, author, title, price, publisher, publication date, category, date of purchase, number of copies on hand, and date of sale. Is this more about penguins than anyone wants to know? Well, I'll pare down later when I see what isn't needed. That seems better than the reverse, to do too little and then find that I have to go back and recover the data.

In the D'Internal warehouse, on my second buying trip, Senhor Manuel recognizes me and lets me wander about by myself. I simply pick up books I like and stack them in an alcove for later delivery.

At Distri-Cultural I am again joined by Bernt. At one point we come to a narrow aisle that holds a section of mass-market porno books. I pause, intrigued as I guess everyone is.

"Maybe you should stock of few of these titles? Ja?"

I hesitate, then shake my head. "I don't think I want my family bookshop to have a porno section."

"Adult books," Bernt corrects me and adds, "I understand your feelings." But then he adds with a bland smile, "Maybe you think about it. We get the lowest rate of returns on these books. Hardly any of them come back."

"Mmm, interesting," I respond and keep moving on to another aisle. When he leaves me for his lunch hour, I pass the "adult books" section again which oddly enough, is right next to a small section of children's books. This time I stop. Should I buy some? I pick up two books to look inside. The writing style seems to be modeled on the "letters" section in the few *Playboy* and *Penthouse* magazines I've seen, all cocks and sucking and bodily fluids. No surprises. I put the books back again thinking, let the hotels do it; it's not what I want. If Distri-Cultural had some better-class pornography, I'd consider scattering a sprinkling of such books through the general adult fiction section. But I reject these particular offerings and head to the children's section. There I gather up as many titles as I can. Children's books in English are scarce here, though I'm told they're coveted by all parents whose children attend Prince Henry College near us (which is not a college at all, but an English grade school). In future, I may need to order a better supply directly from London.

Halfway along on my return trip from Lisbon, the bus pauses at a rest stop, and I proceed toward the restrooms. Centered between the doors of the *Homens* and the *Senhoras* I recognize a familiar large oil painting, a copy of Gainsborough's *Blue Boy*. A most peculiar juncture, all that aristocratic blue velvet and lace on the young English gentleman posed before the WCs of a Portuguese bus station, a site I'm sure Gainsborough could not have imagined.

While cataloging the second shipment of books, I think about the long pull to get this far. The hardest part was not the beginning when the bookshop was still a far-off goal. It was that long drawn-out middle, just before halfway, when my courage deflated like a three-day old balloon and I had to persist because I didn't know what else to do. That stage is now past and. I'm at last working with actual books. Doing it step by step, not the thinking, has saved the enterprise. As they say, God is in the details. The opposite saying, the Devil is in the details, might pertain if one can't get through them, but either way, clearly, <u>something</u> significant is lurking in there.

I call Cynthia Green to ask about two roadside signs I've ordered. In her birdlike English voice she chirps that she has completed the logo using her letters and the griffin portrait I brought back from the States. But she hasn't "quite gotten 'round" to taking the design to the sign maker. I take a deep exasperated pause. Then I say, "I've checked in my journal and it's been two months since I contacted you about signs." Cynthia pleads overwork and promises to get going "straightaway." Meanwhile, we'll have to rig up something temporary.

We have done it! The doors of the Griffin Bookshop are open to the public! I feel so...triumphant at this crest, and I want to savor the feeling. The shop looks wonderfully inviting with books brightening mahogany shelves with splashes of color. The chandeliers glow with points of light. The eight chairs I bought in

Loulé are grouped around two square tables to form seating areas for browsing. One corner marks the children's section with small chairs from the same warehouse and a low round table I painted hyacinth blue with a border of stenciled flowers circling the top. Outside on the front verandah, peach and white umbrellas shade groupings of white tables and chairs set up to attract passers-by.

I can't say that passers-by have actually taken much notice. While waiting for the large road front signs announcing what this establishment is and does, we've been working on an improvised sandwich-board sign with big decal letters. Unexpectedly we are snagged because we can't find the letter "S" in any of the local *papelarias* that stock stationery supplies. Wendy and Nigel relish our dilemma and find a sign that says BOOK HOP a jolly idea but we're not convinced. I'm going out again later today to continue the search for an "S" in Faro.

Aside from lacking roadside signs, we've have an additional impediment to full business activity: on this opening day, Senhor Viegas, our long-awaited mason arrived at eight a.m. to tear up the tile floor of the shop. A number of tiles were damaged in the February flooding and we've been waiting ever since for Senhor Viegas to replace them. Of course, when he finally arrived today, we couldn't turn him away. Much banging, crashing, and cement dust all morning, and the shop entrance embellished by his big truck and tools scattered across the driveway. All in all, this day could be a variant for the magazine column, "Can this marriage be saved?" For us the title might be, "Can this business get started?" Right now the answer looks doubtful, but I take comfort in the thought that this isn't the real opening, just a trial run.

The serpentine search through regional *papelarias* continues. I spend two afternoons seeking an "S" to fill in the words "Bookshop" for our handmade temporary sign. No "S" matches the letters we already bought. I buy a different brand of "S" in Faro but it won't fit. Walter goes back to Faro for a complete set of the second kind and is now gluing them onto our rigged-up sandwich board. We've been open for two days but no one has come, which is just as well considering Senhor Viegas' mess is still prominent. One pleasing note is that when he worked on our house last year he and I could only communicate in French. This year, we speak in Portuguese.

Last night Walter finally got our hand-made sign put together. This morning we set it up in front of the shop and walk up the driveway to look back at our handiwork. It looks awfully small from a distance. I say wistfully, "It would be nice to make at least one sale during our first week," but I am not hopeful. We have books on the shelves, cozy corners for browsing, and change in the cash box, but our improvised sign can't be read from passing cars. People are unlikely to wander in to ask, "What do you do here?" I certainly wouldn't if I were passing by.

"They'll come when the big signs are up at the roadside," Walter says.

"I hope so." We trudge back to the house where I extract the cash box from the closet where we hide it and carry it over to the shop for my morning shift. It's quite pleasant and hardly an onerous workday; the advance preparation has taken far more time, a bit like teaching with two-thirds of the work taking place before any actual encounters with students (or customers).

A while later, Walter waves to me from the front garden where he is raking around tree planting circles. Then he comes to the shop's front entrance. I see him from the sales desk and wonder why he stops in front of the double sliding glass doors. In a moment, looking perplexed, he raps on the glass and I get up and slide the door open.

"Why didn't you just come in?"

"I can't. There's no handle."

A new and ludicrous discovery. The doors have handles inside to let us out, but no handles outside to let customers in. Unless we notice and open the door, anyone who might want to enter would have to press his nose against the glass, like Keats at the sweets shop window. In summertime we can leave the sliders open, but it would certainly curtail trade in cold or rainy weather. Oh well, all it means is seventeen phone calls or four visits trying to find door people.

Two days ago we had our first customer! Wendy came to give us moral and financial support by buying a novel. And since that first purchase, one or two people each day, admittedly mostly friends or acquaintances, stop in to cheer us on and buy something. Nothing spectacular, but satisfying for an unofficial beginning. Besides being nearly incognito, we are also very low tech. Not only did I not computerize, I haven't even bought a cash register. The small metal box with four compartments and a key—one step up from a cigar box—works fine so far. We'll decide later on if the volume of business warrants investment in a proper cash register. All in all, we're learning what we need day by day, and continue to feel very good to have accomplished what we set out to do five years ago. It's two or three years later than we anticipated, but that's Murphy's second law, everything takes longer than you think it will.

The shop's first week ends happily with the installation of the long awaited roadside signs at both entrances to the circular driveway. Like the letterhead, their background is terra cotta color and the droll griffin stands within a circle of bright burgundy letters that announce "The Griffin Bookshop" and *"Livraria Grifo."*

We have taken in 17,590 escudos, or about twelve U.S. dollars. Not a great amount but I am pleased. Most customers are friends or acquaintances but at least there are sales. And I have learned some things. First, I can't figure correct change for purchases in my head, so I must get a small calculator. Second, from now on I must reconcile cash on hand every day. (This time, I waited till the end of the week and even with so few sales, I came up short, and don't know why.) Finally, I need a system of coding the inventory cards to know which books I've already paid for and which are on consignment. I haven't yet gotten into bill-paying yet, but I'll take on that chore when the first bills arrive.

It's August and we walk around taking stock of our garden, which has grown a lot since spring. Some of the plants are lovely, others need tending but at least it's verdant and a complete change from eighteen months ago when everything in sight was barren and

242 MARIANNE GILBERT FINNEGAN

scarred. Many plants are unfamiliar to me, but only one has turned out to be unpleasant—a hedge that runs along the privacy wall right outside our bedroom window. It has waxy yellow flowers that look attractive but give off a surprising and cloying smell of peanut butter.

Our roadside signs look handsome and have attracted attention. The shop is now open five-and-a-half days a week and we have, if not exactly a stream, a steady trickle of customers. I have arranged to carry Ben Edwards' car shades for 400 escudos each, or about $2.50 in U.S. dollars, on a fifty/fifty consignment basis. They do sell, but the number is in the dozens, not the hundreds needed to deplete Ben's inventory. Furthermore, seasonal cycles have warped or cracked the cardboard on many shades so that they no longer fit for sale. The stacks in the Edwards' study-to-be remain barely diminished.

Ben brings Kitty to the shop sometimes for a visit with me while he does errands in town. Kitty spends her time on their mountain top watching the changing seasons, caring for her house, chatting with her maid, and reading books she orders from England as well as those she has started to buy from me. She often refers to her reading and I mention that I hope later to start a book discussion group in the shop. Kitty, however, refuses my invitation to join such a group.

"I never went to university," she says "I can't *discuss* books. All I can do is say "marvelous" or "dreadful.""

"Well, come and say that then. Nobody cares about university credentials and you read more than most people."

"Not my thing," she says firmly. "Besides I can't get there on my own and Ben is busy trying to roof over the guest bedroom before the rains come."

Kitty browses among the shelves, picking up novels, remarking on authors, and singing,

"If you give me your attention,
I will tell you what I am:
I'm a genuine philanthropist
All other kinds are sham,"

and other snatches from Gilbert and Sullivan or Noel Coward. Included in her purchases, I notice, are a number of self-help books on how to combat depression.

By this time, I myself am far from depressed in the Algarve, if anything I am too busy. But I know that were I held fast by someone else's driving schedule, my dominant mood would be a deep gray. I can well understand Kitty's fear of driving in Portugal; my own weeks of learning to shift gears were terrifying. But I couldn't let the terror win out, not due to greater courage than Kitty has, but because the thought of such a cloistered dependent life frightened me even more. I don't feel free to broach the subject of depression with Kitty, because whenever we discuss driving, she insists that if she needs to go somewhere she can always call a taxi, and her life is just fine, thank you.

One day, after Kitty has watched me chat with some tourists, she says she's amazed at how nice I am to people who come into the shop, browse, chat and then don't buy anything.

"They might come back," I tell her. "It's much easier to be nice when they're potential customers."

"I could never do it," says Kitty, "I rather think that my attitude toward most people is despicion."

"Despicion?"

"I made that up; it's a cross between despising and suspicion. Isn't it clever?"

"Mmm, yes it is." I think clever but unfortunately apt; Kitty she does put some people off. It wasn't till I knew her better that I got past that glib surface.

"I was trained, you know, to be a well-bred English girl," she has explained. "That meant being able to speak amusingly in company for hours without ever saying anything interesting."

Her comment illuminates the often puzzling differences we've found here between English and American conversation.

Before the shop opens each morning, I usually spend a quiet hour writing letters or in my journal. For me, it's a means of reflection; writing helps me to know what's in my head. A famous writer once said, "I think with my right hand." Me too, except that these days with word processors, it's probably more accurate to say I think with my ten fingers.

Today I'm thinking about a TV movie we watched last night about an American woman who goes to the Australian outback. After railing against and surviving many hardships she finally comes to love the place. The Algarve certainly isn't a barren waste; in fact it's a vacation dream. Yet I, too, sometimes have felt as though we've come to a place where ordinary life is hard, primitive, and on a near-subsistence level. That old-time stony life continues right next to hotels and villas of great luxury, just as our plot of "hard sandy soil unfit for farming" lies close to the lush Vale do Lobo. Since we evolved from vacationers into residents, we've grown aware how many Portuguese must work all year long to create and maintain a festive facade for those who come for a sunny holiday.

The Viegas family in Almancil is just one example. They run the *papelaria* near the post office. Four family members keep the place open six and a half days per week. The inventory is unwieldy, every nook and cranny is piled with newspapers, magazines, books, paper supplies, film, greeting cards, jewelry, cosmetics, toys, gifts, watches, even suitcases high up on shelves near the ceiling. I can't imagine how they keep track of it all and also serve the constant stream of customers, many of whom don't even speak Portuguese. Long hours and unremitting work go to support the whole family in relative comfort.

Restaurant and bar owners are also ceaselessly occupied throughout the seven-month tourist season with going to market, grilling fish and chicken, serving drinks, returning bottles, disposing of mounds of garbage, cleaning dishes and floors, laundering table linens, and coping with drunken arrogant patrons. The huge hotels, of course, dominate the season, employing hundreds of people to greet and flatter guests, prepare and serve meals, clean rooms, launder mountains of linens, cultivate and water acres of lawns and flower beds, keep driveways in good repair, whitewash walls every spring, maintain sparkling pools, and manage the marinas and extensive golf courses. Who knows how many others work to supervise staff, maintain records, meet payrolls, and publicize all these enterprises. Before I lived here, I never realized that the whole gleaming panorama to keep those tourists happy and coming back each year depends on so much behind-the-scenes toil by so many people.

I wonder where Walter and I, and other former tourists who have now settled here, fit in? Probably somewhere in between, neither tourists nor natives, *ni peixe ni frango* (neither fish nor fowl), pensioners from other lands seeking an inexpensive retirement in a sunny climate or entrepreneurs with modest pioneering skills who start small businesses in hopes of striking it, if not rich, at least comfortable.

Perhaps one of the initial appeals of living in a foreign country is the idea that one can live as one does on vacation, drifting lightly on the surface of a country's life and exempt from its problems. As we have found, living for an extended time in any place is to become aware of its struggles and the various alliances and factions that rule people's activities. A foreign resident, simply by being separate in the midst of community life, is an aspect of local politics, a figure in the allocation of scarce resources, a source of income, a challenge to traditional values, a sign of foreign ways of living and thinking. All those things. The foreigner can hide or be inactive but can never really escape from political intrigue or harsh realities.

In the wake of the worldwide recession that followed the stock market crash we first heard of in 1987, Portugal's annual inflation rate has now by 1990 reached thirteen percent and living here is no longer cheap. So few foreigners now buy holiday or retirement homes that builders and realtors have had to suspend work. We see the skeletons of huge unfinished high-rise apartment towers in Quarteira and Vilamoura, and read about bribery of local officials and the greed of foreign investors that resulted in hasty overbuilding during the earlier boom time. There's no place in the world where politics don't exist, no earthly paradise anywhere.

Yet there are heavenly moments. As I close my journal, pull

up the roller shutters and step outside, I see a perfect blue sky and bright red canna flowers shaded by deep green umbrella pines. I breathe the flower-scented air and am grateful for another beautiful day.

XX
Affiliations

Our friends from dog-training school, William and Sonia, have finished most of their major house repairs, started while they stayed at Vila Gilfinn last winter. With more free time, Sonia has unpacked her watercolors to paint small lovely pictures of local wildflowers while William has fitted out their shed as his carpentry workshop. He is designing cupboards for their kitchen with the help of two American books on carpentry that Walter brought back from his latest trip to the States.

Now William and Sonia stop in at the shop almost every week and repeatedly express their wish to do something for us in exchange. They come unannounced because they have no telephone and though I'm touched by their kindness, their visits are not always convenient. I try to dream up a project. I encourage Sonia to make some greeting cards of her flower paintings. "I could easily sell them," I say with genuine enthusiasm. "I'd love to have some sidelines for the shop and your flower paintings are lovely." I also ask William to make some wooden blocks or toys to amuse little children while their parents browse in the bookshop.

For two weeks we do not see them. Then one afternoon, they appear at the shop. She with a little collection of her cards, he with an assortment of puzzles he's made for children. They arrive as I'm about to interview another prospective gardener after the last two have proved unsatisfactory. As a result I'm unable to study William's or Sonia's creations on the spot.

"I can't do this right now," I explain. "You'll have to leave them with me so that I can look at them when the shop isn't busy." Sonia nods and quietly hands me a little box of her cards. William is slower to understand. "Just let me explain this bit here," he says, taking some wooden shapes from the carton he is carrying.

"I just can't right now, William. That gentleman is waiting to talk with me. Please come back in a few days." I take the carton from him and put it on a shelf behind the sales desk. Clearly disappointed, William says, "Well, er, all right, then," and he and Sonia leave.

After closing hour, I look at Sonia's note cards and find them lovely. The front of each shows two or three hand-painted wild flowers in delicate pinks, blues and yellows. The small Algarvian wildflowers that bloom in the desert have brought unexpected delight to my walks in the countryside. Sandra has captured their subtle delicacy and I will enjoy having her cards in the shop.

On the other hand, William's contribution gives me pause. I carry his carton back to the house where Walter examines the contents. William's puzzles, made to entertain children, turn out to be too difficult for most adults—count the tiny squares in one jigsaw design, count the triangles in another, assemble a set of interlocking rods (Walter spends two days with this one), position pegs in intricate non-conflicting patterns in another one that's way beyond my skill and patience.

When they come back I say (I think for the second time), "You know, William, if children are old enough to read, I want them to look at *books*. It's the little ones I need to distract from flinging themselves down the veranda steps or climbing up on bookcases. Your pieces are beautifully made, but they're just too hard for young children. I'm sorry but I can't use them. I could try to sell them for you, if you like."

William's jaw drops. While he absorbs what I've just said, I tell Sonia that I like her cards very much and she agrees to bring me a list of her expenses so that I can figure out a fair selling price.

"I'll have to think on what you've told me," William says and they leave again.

The next day they return, as they do, like the second blow of a hurricane. This time the shop is quiet and I am glad to talk more with Sonia about her cards but William takes first position, hemming, err'ing, full of concern for his creations. "What you said yesterday," he growls, "was a bombshell!"

I say again, "I'm really sorry. Perhaps I wasn't clear."

"No!" he shouts, striking his forehead with the palm of his hand hard enough to jar his head. "I should have thought. Of course! The older ones you'd want to 'ave look at books. It's the little tykes you're after. But I want to be sure what you want. What is it exactly you 'ave in mind?"

Bit by laborious bit, we settle on blocks. Then we crash into one of those occasional miscommunications between English and American terms. After some verbal gropings, it emerges that William's idea of blocks is painted cubes, whereas mine is of various shapes made from smooth unpainted wood. With that concept in mind, he gets set to construct interlocking shapes for serious building. I again bring him up short by describing an assortment of simple pieces for the random play of toddlers. A long repetitive discussion full of crazy digressions. "Only toxic paints here, can't have them painted," William frets.

"Don't want them painted, not necessary," I repeat. We go on and on. By this time I expect him to come back with something incredibly complex and unusable.

At last I get to Sonia. With a minor pang, I tell her that I don't like her envelopes, faintly blue with tiny white dots that detract from the creamy sheen of the cards' paper. I have some better envelopes and ask Sonia, "Do you mind if we switch them?" and she hastens to agree. We unwrap her cling-wrap from each card to switch the envelopes and I persuade her to leave off the cling-wrap because it makes the cards look too homemade. All through this transaction I feel like a bulldozer compared to timid delicate Sonia. But I wonder why an artist who can create such lovely flower paintings cannot see that card and envelope shouldn't clash.

As far as pricing goes, Sonia has brought a list of her expenses that I asked for—but no per card breakdown. I have more sympathy for that kind of innocence and realize how much experience I've gained in practical business matters, knowledge I assume that everyone has, but they don't. We easily figure out the per card cost, agree on a price that will give both of us a modest profit, and conclude our negotiations enjoyably.

A week later, William comes with a box of little wooden cubes, triangles, and logs that I am delighted to accept. I offer to pay him but he wants his work to be a thank-you gift. The blocks are given a prominent place in our children's corner, near the little blue table with the flowered top. I display Sonia's cards on the sales desk where people can buy one or two as they check out. So far, card sales are modest but steady. They will keep Sonia scouting the fields for wild flowers and painting them to re-stock the Griffin's supply of "hand-painted greeting cards by a local artist."

Nigel and Wendy drop in late one afternoon to tell us that Wendy has just won first place in the Algarve Riding Club's thirty-kilometer competition. The course, designed by Nigel, led riders through all sorts of terrain. Wendy's face is flushed with pride and she shows off a first place rosette and a huge silver trophy cup. She is excited as a kid, having insisted that they both rush here to show off her triumph. We toast her with a glass of wine and photograph her with her trophies and a victory smile. Then she and Nigel go off to a celebration dinner with the other riders. Walter and I wave goodbye, feeling like proud family—*in loco parentis*.

A few weeks ago I ordered imprinted checks for a separate bank account for the Griffin. The new checks arrive imprinted "Marianne Sinnegan." When I show them to Walter, he chuckles, "Sounds a bit risqué, but interesting."

I take them back to Banco Espirito Santo to ask that they correct the error.

"It happens all the time," says the bank clerk with a bright smile. *"Par Exemplo*, we have a client whose name is Mr. Ross, but his checks show his name as Mr. Rose. Is not a problem for us; is a problem for you?"

A bit baffled, I try to explain, "But Sinnegan is not my *name*."

"Oh, we know that," he assures me. "But is difficult to correct spelling. You must go to Faro to request correction from the head office. Maybe not worth the trouble? Why don't you write the F over the S? Is easier and we don't mind."

Seemingly, the computer age has arrived here for setting things up, but not yet for correcting errors. And if a bank (my former model of exactitude) doesn't care, who am I to make a fuss? It's simply one more reminder that we're in Portugal where exactitude is not a virtue. TV shows, for example, start anywhere from ten minutes before to half an hour after the advertised time, and movies may or may not be shown on the advertised day.

I take the checks home and write an F over each S.

One day when Walter and I are both in the shop carding and shelving new books, we are surprised to see our former pool man, Louis, at the door. He steps in, smiles as if his leaving us stranded with a dirty pool and untended garden never happened, and looks around at the partially filled shelves.

"Is good," he approves. "Now you need sales lady. I have cousin, she speak good English. I bring her, yes?"

Louis's family employment agency evidently still functions and I marvel at his aplomb. When I tell him I plan to manage the bookshop myself, he is as surprised by that idea as I am at his reappearance. He decides to ignore my statement. In his experience, English s*enhoras* in the Algarve do not run businesses. "When you need, I send my cousin," he promises as he leaves, and I suppose, as he did for our pool, he will return periodically to repeat his offer.

Actually, Louis is mistaken about English Senhoras. Fiona, my fellow-student at Portuguese language lessons, has started an Algarvian professional women's network that holds monthly luncheon meetings. Fiona herself is an independent consultant who works with multi-national corporations who send executives to Portugal. She helps the families to find housing, schools and medical services, as well as advising them about cultural customs and expectations. The association she has started is drawing together active women from across the Algarve, not only English and expatriate business and professional women but Portuguese nationals as well.

I have gone to several "Network" luncheons and met several women who own shops—cane furniture, interior design, fabrics, resort clothing, and second-hand villa furnishings. I also met the owner of a riding stable, a copywriter, two graphic designers, a caterer, the owner of a yoga and fitness center, a bank manager, a psychologist, and an attorney. So many diverse occupations and interesting women of all nationalities, and I haven't yet had the chance to speak to everyone who attends.

Through several such contacts, and mostly through my work with the Griffin, I grow aware of informal and mutually supportive relations among small business owners. I regularly eat lunch at Megan's Bistro, and engage Jessica to restore our garden after each winter's damage. Maria, the interior designer in Almancil, made our new curtains; Joanna from the wallpaper and paint shop stenciled the flower border for the shop's children's table. We frequently recommend Vila Bonita to tourist customers. All of these people attend events and buy books at the Griffin.

When I left my previous jobs at cultural agencies and the college, I feared I would miss the camaraderie of fellow-workers. "Sole proprietor" to me was essentially synonymous with lonely proprietor. Now I'm finding that's not the case at all. My ties with colleagues are looser but good will is strong. When I need advice, I can pick up the phone and talk with someone with relevant knowledge who is willing to advise me. Even though we run separate businesses, we are all trying to make a living. The sense that we are in this together sustains us.

I don't hire any more of Louis's "cousins," but am able to increase Mafalda's work time with us. She spends her usual two afternoons in the house, and two additional afternoons in the shop where she washes the floors and windows, sweeps the front walk and terrace, and dusts the books. At the start of each month she begins with the "A's" of English general fiction; by the month's end, she has worked her way around to the "Z's" of Dutch travel guides and is ready to begin anew with the new month.

As each dusting cycle concludes she sighs, "*Nao bebe, esta mes*,"(no baby this month). She has been going for medical tests for some months to see why she isn't getting pregnant again. No reason has yet been determined, but she is taking extra vitamins and hormones. Still months have passed with no baby expected.

Then one day, I hear her come into the house and start to work without her usual friendly, "*Boa tarde*, good afternoon, Madame." A while later, I look for her. She is on the terrace hanging out laundry.

"*Boa tarde*, Mafalda, I say. "*Tudo bem*? Everything all right?"

Looking stricken, she shakes her head and tells me she has just come from her doctor who has tried all locally available diagnostic tests and equipment but can find no answer about the cause of her present infertility. He has recommended that she go to Lisbon for a more sophisticated diagnosis and possible treatment. I know how disappointed Mafalda is that she hasn't gotten pregnant, but I can't quite grasp why she is so acutely miserable now. I ask if the new tests in Lisbon would be very expensive. She doesn't think so because they would be covered by the *Caixa,* the national health insurance. Then I ask why doesn't she just plan to have the tests?

"Is not possible for me to go to *Lisboa*."

Her flat statement baffles me. Lisbon can be reached in three and a half hours by car, bus, or train. Walter and I now drive there every two months to refill the Griffin's shelves. Our friends also go regularly to shop, sample hotels and restaurants, and attend dance performances at the Gulbenkian.

"Lisbon is not very far away, Mafalda. Why can't you go

there?"

But she says again, "Is not possible." When I repeat my question, she explains, "Is necessary stay there. One night, maybe two nights."

She looks at me in misery and I can see that the very idea of Lisbon looms before her like a huge frightening maze. She can't imagine how to get there, and even if she were to reach it, how to find her way about the city, how to find a particular address like a hospital or clinic, or a place for meals, how or if she would ever emerge again to return home. As for spending one or more nights in a hotel, the prospect is unthinkable. Not only is the cost unimaginable to her, the very idea of a solitary anonymous stay among strangers holds the terrors of a visit to hell. All the arrangements of travel, which for us are routine, are *terra incognita* for Mafalda. No wonder the doctor's report is a grim verdict for her. She contemplates a three-hour trip and a three-day stay in Lisbon as I would face a three-month sojourn on the moon. Since even talking about the city upsets her, I say no more about it to her at the moment. But I keep worrying about her and wondering what might be done about the impasse.

In the following weeks, I try to persuade Mafalda to consider Lisbon. I tell her it is a lovely crumbly old city of neighborhoods clustered around seven hills. People sit on front stoops along winding narrow streets, bird cages and flowers brighten their windows, women push baby strollers, young people go to work in the mornings and fill the smoky cafes in the evenings. A million people live in Lisbon, thousands of visitors come and depart, and (since the earthquake of 1755) they haven't disappeared from the face of the earth. I stress that the three-and-a-half hour trip to get there might bring help for Mafalda's childlessness, but her fears bar the way.

"It seems such a shame," I say to Walter.

"She could ride up to Lisbon with us next time we go to buy books," he suggests.

"But then what? She won't stay in a hotel." Walter thinks for a while and then reminds me of our experience with local workmen.

"Everybody in the Algarve goes to funerals for uncles in the north. Maybe Mafalda or her husband have some relatives near Lisbon."

A promising idea. Sure enough, when I ask Mafalda she admits to an uncle and aunt in Palmela, just forty minutes south of Lisbon.

"You could ride up and back in the car with me and Senhor Walter," I urge, "And you don't have to go to a hotel, you could stay with your relatives in Palmela."

A faint ray of possibility dawns in her eyes. "I will ask José."

When she comes again, she does not mention Lisbon. I corner her at a bookshelf. "What did José say?"

"He say is too far for me to go alone."

"Well, he could come too. That would be good; he could be with you at the hospital."

"I will ask," Mafalda agrees again.

But José refuses again. "Is too far," Mafalda reports. "Jose say he cannot go. He must work." She is stoic, resigned. Though she has humored my appeals, she herself has no faith in her ability to undertake the trip to Lisbon and won't pursue ways to make it feasible. Practical solutions are no match for psychological barriers. I cannot find a way to persuade her.

Mafalda continues to clean our house and the bookshop. She washes our clothes, tends our flowers, brings us figs and little cakes she has baked. In autumn the large carob tree at the edge of our driveway begins dropping a few pods. Mafalda asks if we will allow her father to harvest the tree for feed for his pigs. We agree at once, pleased to find a use for the six-inch long pods that litter our parking space. The following Saturday Mafalda's father and José come with long sticks and beat tree branches while pods clatter down to the ground. The men rake them into piles, shovel them into large plastic trash bags that they pitch onto the back of their truck, tip their Fedora hats to us, and drive away. A few days later, as thanks for the carobs, Mafalda brings us a traditional Algarvian delicacy—oval croquettes made with *bacalhão*, the salt cod that is a staple of the Portuguese diet. They can be served hot with meals but are more often served cold as appetizers or snacks. We find them delicious and anticipate an annual exchange of carobs for *bacalhão* croquettes.

Mafalda's father and husband return about once a month to pluck snails from our outside walls, another delicacy I might eat in a restaurant but can't bring myself to cook. We give Mafalda any clothing we no longer wear to pass on to various relatives. She brings us figs and almonds. Thus the basic contract of our paying Mafalda for her work has become embellished by an expanding web of reciprocity between our family and hers.

Yet the unsolved problem of the longed-for baby has taught me that we still live in different worlds. The differences in our income, nationality, education and background are obvious. On the other hand, the Algarve is changing. Even the most remote crumbling farmhouse has a television aerial affixed to its tile roof, and the entire population seems enthralled by the latest hour-long *telenovela*, the daily soap opera imported from Brazil. The people also watch news programs and movies from all over the world, more accustomed to reading sub-titles than Americans are. Most Algarvian men now drive cars or motorcycles to work. Many women like Mafalda are maids in homes with radios, stereos and TVs, where they use washing machines, dishwashers, and vacuum cleaners. The work of both men and women—in restaurants, shops and luxury hotels, as well as at marinas and golf courses— brings them into contact with jet-age tourists from all over Europe. Some Portuguese who emigrated to find work in France, Germany or even Brazil, have returned with modern ways. New highways are being constructed throughout the country; computers are commonplace, and hospitals gain new technological equipment. But this era of rapid progress has brought odd discrepancies. Local doctors still sometimes set broken legs without anesthesia, most homes outside of cities lack central heating, and the new highways carry high-powered Mercedes that must snake around plodding donkey carts.

Through Mafalda, I learn that the minds of Algarvian country people harbor similar discrepancies. A trip to Lisbon holds unknown perils that outweigh her paramount desire in life, to have a child. We might gradually have persuaded her to face those perils in our company, but her husband forbids it and his word, traditionally, is her law. Though it saddens me, we have to accept her decision. She has tried every modern remedy within her reach but can go no further. On her next afternoon with us, she tells me that she and José have resigned themselves and have begun to speak about the possibility of adopting. I nod, pat her shoulder, and say no more. As weeks pass, we do not return to the subject.

Then one day Mafalda rushes into our kitchen breathless and beaming.

"Madame, *bébé!* José and me. We get *bébé*."

My first thought is that they have found a child to adopt, but her news is more thrilling. Her doctor has just confirmed that she is pregnant! Her infertility has been beyond the help of Algarvian medical science but blessedly not beyond the kindness of nature. I rush to the study and bring Walter to come to hear her news. We both hug her and shower her with *Parabems* (congratulations). Jubilation all around!

XXI
Hail and Farewell

On my early morning walk with Caesar around the periphery of our property, he hurtles down the hill and gets a toenail caught in the fence. He pulls to get loose, thereby tearing a section of fence off its pole. This, the day after Walter has spent a morning patching a big hole Caesar chewed in another part of the fence. I decide on the spot—no hysterics, just a cold shutting down—that's it. Enough.

I march back to the house and burst in on Walter who is shaving in the bathroom. "Caesar just ripped down the fence in back and I can't stand it any more. I'm taking him to the kennel." Walter takes a deep breath and continues shaving. I march out again, put Caesar in the car and drive him to the kennel. There I tell the owner that we will be back for him but that we want to sell him or give him away. At home, Walter and I go silently through the day. He hasn't objected, tacitly relinquishing the decision and required actions to me. That leaves him the Pontius Pilate way out. All day, my accumulated anger rages like a bonfire in my chest. Walter wanted a dog, picked out a great huge one without knowing anything about the breed; left everything to do with the dog to me, and finally refused all action or responsibility when I repeatedly said (and screamed) that I couldn't stand it any more. My last screaming fit was a week ago when Caesar again tore asunder the bougainvillea on the terrace. After that, I decided no more screaming, the next thing he destroys, off he goes. Funny that it should be an ugly wire fence I don't even like that much.

What has brought me to this pass is never knowing what flower bed, or vine, or bush, palm tree, rug, blanket, cushion, or item of clothing is going to be torn apart next. Every morning I step outdoors in suspense to see what growing thing might still be there and what is a shredded killed mess. I've grown afraid to enjoy or get attached to any single garden plant or flower because it might not be there next time I look. So finally I'm done and Caesar will go to other owners who perhaps can manage him better than we can.

Even in the midst of my anger, it troubles me to be responsible for a failed dog story. There is no such genre. Starting in my childhood, *Lassie Come Home, Lad, a Dog,* and *White Fang* all featured heroic dogs and loving owners. Books and movies celebrate the bond between owners and their faithful canines; in some stories a character who at first doesn't like dogs improves as a human being by growing to love one. Not only have I not improved, but instead seem to have lived the only documented owner/dog failure story, a distinction I'd rather not have. Dorothy adored Toto while the wicked witch cackled, "I'll get you my pretty, and your little dog, too." And now I'm the wicked witch, turned putrid green.

Two days later Caesar is back. After I left him at the kennel Walter was so quiet and downcast, just sitting in his armchair staring into space. I felt as if someone had died or, more exactly, as though I'd murdered someone. Even though I knew the cause, I asked, "What's wrong?"

His answer was listless. "I'm sorry I'm so dull, but I feel like the lively spark of our place is gone, and right now I'm just not interested in doing anything." He kept on sitting there looking mournful.

I tried to ignore it, telling myself that his dark mood will lift, but he got to me. Since Walter is so seldom depressed, I take it very hard when he is, and if I have caused the depression, I feel even worse. So I agreed to try again and the "lively spark" has come back once more, at least temporarily. Walter picked him up yesterday with the idea that we will keep him in his pen at night so that he can't tear up the garden. I've had to get out his dish and sleeping mat which I had bundled away as quickly as I could. Now that he's here, I've taken up caring for him once more, but not with good grace. Grimly, I play with him on the lawn, pick burrs and ticks off his coat, and wipe up after his sandy pawprints all over the floor. I'd really thought not to see him again. I am resentful, weary, and disgusted with this whole drama.

A week later, Caesar has ripped out two bushes beside the house. I drive to Wendy's house for tea and sympathy and she is great, pledging to ask around for people who might give him a good home. Again, Walter and I say he is to be kept in the fenced pen or on a tether, given regular walks, and not allowed to run free through the garden. We make resolutions: I'll try not to get upset and Walter will try to control the dog, and so we'll muddle on.

The issue keeps causing problems for us because we perceive it so differently. I mourn for all the spoiled flowers, hedges, and ground cover, and I miss the peace and quiet of former times. Walter sees the destruction as minimal and finds the dog's friendly antics lovable and diverting. When he looks at the garden he sees some nice trees and flowers separated by a few sandy tracks and bare spots. When I look at it, I see Carthage after the Romans have marched through. And neither of us can understand the other's reactions, though we try to respect the feelings involved.

I no longer believe that it's puppyhood that causes the difficulties. Caesar is almost two years old. The vet told me recently that he had opposed the breeding of Schnauzers here because he sees the breed as "stubborn and unruly" by nature. This made me feel somewhat vindicated at our failures in training. How I wish that this dog had never come into our lives. No matter which way we resolve the problem, one of us will be unhappy about the outcome.

A few weeks later we at last agree that this dog situation can't continue. No matter who is right or wrong, it's not working for us and we must find a way out that will restore us to harmony with each other while also finding a more suitable placement for Caesar. Wendy has spoken to friends in the local horse and dog community. I have told the kennel owner and also posted an ad on the bulletin board in the vet's office. So far no response.

Now that Walter and I have agreed to find another home for Caesar, I've calmed down and am chagrined to realize that life with him isn't so bad any more. The little palm tree in the center courtyard is recovering from his attacks and has new growth. The dog clearly no longer wrestles with it at night. The bougainvillea beside the pillars are in flower and stay there even though Caesar sleeps nearby. His sandy tracks honeycomb the garden but he bounds along those he has already worn and doesn't try to make new ones. The rest of the garden is thriving.

He only needs tying up in late afternoon so that he won't run and bark himself into a frenzy when the Vale do Lobo workmen cycle past on their way home. After that I play with him on the back lawn and then it's supper time. In the evening he comes inside and first comes to me for hugging and being told he's a good dog. Then he sleeps on the living room floor while we read or watch TV. Around ten p.m. I give him his bedtime carrot and take him outside to the terrace. He plods willingly to his mat which he no longer shreds and stays there quietly through the night. All in all, the monster Caesar is on his way to becoming a manageable dog, except for his inability to walk with anyone and his major remaining vice of chewing holes in our fence and slipping out, forcing Walter to spend some hours each week repairing the damage. Caesar never goes far, but whenever we see him loping into the driveway from the street, we know that there's a new hole in the fence.

Unexpectedly, we have a response to our ad. The vet has given me a phone number of people who are looking for a large dog; Walter and I hesitate before placing the call. We have one last talk about what to do. As Caesar's behavior has changed, my feelings about him have gradually shifted and we wonder if, after all, we should keep him. Then we think of never knowing how to care for him during our winter weeks in Saratoga and I pick up the phone.

And so we meet Paul and Jane Vernon, an English couple who own "Jumpers," a pub in Almancil, frequented by British tourists. Paul Vernon is a tall "skin-head" Brit with tattoos on his arms and fingers, a facial tick, and regional speech hard for us to understand. Despite this tough appearance, he seems a pleasant sort. His wife Jane is small and squashy-looking.

"Do you run the pub together?" I ask, trying to make pleasant conversation during their first visit to our place.

"Oh, 'e does the bar, and I do the cookin'" Jane shyly smoothes her skirt.

I feign enthusiasm. "How interesting, what sorts of dishes do you make?"

Jane looks alarmed, "Oh I'm not a chef, I just cook. Simple food. Chops, sausages, spuds, mostly."

The Vernons own Caesar's brother, Cassius. They tell us Cassius was sold as a six- months-old puppy, just as Caesar was, but his owners went back to England. They returned him to the kennel and simply left him there without paying for his board and keep.

"'E was in terrible nick when we got 'im," Paul says, "a near skeleton and cringin' in a corner."

The kennel owner had vented her anger at the defaulting owners by starving the poor dog, an incomprehensible act by someone who keeps a kennel. It's also poor advertising in a place like this where all the ex-pats know everything about each other. Paul and Jane have brought Cassius back to near health and now want a pair of dogs to guard the restaurant at night. After a bit more conversation, we agree that the Vernons will come to our place twice a week to let the dogs get acquainted.

When they arrive for the first visit, we see that Cassius is a bit taller in the rump than Caesar but still painfully thin. A very timid spindly-legged dog who growls and barks at Caesar with fake bravado but backs away and hides behind Paul when Caesar responds. Caesar, well fed and healthy, is dominant on his own turf and clearly distrusts his brother. We owners spend three afternoons together by our pool, which Caesar feels obligated to defend from strange animals, though not from strange humans. He demonstrates this by repeated barking, challenging, stalking, and barring Cassius's way. And Cassius, poor kennel-confined neglected orphan, gives way every time. After the third such visit, we decide that next time Paul will take Caesar back to the pub to try the relationship on Cassius's turf. I hope that will work because after hearing about Cassius's experience at the kennel, we certainly won't ever leave Caesar there again.

Paul takes Caesar for an afternoon at their place without us and that seems to be fine. Then for an entire day. And now, Caesar is spending the weekend there. Our place seems quiet and empty without him, even for me. Walter and I speak about changing our minds.

"Maybe we should just keep him?" I half-suggest, half-ask.

Walter doesn't take up the implied offer. "I don't think so. I liked thinking of you having a dog when I'm back in Saratoga but that hasn't worked out well. And then, we're both going home for the winter holidays."

"Well, we wouldn't put him back in that kennel."

"Damn right." Walter says. "He'll have a good home at the pub. All those meat and potatoes leftovers every night."

"And his brother for company."

Consoling ourselves with visions of Caesar's happy new home, we agree to go ahead with the adoption. At least Walter and I are together in our feelings this time, not bitter or angry or upset with each other.

Caesar has been gone for two weeks and I've been surprised by how much I miss him. How ironic, in view of my miserable history with the dog. In fact I think I've missed him the most because Walter left for Saratoga right after Caesar moved to Jumpers whereas I've stayed in place. While I go through my solitary routine, I remember how Caesar was so delighted every morning when I came out to untie him and I wish I'd known that his puppy destructiveness wouldn't last forever. I keep thinking, "that dog loved me," and regret having arranged to give him away before I realized how nice he was getting to be.

Late one afternoon I drive to Jumpers where Caesar now lives. All closed up, the dogs evidently inside because I hear Cassius barking as I walk around back and peer in windows. A shabby littered small space; I feel sorry for Caesar shut up in there all day long.

I go back again around seven p.m. to bring his pedigree papers and some Heartguard pills since he's due for one at the beginning of next month. By this time the place is open and looks a bit better by lamplight, dim and cozy in the way of small-town English pubs. The two dogs are nowhere in sight. Jane, busy with setting tables, doesn't look up at first but then greets me pleasantly. She responds a bit nervously when I ask how the two dogs are getting on.

"They had one fight, after Caesar moved in, bit o' snarlin' and growlin'" she admits, but then smiles, "By now they've sorted it out."

Then Paul joins us and essentially echoes her words. He says he walks the dogs every day, hasn't yet let Caesar off the lead because he's not sure he'd come back just yet.

"He's jumped over the fence a couple of times. I'll 'ave to raise it higher." But Paul insists the dogs are getting along very well. "A bit of a nip or a growl here or there, but they get on, even lick each other."

I ask if they are glad to have Caesar and they both quickly answer yes. Then I tell them Walter and I are glad he has found a good home. I give them the Heartguard and the papers, we shake hands and I leave. They haven't offered to let me see him and I haven't asked. Walking across the road to my car, I feel desolate and forlorn, my eyes stinging with unexpected tears.

I guess partly I must have been hoping that Paul and Jane would say it hasn't worked out and that I'd take Caesar back home with me. But it's done now and I have to let it lie.

As I drive home I realize that Jane and Paul were nervous, perhaps afraid that I had come to insist that they give Caesar back. Like parents who have adopted my child, they still fear it won't be permanent. And as for me, I understand how biological or surrogate mothers feel, having thought they could just hand over the baby, be relieved of the responsibility, and walk away without a backward glance, feeling fine. And then when it's done, it feels awful. Something decided upon in one frame of mind and in one set of conditions, takes place later when the context has changed and then reverberates in an aftermath of longing and regret. And if I can feel this way for a dog, whom I disliked for most of the sixteen months we lived together, how much more piercing must be the regret about a child of one's own body and soul.

Now I shall try to enjoy the easy routine I had before there was Caesar. I can get up when I want. Go away from the house when and for as long as I want without worrying about him. The floors are not covered with sandy pawprints. The garden is growing over Caesar's web of tracks. And I can look ahead to vacations without the recurring worry of what to do with the dog.

But all is not perfect this way. I miss the evening companion stretched out on the small rug in the living room, and the pleasant ritual of giving him a goodnight carrot before bedding him down on the terrace. I miss the morning greeting, giving him a mid-morning buttered roll while I have a second cup of coffee, his silly running around with the torn blue blanket, and the welcome when we come home on late evenings and a sleepy black dog trots over to say hello. And while Walter is away, I miss Caesar's misleading fierce image scaring off intruders.

And I also miss Walter and write him a note of apology. "Thank you for not reproaching me for Caesar's leaving. I'm sorry that I had no idea that I would come to love Caesar too, and even sorrier that I found it out too late. I guess now we'll just have to miss him together." I remind myself that during our trips to Saratoga we'll be glad that Caesar has a good home. But right now, I'm just aware that he is gone, through my fault, through my fault, through my most grievous fault.

Well, there I was all mournful and forlorn about Caesar's absence, and even talking about my rueful feelings with friends on a Sunday afternoon at the beach. I get home around five o'clock and within ten minutes the phone rings. On the line, the voice of a Portuguese boy asks about "*dois grands caes pretos*," (two large black dogs). A bit befuddled, I say that I don't have two dogs, only one dog, and he is now living elsewhere. The boy keeps trying to explain something about "*campo de futebol*" and I suddenly grasp that the "*dois caens pretos*" in question are at the football field. The boy has found our phone number on Caesar's collar tag. So I say I will come, untie the gate, and jump into my little red Citroen. I speed down the Quinta do Lago road, looking each way for two large black dogs and quite excited at the thought of seeing Caesar again.

Sure enough, near a corner of the *campo de futebol* I glimpse some boys holding the two panting and docile dogs. I pull over, leave the car, and crouch down by Caesar who looks quite scruffy, having gotten his fur all covered with burrs. He receives me with no great enthusiasm. Both dogs willingly let me put them in the car, not an easy feat since Cassius wants to sit in the driver's seat and I must shove him to the passenger side, and Caesar has to be hauled up into the rear space through the hatchback. But we manage to get them both in. I thank the boys and drive off, happy with my booty.

But what to do with them? The decent thing, I realize, is to try to bring them to their home at Jumpers. I drive there but find no sign of light or life. Pleased to have Caesar back for a while I drive back to my house. Once out of the car, both dogs trot around the house directly to the pool at the back where each drinks some water. Caesar clearly remembers the pool because he moves down two or three steps to sit in the water as he used to do. Then they both lope around the place while I go into the house to try to phone Paul and Jane. A series of whimpers at the kitchen door, so I let the dogs in. I search through the phone book, but no number for Jumpers or for the Vernon's home. Dogs padding in and out, Cassius actually staying closer to me than Caesar who is busy rediscovering his former territory. I try setting out dog food in two bowls separated by an expanse of lawn. A spate of growling so I remove the food. While Caesar is outside, I take Cassius into the kitchen and feed him, thinking I'll switch the process a bit later on. I find it odd that Cassius (who has never been alone with me before) stays close to my side, whereas Caesar (whom I have pictured as pining away for his dear mistress) hardly gives me the time of day. He lets me pick the burrs off his coat, but shows no joyful recognition at all. I start to wonder what I'll do with them during the night and decide that in the morning I'll telephone the vet who has the Vernons' telephone number.

Then the doorbell rings and there's Paul. He has been looking through Almancil for more than an hour and finally decided to try here. I am relieved to see him, and he is relieved to see the dogs. Caesar is happy too. When Paul walks over to him, he rolls over on his back, waiting to be stroked, as he used to do for us. I give Paul a beer and we sit in the living room while both dogs stretch out at our feet and sleep on the floor. Paul and I review our adventures, how Caesar led Cassius astray by leaping over the fence behind the restaurant, how I was called to pick up the dogs, and first went to Jumpers and then tried to phone, how Paul has been driving around to search. Then we talk about the dogs' temperaments and their life at the restaurant. Quite a pleasant chat which has no overt point but which comfortably settles the fact that both dogs now belong to Paul and Jane, and if they should get out again and be brought to me, I will return them to the Vernons. I think our talk allays Paul's nervousness about our possibly reclaiming Caesar, and I feel that if we ever want to visit him, he won't be inaccessible to us. Somehow, this whole episode has confirmed the adoption.

Clearly, in just these few weeks, Caesar's affections have shifted. He is attached to his new owners, he gets along with his brother—the two stuck together during their expedition—and he is quite simply no longer my dog. I feel somewhat hurt by this dose of reality, that the shift of loyalty has happened so quickly, but no doubt such flexibility enables Caesar not only to survive but to engage the affections of what may be a series of owners in the course of his life. And with him not pining for me, I realize that I have to stop pining for him. I'm glad that the dogs' run-away adventure brought them to my house. It has given me the chance to separate from the ideal Caesar as well as the real one.

I walk Paul to the car and he puts Cassius in the back seat. I call Caesar who actually comes when I call. Then I hold him till Paul gets the hatchback open, and up and in he goes. They drive off. I close the gate, walk back up the driveway, enter the house and close the door behind me. It is over.

XXII
Kitty's Calendar

Kitty Edwards hates tourists. Whenever we approach a hub of tourist activity, she has little fits of Pukha Sahib disdain about how perfectly frightful the new people are. "There's nasty Vilamoura with its dreadful marina... drive quickly past that ghastly petrol station...Imagine someone building that vulgar house...." At first, when we drove anywhere with her, I tried to avoid areas of obvious sprawl, but that is difficult here. Now I begin to see that Kitty enjoys making fun of tourists just as my mother enjoyed picking out someone at the next table in a restaurant and ridiculing that unsuspecting target's clothing, hair style, gestures or laugh. Elke never modulated her voice and felt ever so witty and superior while I cringed behind my menu. In just that way, Kitty feels tasteful and refined in her beautiful restored *quinta* in the hills. It is indeed beautiful. But the Edwards too, though they do so with care, are changing the Algarve from what it was into something new and foreign to itself. As are we. We are all tourists.

One day I happen to mention to Kitty that several English customers have asked for appointment calendars or what they call "diaries," that I don't stock in the bookshop.

I wish aloud for a large wall calendar with pictures of the Algarve and a grid that shows both English and Portuguese

holidays. "I'd love to be able to sell a calendar like that.   I'm sure
it would appeal to tourists looking for souvenirs, and even more
to expats like us, don't you think? I don't know how many times
I've been caught off-guard when everything closed on Portuguese
holidays that I've never heard of."

In a thoughtful tone, Kitty agrees. "Quite."

A few days later she telephones. "Marianne, I've been
thinking," She sounds tentative, then plunges on. "I've taken
scads of photographs in the three years we've lived here. I wager I
could find twelve good ones for a calendar. Will you look through
them with me? If you think they'll do, I might try making your
calendar meself." She admits she knows nothing about it, but is
eager to try.

Soon I drive up to Kitty's house to see her photographs.
There are no pictures of cultivated golf greens, luxury yachts,
palatial oceanfront hotels, or time-share villa complexes.   Kitty
has simply ignored the luxury building boom created by swelling
seasonal tides of tourists. Instead she has used her camera within
walking distance of her home to record country people and the
landscape: hillside almond trees arrayed in their delicate February
blossoms like ballet dancers; narrow cobblestone village lanes;
sunlight shimmering through wide umbrella pines; peasant women
carrying baskets on their heads; farmers using long sticks to beat
down the fruit of olive, almond or carob trees; old farm houses
with their small deep windows and narrow double doors painted
bright red, blue, or yellow; herds of sheep grazing along grassy
slopes and dainty brown and white Algarvian goats wearing red
ribbon collars with bells. The photographs preserve scenes from
the lovely old Algarve that lured foreign residents to live here, and
that we hope tourists will want to remember.

When any of us are tourists, we are often in love with the past,
especially the past of other places. We discount the hardships
of bygone days and seek reminders of historic traditions that
bear no resemblance to our daily lives at home and, in fact, little
resemblance to the current lives of most of the country's citizens.
To me, Kitty's photographs bring back the romance that now too

often lurks in the Algarve's hidden byways. I think them ideal for our venture.

"I think these are wonderful, Kitty, just perfect."

"Oh, grand. I'm ever so pleased you like them."

We choose one photograph for each month. In our enthusiasm, we expand our concept to include American, as well as English and Portuguese holidays. Kitty gets set to discuss the project with Cynthia Green, who designed the Griffin's stationery.

In a few days Kitty phones to tell me that the estimated price tag is alarmingly high. She wants to print only two thousand calendars and the per unit cost is far more expensive than she imagined. Her courage falters, and we decide that she should seek advice from Marvin Wilson who is familiar with most English language publications here. Afterwards, she comes to report that Marvin asked her a string of questions and then advised her against proceeding. According to Marvin, the small print run would make the calendar too costly for the potential market. He also pronounced his judgment that her photographs were not quite good enough.

"Quite set me back, that did," Kitty admits and before I can respond she glides across the room singing:

"Oh don't put your daughter on the stage, Mrs. Worthington, Please don't put your daughter on the stage."

Marvin's advice, though well-meant, reminds me of the Portuguese Chamber of Commerce in New York whose director warned me about opening a bookstore here, "Don't do it for the English, Senhora, they don't read in the Algarve. All they do is get drunk and fall out of hotel windows." Since then I have met many English with different pastimes. While it is too soon to tell if my Griffin will be profitable, more customers come in each month. If I'd listened to that early warning, I wouldn't have had this whole experience, which, despite all its ups and downs, I wouldn't have missed for anything.

But I try to be careful in applying my views to Kitty's project. Will a calendar be profitable? We can't be sure, and the real financial risk argues against it. On the other hand, it engages Kitty's interest, brings her down the mountain, involves her with people, and lifts her spirits. With this in mind, I encourage her to go forward. I don't know how heavily my opinion weighs, but she does decide to continue. She rides along each time Ben drives to Almancil. While he does his errands, she conducts her business about the calendar. Sometimes she also comes to visit me at the bookshop. She mentions meetings with various people about the calendar, but shows me no samples or proofs. I assume she wants this to be her own project.

Then one afternoon in early September Ben brings Kitty to the shop and she proudly presents me with the Algarve's first bilingual, tri-national, illustrated appointment wall calendar.

"A jolly good piece of work, if I do say so meself," she beams as I congratulate her.

The calendar's cover is attractive with paired photographs, one of an Algarvian farm woman garbed in black and the other, in bright contrast, a spray of wild red poppies. Inside, each month's full-color photograph displays a traditional scene. The cover's title is printed in both English and Portuguese. I note with a slight pang that Kitty's proofreading has not caught a misspelled word and the English reads "Algarve Calandar." We hope that people won't notice the misspelling or won't care.

That evening Walter admires the photographs, notes the misspelled "Calandar," and points out that the grid opposite each month's photograph begins each week with Saturday.

"I couldn't use this," Walter confides to me, "I've grown far too used to calendars that start weeks with Sundays."

"Maybe that's just an American thing," I venture. Just the same, I telephone Kitty to ask why she's laid the grid out to start with Saturdays.

"Oh, does it? I hadn't noticed. Cynthia must have done it."

It doesn't matter to Kitty nor presumably to Cynthia. Walter and I may well be out of step. Perhaps English calendar grids do begin with Saturdays. Customs vary. The Portuguese, for example, run their grids with days of the week down the left side instead of across the top of the page as we are used to, a format as disorienting to me at first glance as a trick watch I once saw with number six on top and twelve at the bottom.

Despite any flaws, we are all pleased with the calendar. The splendid photographs will appeal to tourists as well as English-speaking residents and the grid will be useful to the latter. On appropriate squares, tiny pen-and-ink drawn flags of Portugal, the United States, and the United Kingdom mark the various national holidays. Kitty's calendar seems a perfect souvenir to take home: attractive, distinctive, lightweight, flat, easy to pack, unbreakable and presumably inexpensive.

We now need to set a selling price. Kitty's weeks of negotiating with designers and printers have left her uncertain of the final cost of her print run.

"You do need to know that," I advise.

"Why, whatever for? As long as I settle up accounts each month, the bailiffs won't come to get me, will they?" She flashes one of her brilliant smiles.

How wise and experienced I feel. "You need to know the entire cost so that you can figure out the per unit cost."

Kitty looks blank.

"If you don't know what producing each calendar cost you," I explain. "You won't know how to price it for sale."

"Blimey," Kitty says. "I'll have to go home and look through the bills, won't I?"

The next day she returns with a fistful of bills and we go through them. Our first total comes to an alarming three million escudos for the run of two thousand calendars, meaning that each individual calendar cost her fifteen hundred escudos, or about nine U.S. dollars, to produce. Even with a minimal profit for her, shops that might carry the calendar would have to charge the equivalent of eleven or twelve dollars, a prohibitive price. We would have to hope that tourists, at least, wouldn't translate the escudo price into their own money.

Then Kitty thinks again. "I don't understand how it could all have cost so much." We look more closely at her bills. Reprieve!

She has separated the duplicate invoices customary in Portugal and therefore we added everything twice. The true total is still a hefty investment of nine thousand dollars, but at least that means we can peg the calendar at a reasonable price. The basic per item cost was 750$ escudos. I advise Kitty to add a 300$ escudo profit for herself, another 150$ for the retailers, and then sell the calendar for 1200$ escudos or about $7.50 U.S.

Kitty resists. "I don't need a profit, I just want the buggers to buy it."

"You've got to have a profit or it's not a business. *I'll* want a profit when I sell it."

"Right. I don't mind if you take a profit but I want to keep the bloody price down. I'll take one hundred escudos."

"That's not enough. What about all your time and work? You're hardly paying yourself for all that. At least take two-fifty."

I plead but can't persuade Kitty to take more than one hundred escudos, about sixty cents, per calendar for herself. She has never thought of anything more than recovering her investment. Unfortunately, in her scheme of things that means sales of the entire stock.

The final price I put on each calendar for the shop is 1100$ escudos which corresponds to the six or seven dollars charged for illustrated calendars in America. I take fifty calendars on consignment to sell in the bookshop. My nearest competitor, the lady who owns the Beanfeast restaurant and bookshop in Almancil, takes twenty. Martha Stimpson from Porches takes another twenty for her books and art supplies shop. Kitty herself gives twenty or so to friends and promising contacts. She offers four to editors of Algarve newspapers in exchange for printing her press release. And there matters stand. Out of a print run of two thousand, Kitty has placed one hundred and fourteen calendars. Beyond the news release, she has no plans or ideas for further outlets. She does not drive and she has eighteen hundred and eighty six undistributed calendars stacked neatly in her storeroom/study, right next to Ben's forty-eight hundred remaining car shades.

I cannot bear it.

Kitty stands to lose a million escudos on her project and I urged her to go ahead where wiser heads counseled against it. It isn't even the fault of the calendar itself. We just didn't figure out any marketing plans. I feel terrible.

Despite my distress, Kitty herself seems oddly unconcerned and remains proud and pleased with her achievement. "Best thing I've made on me own other than lemon tarts," she crows," and for those part credit goes to the lemon tree."

I try to bring her down to earth. "Do you really think a news release will bring throngs of pilgrims trudging up the mountain to your door to request the calendar?"

"No, I expect them to drive to your bookshop to ask for it,"

Oh Lord, my little out-of-the-way bookshop that hasn't even opened officially yet and is lucky to see one hundred customers in a month. The Griffin alone could never sell her two thousand calendars before the end of the year.

"This needs a blitzkrieg," I decide. "You've got to place it all along the coast."

"Can't do that; I don't drive," Kitty reminds me.

"You could hire a distributor. I've got people who come into the shop wanting to leave lots of things on consignment. Artists give them a commission for distributing their stuff. You could do that."

"I shan't give it out on consignment because I wouldn't get me money." Kitty announces this as a given, like the weather or an act of God. "The small Porgie shops don't pay their bills by post and I can't drive 'round to them to insist."

"But the distributors go to all these places to do the collecting as well."

"Ah yes. Well. And what's to make them pay _me_?" She is adamant.

I picture how she will feel next February when she still has the stack of eighteen hundred unsold calendars at a loss of a million escudos.

"I'll give you a day's driving," I resolve. "Walter will mind the store. And I'm sure he'll give you day's driving also," I recklessly volunteer him as well as myself. "We can at least get to the big tourist hotels."

"That is enormously kind of you," Kitty accepts my offer in a solemn tone. We shake hands to formalize the agreement, and fix the following Monday for our expedition.

A fine team, I think as I watch her leave the shop. I, the world's most reluctant sales person, and Kitty, the world's least experienced business person.

"How many should I bring along?" she asks when I arrive at her house for my day as chauffeur. "Fifty?"

"Good God, no! Bring a thousand," I am fiercely optimistic.

Ben helps us load the boxes into my car. A thousand calendars weigh down my little red two cylinder Citroen as might two corpulent rear-seat passengers, but we rattle non-stop down her mountain to the ocean front and along the highway to Vilamoura which boasts three major resort hotels. Our first stop is the Dom Pedro, a white behemoth with balconies, and tall brass flagpoles with the usual tourist banners. Bearing several calendars, Kitty and I spin from the revolving door into a huge green marble and gilt lobby tended by green-uniformed hotel staff.

"What do we do now?" Kitty whispers.

"We ask for the sales manager's office."

"I'm not going to speak to some flunky sales manager, " she hisses. "I know how these things work. You've got to go straight to the top." She flags a passing bellman. "Please direct me to your president's office."

He looks startled but bows smoothly. "The Senhora must inquire at the Reception." He escorts us to an enormous mahogany counter and glides toward distant marble halls.

A young woman behind the counter asks our wishes.

"My wish is to speak to your president," Kitty announces.

"The president of the Villalux hotels lives in London, but the general manager of our Dom Pedro Hotel is Senhor Mario Horta e Costa."

"Then I wish to speak to him."

"May I inform Senhor Mario of the matter you wish to discuss?"

the clerk is pleasant but firm.

"No thank you, you may not. I wish to speak directly with him."

"The young woman nods and turns to murmur into a telephone. In a few moments an imposing lady with a lacquered blonde coiffure emerges from an inner doorway and approaches.

"I am the secretary to Senhor Mario. May I assist you?" She bestows a tight professional smile.

Kitty raises her chin and counters with her own debutante smile. "I wish to speak with Senhor Mario himself."

"He is not here." The lady flutters long red fingernails to keep her smile from freezing. "Perhaps you might tell me what you wish and we could arrange for an appointment."

"It is a personal matter, I shall write to him," Kitty snaps. She turns on her heel, grips my elbow and marches us back through the green marble lobby and out the door.

"<u>Why</u> didn't you tell her what we wanted?" I wail when we are back outside.

"That silly cow? I'm not telling her anything."

"But secretaries are <u>important</u>. The manager isn't going to see you if you're not nice to his secretary," I hear myself getting shrill as I glimpse potential disasters still ahead on this day. "The secretary guards the gate; that's her job. If you're nice to her, she can get you in."

"She's an officious cow. I won't waste me time with her."

I subside and try to figure out how to proceed.

When we reach the car, I suggest, "At the Hotel Atlantis, let's first try to find out who makes decisions about stocking the hotel gift shop. I'm sure that isn't the president of the whole hotel. Maybe if you know who's in charge of the buying, you can go directly there."

Somewhat chastened by our first encounter, Kitty agrees to the new strategy. At the Atlantis we go straight to the gift shop where we find a Portuguese woman setting out newspapers. I take the lead this time and ask to see the shop manager.

"*Nao esta.*" (He isn't here.)

"When does he come in?"

"*So Seixta Feira.*" (Only on Fridays)

"Does he decide what this shop sells?"

Yes he does. Senhor Manuel Martines make the inventory decisions. She just sells the items. But he manages other shops as well and comes to this one only on Fridays. Kitty and I confer and then I continue. Perhaps since Senhor Manuel comes only on Fridays, some other hotel official might consider our attractive calendar. No, Senhor Manuel is the only one who makes all decisions. On Fridays.

Clearly this calendar venture needs not one or two but many days of driving, letter writing and telephoning for appointments in advance.

We drive on to the third luxury hotel in Vilamoura, the Marinehotel, a newer even more imposing structure with a lobby the size of an airplane hangar. The gift shop at one end is closed. I persuade Kitty to let me try some charm on the reception personnel to see if we can at least get to a sales or promotion manager. We show the calendar with its bright photographs to an attractive Algarvian girl at the reception desk and she looks through it with genuine admiration. Success. After a few in-house telephone conversations we are conducted to a suave gentleman in his glass office stocked with kidney-shaped white leather furniture.

Kitty takes a deep breath, flashes her smile, and makes a sales pitch. "This is the first English-Portuguese calendar for the Algarve." She displays the photographs and then points to the printed flags that identify national holidays. "Isn't it super? And useful too. We think your hotel guests will like it as a souvenir of their holiday here." She hands it to him with a flourish.

He leafs through the pages. "Very nice," he hands it back to Kitty, "but we cannot use it."

"Why ever not? It's a perfect souvenir—lightweight, easy to pack, with lovely photographs."

"But no photograph of the Marinehotel."

"Oh, um, perhaps we could add one on an outer cover," I interject.

"No. It would need a picture of the hotel for every month. Perhaps different views. Some of the front entrance in the morning, some in the evening with our lights over the ocean..." he warms to his subject.

Kitty clutches the calendar. "They don't want pictures of a tourist hotel that could be anywhere in the world," she blurts out. "They want the real countryside, the Portuguese people." She pauses and struggles to recover a pleasant expression. "The unspoiled Algarve is still beautiful and ever so picturesque, you know. That's the reason people come here," she says in a softer tone as though she and the manager share a secret.

"Perhaps." The manager is unyielding; her secret is not his secret. "Perhaps Madame can made a new calendar for next year with photographs of the hotel also." He rises, bows and shakes our hands. The interview is finished. We leave quietly. Five thousand pairs of huge cardboard sunglasses shade my thoughts. We have repeated Ben's mistake. With hotels, everything evidently comes down to advertising. As we walk back through the enormous lobby, Kitty's pace quickens with indignation.

"That man is going to steal my idea. He's going to spend millions on a calendar and plaster it with photographs of his beastly hotel."

"Well, let him. Nobody will buy it. Maybe we should try the *papelarias (*news-stands*).*

"No, I'm not leaving my lovely calendars in the hands of Porgies I don't even know. I'd never see them again, or the money either."

I'm getting exasperated. "I wish you wouldn't say Porgies."

"Why not? You say Brits, I say Yanks. Porgies is just shorter."

"It doesn't sound like Yanks. It sounds like Frogs, or Wogs, like the Pukha Sahibs talked." We revolve out of the door and into brilliant sunshine.

"Frogs is perfectly respectable."

"Is not. And it isn't any shorter than saying French. Anyway I think Porgies is insulting."

"Do you really? I certainly don't intend it to be." We get into the car.

"But you wouldn't say it directly to a Portuguese, would you?" We bicker on as I put the car in gear and we drive to our next stop.

We bicker in and out of hotels, in and out of the car, back and forth along the Algarvian coast. By two o'clock we reach Carvoeiro, a lovely cliffside town, where we stop for lunch at a small café. The rear of the Citroen still sags; we have placed not a single calendar. In the afternoon, since Kitty refuses to enter any more hotels, we change strategy. We try two Anglo-Portuguese riding clubs. The managers see no market among their members for a calendar that doesn't emphasize horsemanship. By five o'clock we have run out of ideas and energy. In silence we toil back up the mountain in low gear and then along the sandy lanes to Kitty's home. Ben refrains from comment and unloads the thousand calendars we started out with that morning. When they are stacked back in the study, he tactfully excuses himself to continue plastering an upstairs room.

Kitty makes tea while I stand by her window and gaze dully across the Algarvian hills toward the distant sliver of ocean on the horizon. I can't think of what to do next. Kitty refuses to go to more luxury hotels for fear they might steal her idea, she won't contract with distributors, and she won't leave calendars with the Portuguese newsstands for fear they might steal her money. With these restrictions, another day of driving either by me or by Walter seems pointless. I feel stymied and discouraged, but Kitty herself, though also tired from our long day, does not seem upset. She clatters cups and saucers, singing softly,

"If I were not a little mad and generally silly
I should give you my advice upon the subject willy-nilly..."

As she pours tea into our cups she breaks off her song to say "don't fret," quite gently to me "I shall simply place more adverts in the *Algarve News*. I shall say that people can either purchase these splendid calendars at the Griffin Bookshop or I'll fill orders straightaway by post."

It is what she has wanted to do all along. I nod quietly and sip my tea. I have minded her business long enough, and probably too intrusively. She has to do this her own way, whether or not it succeeds, and I have my own business to run. I cast a last glance into the study at the new stacks of calendars beside those of Ben's car shades, and take twenty more calendars back to add to my supply at the shop. Then I rattle back down the mountain in my newly lightened car.

Financially, the venture threatens to be a disaster which will prove that our editor friend Marvin's advice was right. I'm glad that the failure of her investment doesn't seem to be a bread and butter issue for the Edwards. Nevertheless, I feel guilty and responsible for her monetary loss. Chastened, I vow to give no more advice based on hope and emotion rather than on hard-headed business sense, especially when it doesn't include market research. And no more advice that doesn't take into account a person's ingrained habits and character. I have been so eager to help Kitty emerge from her isolation that I didn't pay enough attention to how strongly she clings to her chosen ways.

And yet who can tell? Kitty may never make another calendar, but she doesn't seem to regret having made the one. As I sell a mere two or three a week, she continues pleased. "First important thing I produced since I had me son thirty-eight years ago," she maintains in her music-hall exaggeration of British speech. "Since me youth, I haven't had work of me own. Merely traveled about with one or another husband to their postings in India or Africa. Come to think of it, I've spent most of me life as someone else's luggage. Now I've made this calendar and I'm jolly proud of it."

As the late autumn evenings grow chill, the stacks of Ben's car shades gradually shrink as they provide excellent kindling for the Edwards' now completed fireplace. A few more winters may also deplete the eighteen hundred unsold bilingual tri-national calendars.

Then one day, Kitty announces plans to rent a flat in London for six weeks next spring to take driving lessons. By summer she may come down from her mountain after all.

XXIII
The Griffin Flies

This has been a quiet time while Walter and I have tested ourselves as booksellers. We share the six-hour workday when the white wrought iron grills and glass front doors stand open, and chairs and tables with striped beach umbrellas are set out on the front terrace to invite potential customers. Generally, I take the morning shift while Walter drives to Almancil for the mail and the *Herald Tribune*. On some days he continues on to buy fresh fish and produce at markets in Quarteira or Loulé. On other days he may see a patient or two. At one o'clock, I furl the shop umbrellas and close the gates. We have our lunch at the house, read the *Tribune*, writer letters and relax during the two-hour break that soon seems a far nicer custom than our American lunch-on-the-run pattern. At three o'clock Walter re-opens the shop for the afternoon shift, while I do my own errands in town, household tasks and the behind-the-scenes shop work of ordering books and keeping sales records. At six, we close the shop doors, roll down the shutters, carry the metal cash box to the house, secrete it among tools and hardware in the kitchen closet, and begin preparations for dinner.

It is an easygoing work life: light hours, no commute, no tedious committee meetings or political wrangles. My earlier fears of starting my own business evaporated like wispy ghosts on the day we opened. We have come through infestation, burglary, flood and fire, survived bone-chilling cold, repeated equipment breakdowns, an unruly dog, and precarious connections to the outside world. The shop is like a pleasant book-lined study where our time of reading, writing, and arranging shelves are enlivened by short visits from friends or passers-by who stop in for a chat and might even buy a book once in a while. Still we must face the fact that this enjoyable pastime cannot yet be called a business. We lack the essential ingredient: an ample supply of customers. It is time for our long-delayed official opening celebration.

Excited at the prospect, we gather the names of everyone we've gotten to know since we first came to the Algarve—builders, artisans, merchants, restaurateurs, neighbors, friends, friends of friends, a total of one hundred and fifty people for our invitation list. But what to invite them for? The basics are obvious; they will come to see the shop, sip a little wine, munch some canapés, browse, chat, and wish us well. But I want something more interesting, something to distinguish our opening from that of a supermarket.

During our weekly lunch, I brainstorm with Wendy, "What do bookshops do besides sell books?"

She puts down her menu and looks at me over the striped pink and purple frames of her reading glasses. "In the States, they hold readings and book signings by famous authors."

"We're a little short of famous authors here." I begin, then— "Eureka! That doesn't mean we can't have a reading, does it? We'll issue an open invitation for people to choose some favorite excerpts and read them aloud at the Griffin's opening."

"I'm sure Robert Middleton would agree to read," Wendy catches my enthusiasm. "He hasn't performed since the Old Vic and it would be fun for him. And Marvin and Pepper Wilson used to do regional theater."

"Or if people prefer they can come just to listen to their friends and neighbors read." Caught up in the new plan, we chatter on, describing talents among our friends.

In the following days, to guarantee a few readers *pour encourager les autres,* I take Wendy's suggestion and ask Robert

Middleton, the handsome young actor, to read. I also secure the talents of Marvin Wilson and his wife Pepper who come from Idaho. Walter and I first met Marvin when I worked on Salir for *Algarve Magazine* which he edits. We later met Pepper at a dinner party hosted by Wendy and Nigel. At the time I thought Pepper a bit silly. She is bouncy, curly-haired, and given to baby talk when near Marvin, who is about twenty years older and invariably paternal. But her antics and their regional theater experience may prove valuable.

I'm grateful to find that the Wilsons look forward to performing at the Griffin. Not only have they agreed, but they also offer to bring a promising young Portuguese poet who has recently published his second collection. When I next see Wendy, I'm thrilled to announce, "We'll have a real author after all for our celebration." He will read in the Portuguese language, thereby embodying our appreciation to our host country. My spirits rise at this constellation of talents. We also have promises from a few more friends who are searching their libraries and polishing their elocution. Other readings (five minutes each) will be supplied by our audience in whatever language each reader chooses. We're anticipating a delightful time.

In between regular bookshop duties, I make arrangements. Megan Buckley, who owns the Bistro where Wendy and I lunch each week, will do catering for our opening. She comes to the shop to decide on placement of her food and wine tables and we discuss the menu. I hope people will want to look through the books as they arrive, again during a half hour interval, and once more after the readings close. This means that Megan's canapés should be tasty without causing sticky fingers, and we agree on several kinds that won't leave smudges on books.

Megan will bring sixty stacking chairs for the audience. When my ingeniously designed moveable bookcases are rolled to the side walls, her sixty chairs will transform the bookshop into a small theater. We'll leave space for a center aisle and set up the performance area near the sales desk. Greetings, conversation, and refreshments will be on the front terrace. Fortunately, autumn afternoons are almost always pleasant and sunny.

One morning a young man steps into the shop, says *Bom dia, Senhora,*" and gives me his business card which identifies him as Distri-Cultural's sales rep from the Faro branch. We shake hands and he moves toward the bookshelves. At the end of each row of books, he shakes his head and sighs heavily, signaling that he is not pleased. I wait. After completing his circuit, he returns to me and states the cause of his distress.

"The Senhora does not have a good selection."

"Oh? Are you looking for a particular book? " I'm still waiting for the purpose of his visit. "Many of these titles are recommended by your main office in Lisbon."

"But you do not have the best books. If you want to sell many books, you need to have the best ones. *Um momento,* I show you."

As he bounds outside to his van his purpose becomes clear. He comes back with two cartons of a hundred or so mass-market paperbacks with lurid covers. "These are the books you must have, the best books people want."

I look through the stack of bodice rippers, gory murder tales and adventures with space aliens, and I think "beach books." Not my taste, but I'm glad to try selling them. My "best books" as a reader may not be my best books as a bookseller. And the sales rep is right about one thing; I do need more books on the shelves.

"All right, I'll take these if I can get them on consignment."

He agrees at once; it's what he has intended all along. "*Esta bom,*" (that's good), he says and hands me a pricing list. "I come back with more every month. You give back what you don't sell."

We agree to the deal, both of us pleased. With him stopping in regularly, I won't need to go to Lisbon for light summer reading. I'll still want to go twice a year for books with greater appeal for me and I hope for others.

A galleon of a lady sails into my shop one Friday with pennants flying. Aged about sixty-five, large, plump, and topped by a towering nest of exceedingly bleached hair bedecked with bangles, dangles and bows. She proclaims herself to be Tamara Nelson, poet and painter, wants me to sponsor a signing for her books, and offers to do all the publicity herself. I hedge, say I'd like to read the books before deciding, and she graciously leaves three volumes with me.

With some trepidation, I look through her books in the evening after dinner. Oh my! The first is all about the Queen and the royal family, written with the spanielly devotion of a loyal subject of the Crown, in metered verse forms that compel singsong clumping oration. There are also accompanying royal portraits executed by the loving hand of Tamara Nelson herself.

The next two volumes are parts one and two of a forthcoming six volume history <u>in verse</u> of World War II. Sonnets, rhyme royal, and ballads with anguished invocations against the horrors of war. This series is being funded by a royal military benevolent fund, which will realize all the profits (such as they may be). I ask myself, why is she writing so devotedly about World War II? Perhaps a father or brother in the armed forces? In any case, here I am with this remarkable tome. What to do? Walter agrees that the poetry is dreadful but sees no harm in letting her have a signing here during our Grand Opening. Reluctantly I agree, figuring that she will surrounded by many other readers. Who knows, she may find some kindred anglophiles among the audience. It's alarming to visualize this large verse-making machine churning out page after page like sausages. All headed for the Griffin Bookshop.

Each day holds some surprises. Yesterday, a woman came into the shop buy some novels for herself and sent her small blonde daughter over to our children's section to pick out a picture book. But the child didn't want a book; she wanted the hyacinth-blue children's table. Neither her mother nor I could make her understand that it was not for sale. The table was what she wanted, not some stupid picture book, and she flung herself across it, and clung to the edge with chubby little fingers. Finally, she was detached and carried off, screaming and sobbing while I stood by helpless. Incidents like this can't be predicted but their variety keeps me eager to open the shop each morning.

After much thought and several conversations with Walter and friends, I decide to send mailed invitations for the Griffin's opening and not advertise it more widely. Though I probably misunderstand my market potential, I worry about unexpected hordes of avid readers overwhelming our limited seating space and laying waste the finite quantity of our refreshments. After the celebration, I'll definitely place ads in the *Algarve News* and other publications. Meanwhile, as a kind of compromise publicity we'll pass out announcement fliers to any new customers who might wander in.

"Remember when we thought we'd walk through parking lots up and down the Algarve to put fliers under windshield wipers," I ask Walter during our leisurely two-hour lunch break.

"I don't think I'm quite up to that," he cautions.

"Me neither. But it seemed like a good idea a year ago."

"Yes it did, but right now, it's not too appealing."

I agree; seen close up the parking lot idea is not attractive. And I think back to another early vision we had of ourselves as booksellers.

"Remember our donkey bookmobile plan?"

We both laugh. At one point before we settled here, we talked about advertising the shop by hitching a donkey to a colorful wagon full of books and moving it from place to place like a picturesque bookmobile. Fortunately, the prospect of full-time care and feeding of a donkey stopped us in those tracks.

"Still seems like a good promotion idea," Walter says and then, ever the optimist, he startles me by adding, "it could be fun owning a donkey."

"Yeah, fun," I mutter, having only recently survived Caesar and picturing cleaning out the donkey's stable. I decide to deflect the whole discussion. "But no donkey for opening day, right?"

Walter smiles, pats my hand, and puts his donkey dreams on hold.

I worry on, as is my wont. Even the number of invitations sent out worries me. I imagine dire results. If all one hundred and fifty come we won't be able to seat them, they'll finish the wine and canapés in ten minutes, and then leave in a huff. Surely, I tell myself, they won't all come; no invitation results in one-hundred percent attendance, especially not invitations to public occasions of little interest to most. Maybe the majority will stay away, with only staunch friends willing to appear. But what if they have some other more compelling engagement? What if only ten people show up? Or what if that Sunday sees torrential rains, and a hundred people come with dripping umbrellas, we can't set up any refreshments on the terrace and have to cram everything and everybody inside? What if, as often happens here, all the lights go out when people are trying to read aloud? What if? And so I fret on. While during daylight hours we are excitedly preparing for a successful day, late at night I am busily engaged with matters that occupy what Walter terms my "worry slot," imagining everything that can possibly go wrong.

We spend an afternoon at Vila Bonita to share plans for our opening. Summer has ended and tourists are few so that Mike and Odette have time for lemonade and a chat with us. We sit at one of the poolside tables and reminisce about our first summer as their guests. "We had a wonderful time here with you," Walter says. "And you took good care of Marianne when she was here alone."

"It seems quite carefree now, when I look back," I say. "I remember all the nice young couples on holiday here with nothing to do except amuse themselves. And all I had to do was watch the construction and learn to drive."

We linger for a while in the sunshine and as we gather our things to leave, Mike and Odette offer to help by serving wine at the grand opening.

I stock some German and French books to appeal to nationalities that visit here, pleased to think that the Griffin will be international. With that in mind, I decide that we should have some books in Portuguese. I can't compete with several fine Portuguese bookshops in Faro, but as a courtesy I'd like at least a sampling of books in the native language. Our Portuguese poet may bring several other Portuguese guests and they should find some Portuguese titles here. To find out how I might purchase them at the usual bookseller's discount, I visit *Livraria Bertrand*, the largest bookstore in Faro and part of a national chain. Unfortunately, the clerk is one of the "lemons" among Portuguese people, a chilly unsmiling woman who listens impatiently to my halting Portuguese.

"I am a bookseller in Almancil," I begin. Though she regards me as she would a blank wall, I continue. "I wish to stock some Portuguese books. To sell in my shop. Do you know where I could buy them at the bookseller's discount?"

"No, Madam, I don't. I sell the books that you see here."

"Well, do you know where *Livraria Bertrand* buys the books you sell?"

"I know nothing about that, Madam," she replies, and starts to turn away.

"Can you direct me to someone who might know?" I persist, steeling myself to maintain a pleasant expression and voice tone.

She is exasperated but to get rid of me steps to the sales desk, writes rapidly and hands me a slip of paper with an address.

"That is the *Bertrand* distributor in Faro, perhaps you can ask there."

I thank her and leave. I consult the map of Faro I keep in my car and see that the street name the clerk has noted is only a few blocks away. When I get there I realize that the address shows no number. I search for a while, hoping to find a sign for the distributor, but without success. It seems a fruitless pursuit and is taking time I do not have. Frustrated, I walk back along cobbled streets to my car, thinking I'll have to return to *Livraria Bertrand* and buy some Portuguese books at retail price.

Before doing so, I drop in at Distri Cultural's Faro warehouse to pick up some coffee-table garden books I've ordered. The shiny covers have gorgeous color photographs of red, pink and yellow flowers that will embellish the large slanted bottom shelves of the Griffin's bookcases. As usual while in the warehouse I wander and browse along the aisles and, as though guided by some minor goddess in charge of booksellers, I find a cluster of Portuguese books that I've never noticed before. I don't know if they're good or bad, but they are written in Portuguese. Amazed and delighted I mutter, "Your loss, *Livraria Bertrand!*" and snatch up one of each, thereby secure thirty volumes for my opening.

Two days later, I agree on a contract with Leonor, the lovely artist we have met at the *Centro Cultural*. Leonor fashions pressed flower petals and leaves into bold and imaginative designs nothing like the kitsch seen in tourist shops. She brings a dozen of her pictures to hang in the shop. I have them on consignment; if I sell them I will get a percentage; if not, they go back to Leonor. This way she will have exhibit space and we can adorn our shop with examples of an unusual and indigenous Portuguese art form. At sixty or eighty thousand escudos each, the pictures may be too expensive for a shop where people come expecting to spend three or four thousand for a paperback book. But any sale is possible for wealthy tourists at Vale do Lobo, if an item catches their fancy. I am proud to have the flower pictures as an elegant sideline, especially because they look so lovely on the walls.

Kitty Edwards comes in to help catalogue the latest shipment of books. We chatter throughout the morning and then go back to the house for a long lunch hour. All of this is fun but the skimpy pile of books we get done persuades me not to ask for her help again until after our grand opening.

Susan Lester, wife of one of Walter's golfing buddies, also comes to help on another day and even offers to volunteer for an afternoon each week. She is more efficient than Kitty and her first-hand knowledge of beach books could be useful in the future. I accept her offer with gratitude but during her first afternoon I have second thoughts. Susan presents such a torrent of suggestions that

I grow weary. After two hours, I say that I will welcome any idea if she herself wants to put it into action. That quiets her for a bit. After her shift is done, though, I'm remorseful and think I really should find a way to take advantage of all that energy. One idea of Susan's is for me to rent a photocopy machine to bring people in. I've asked her to research it, but I'm not really keen. With the rate of machine breakdowns here, I think I'd rather continue with Sonia's greeting cards and Leonor's flower pictures.

All in all, this season has not been bad, with the fewest routine breakdowns and misfortunes since we first set up housekeeping at Vila Gilfinn. An outfit called "Mr. Fix-It," run by two Englishmen, has promised to get some outside door handles for us so that customers may enter the shop at will. Mr. Fix-It will also lower the high axle-scraping bumps in the driveway. I'm hoping that can be done before the opening.

Fernão telephones to report that they have a houseguest, a visiting author from England, Gerda Baker. He and Daphne wonder if we would like her to autograph and sell her book, "*Shadow of War*," during our opening evening. I'm happy to say yes. The Griffin's opening will now have <u>two</u> real authors, just like a proper bookshop. And then, of course, there's the added attraction of the imposing Tamara....

One day before the opening the shop is open only in the morning, as is usual on Saturdays. Just under the wire, a greeting card salesman who travels up and down the coast happens to come in with samples. I buy twenty packs of twelve cards each for 15,000$. Unlike Sonia's delicate note cards which are blank inside, these are pretty garish but cover a variety of holidays and occasions and the salesman promises a one hundred percent mark-up. That's a lot better than the thirty to forty percent I get for books. What luck that he appeared just in time.

In the afternoon, with the shop closed, William comes to help us roll bookcases against the side walls. The chairs won't arrive till tomorrow morning when Megan can spare them because her

Bistro is closed on Sundays. I set out the new stock of greeting cards on the sales desk and rearrange the books to display the most attractive covers and titles at eye level. Our largest and most varied collection is in English where we boast appropriate signs for separate categories of fiction, mystery, biography, travel and restaurant guides, self-help, gardens, "cookery" (as the English say), interior design, and children's books. German is represented by several cases holding an interesting collection of second-hand German classics and splendid art books from my mother's library. Smaller collections round out the inventory: French and Dutch paperbacks in a separate case, and my thirty new Portuguese books prominently placed on two shelves near the entrance. When I'm done arranging, Walter makes a few adjustments, and then we look around the two connected rooms with pleasure. The Griffin, all dressed up for company with its four large chandeliers glowing, is an attractive and well-stocked bookshop.

"Well, Patoot, you've done it." Walter says and puts his arm around my shoulders.

"*We've* done it." I hug him and we stand for a while savoring our achievement.

There were many moments when I doubted this day would ever come but now it's here and we are immensely pleased to have gotten this far. We congratulate ourselves, turn off the lights, close the doors, and drive to Loulé to celebrate with a delicious dinner at *Aux Bons Enfants*, where the young owners wish us luck with a complimentary after-dinner cordial. As they serve other customers, Walter and I smoothly switch full and empty glasses.

Sunday dawns clear and pleasantly warm and stays that way. In late morning Megan, true to her word, brings the chairs and we set them in rows. A bit later our neighbor Dola Van Riin appears carrying a huge vase of red carnations, which add a splendid blaze of color to the sales desk. William and Sonia arrive an hour before the announced opening time. He has fished through all their bags and boxes to unearth some strings of Christmas lights, which he winds around the four front pillars to add a festive touch. As a bonus, the extra light points don't short out the electric power. Several more friends also arrive early to help set up. Fiona, my fellow student at Portuguese lessons, will help to greet people, and Mike and Odette are on hand to staff the wine bar. How generous and sweet people are to us on this day! With this little group already here, we chat and laugh without the usual tense moments of waiting for first arrivals

At the appointed hour of four o'clock the first cars pull into the shop's small parking lot or park by the roadside. Their occupants stroll up the driveway to our entrance and within twenty minutes the terrace is full of people and the hum of greetings. Soon we call them inside to begin the Reading Aloud.

Walter, as emcee, introduces Marvin Wilson, our first reader. With his stocky frame and short gray beard, Marvin looks like a smaller Ernest Hemingway and, fittingly, reads from Hemingway's essay on writing. Courteous applause follows. Then Pepper steps up to the lectern, tosses her extravagant blonde curls, scrunches up her face into a glowering pout and wails a tirade of childish fury at having been denied the starring role of a daffodil in a school play. Our dominantly English audience is baffled at first, then a laugh here and a giggle there puncture their reserve. Within a few moments, they are clearly enjoying Pepper's spoiled brat, and I relax.

Just as the next reader steps forward, I hear a commotion outside and a loud Germanic voice, "Ja, this is it. And here is Megan with the wine. Ho? What? Everyone inside? Well then, ve go in." And Gunnar Nielsen, carrying a large green plant, bursts into the shop followed by his graceful blonde daughter, Ingrid.

"Hallo Walter! Hallo Marianne! Here ve are." Gunnar booms as I rush toward them and murmur, "So glad you both could come. Thank you so much; the plant is spectacular." I take it from him and set it on the sales desk. "Won't you come and sit down? We're having a reading…"

"A reading? What are you reading? I get a glass of wine first, Hallo Senhora, *boa tarde* Senhor," he calls and waves to people he recognizes.

I draw him outside, explain that the wine will be served in a little while and again urge him to take a seat.

"I vait here," moves across the terrace to the bar table and smiles. I signal to Megan to give him some wine, and then I go back inside to attend the next reader, Dola van Riin.

She opens a book and smiles sweetly at her audience. Most, having been distracted by Gunnar's interruption, are now busy chattering to each other. When they realize Dola is waiting, they quiet down and listen politely.

"Marianne said we could read in any language," Dola begins, "and I am reading this story in Dutch, but it is a Portuguese story." She first outlines the story in her careful English and then reads in cadenced Dutch the tale of Inês de Castro, a lady of the Portuguese court during the middle ages who was loved by Dom Pedro, the crown prince. Inês was murdered by jealous nobles who didn't want her children to succeed to the throne. But when her lover became king, he found a way to foil the plans of the wicked nobles. He had Inês' body exhumed, dressed in royal robes, and seated on a throne beside him. Then he forced all the nobles in public procession to swear fealty to her as queen, thus assuring their children's succession.

The gruesome tale of Inês de Castro is familiar to every Portuguese school child and though few among the Griffin's audience understand all of Dola's words, her earnestness and musical voice compel attention and she gains enthusiastic applause for her performance.

A string of short readings follow. An English gentleman, pink and white like a plump overage baby, reads a comic poem of his own devising, very arch, suggesting that ladies who desire equal opportunities are decidedly ill-advised to seek them in a world too harsh for their frail fingers and brains. I catch Wendy's gaze through this little burst of malice and we keep our faces bland through the polite applause that accompanies the reader's return to his seat. He is followed to the stage by another Englishman who recites from memory in a voice booming with gusto the entire delightful text of "The Walrus and the Carpenter." Good humor is restored.

By this time the audience is warmed up, receptive to whatever comes next. Though Walter and I have our doubts, what comes next is Tamara Nelson. Walter introduces her as "this fine lady who generously donates the proceeds from her rhymes toward support of the British Foundation which clearly holds her in high esteem. She will read from her work in progress, a six-volume history of World War II in verse. Ladies and Gentlemen, Tamara Nelson."

Tamara rises from her seat and sweeps toward the lectern, trailing scarves, ribbons, and her small pale husband who carries her books and papers. He hands several pages to the poetess as directed by her majestic finger flutterings. She stands before her stunned audience, her golden hair in a tower, her carriage regal, her frame large and overflowing her short flowered dress which, to us at the side of the podium, displays an inch of slip and stockings rolled above doughy knees. She smiles upon us all with great benevolence, then arranges her features into solemn reverence. She gazes down at her papers, then imploringly up at the ceiling, and declaims,

"To thee, most royal monarch of this verdant isle..."

From my seat I can see both speaker and audience. As Tamara warms to her oeuvre, an invisible curtain seems to descend over the faces of her listeners as they sit motionless before the swells of rime royal.

After some time, a pause, a shuffle of papers from small husband to large Tamara who proclaims, "That section concludes volume one of my history. Now in volume two I address the Battle of..."

Walter and I exchange desperate glances and both surreptitiously look at our watches. Seven minutes have passed, then eight, ten, twelve. The gallant battle has hardly begun; the flower of English manhood is about to be decimated. So is our audience. Walter, my hero, stands up and steps quietly to Tamara's side. A few more stanzas and she has to acknowledge his presence. She looks at him sideways through blue eyelashes and pauses. Walter seizes the moment.

"Thank you very much for that moving reading, " he says, "it was truly unforgettable. Those who wish to read more for themselves have the opportunity to purchase the volumes that you've kindly brought along today. Isn't that right?"

"Yes, absolutely," Tamara agrees. "But I thought I would just read the bombing of London before closing…"

"I'm sure that would be very powerful, " Walter is regretful but firm. "But we have many more readers waiting in the wings, so we must make way. And right now, we have scheduled a brief interval when we may all have some wine and refreshments."

He gently takes Tamara's arm and guides her toward the terrace. The audience applauds with only barely perceptible relief, then rises as one. As people move rapidly into the center aisle and out to the terrace bar, Fiona, my fellow student, catches me. "My sainted aunt! Wherever did you find her?" she mutters from behind a cinematic smile.

"She found us. Truly remarkable, isn't she?" I agree with a corresponding smile as we move outside to help the servers and mingle with the guests. Most stay on the terrace in the fading late afternoon sunshine, but a few drift back inside to study the bookshelves. Pepper is stationed at the sales desk doing a brisk little business in greeting cards. Megan and her two assistants circulate with trays of snacks on toothpicks-- pigs-in-blankets, spiced crab balls, cheese or pâté squares—all small enough to be consumed in one bite. We've got a good crowd, about seventy people who make the shop and terraces look bustling but not uncomfortably crowded. Twilight deepens and the conversational level rises as the wine supply lowers.

Toward the interval's close, Mike takes a break from serving the wine and pulls me aside. I've fancied that he and Odette would be pleased by the size of the crowd but Mike still worries that my bookshop won't make any money. "What you ought to do, Marianne," he urges, "is try for a Tottolotto concession." He grasps my arm for emphasis, "People who have those machines get two million escudos a day. Two million a day, Marianne!"

I've seen the loud Portuguese lottery salesmen hawking tickets with their bullhorns on many street corners and at the markets. Imagining them in my driveway, I can't quite manage Walter's strategy of saying it's a good idea and I'll consider it. "Well, Mike," I demur, "People don't usually go to a book store for those tickets. Usually a *mercado* or a *papelaria* where they sell newspapers," my voice trails off and I try to recover my good manners. I promise Mike that I'll think about it, and flee to join another group.

Actually I know that I will add his suggestion to those of other well-wishers in the past two years. It is remarkable how many I've had. In New York, the director of the Portuguese Chamber of Commerce thought I should add a bar with brandy to bring in more trade. Kitty has suggested that I serve cream tea. Susan Lester thinks a photocopy machine might help. One customer urged me to display book jackets at the roadside. No one seems to believe that people might come to the Griffin simply to buy books. Or at least no one thinks I can make a living from selling them. They might be right. Who knows? I have some talents but a talent for making money hasn't been one of them. Maybe one of these schemes that I reject could make me millions—two million escudos a day as Mike says. For the moment, though, I am satisfied to see my bookshop filled with people, with some lined up at the sales desk to make purchases.

When the customers have been served, it is time for the second act. Feeling like Broadway impresarios, Walter and I switch lights on and off to indicate that we are ready to resume, and people radiate enjoyment as they file back to their seats. Amazingly, we have lost only three or four, Gunnar Nielsen and his daughter among them. Listening to people read was obviously not to his taste, but I appreciate his having come to wish us well.

The first reading after the interval is a passage in German by the former showgirl who comes to Walter for counseling. With his help, she is slowly regaining a sense of worth, and has chosen to read a passage from Herman Hesse that exhorts faith in the future. Though we have only a smattering of German listeners today, Walter and I admire her courage and willingness to add to our multi-lingual readings.

Next we return to English for a while with Gerda Baker reading from her memoir *Shadows of War.* Her childhood as a refugee from Germany to England was clearly filled with hardships, and her description is genuinely moving.

Kitty then steps up to read from Gerald Durrell's *My Family and Other Animals.* It perfectly suits her clipped English voice and brings smiles of recognition. She is followed by a multi-national mini-troupe of actors, Robert Middleton and Nigel from England, Wendy from the United States, and their visiting Canadian houseguest, all careening through a scene from *Twelfth Night* in a boisterous jumble of English pronunciations. They take many exaggerated bows in response to the audience's appreciation.

It is nearly time to end. With some words of appreciation for Portugal's hospitality to us and our fledgling Griffin, Walter introduces the young Portuguese poet, Manuel Netos dos Santos, who will close our readings. Wiry and intense, he reads several lyrics from his newest collection. Though most of us don't understand every word, his fervor and dignity compel respect, and the presence of a serious Portuguese writer seems a fitting close to our celebration. I see it as a kind of mutual tribute, to him for agreeing to represent Portuguese art and culture for this band of listeners from other lands, and to them for coming out of separate groupings to encourage an international community.

When Senhor Manuel has finished, Walter and I both rise to thank him and also thank the congenial audience of new friends and neighbors for joining us for this occasion. We invite everyone to the house to share a light supper catered by Megan. For Walter and me this is an evening of glowing warmth. The long phase of planning and building has ended; the dream of opening a bookshop in the Algarve is accomplished. The Griffin is flying and his wings are strong.

While I mingle happily with our guests, I also look to the future. I can think of many activities for the shop, but I'll have to consider whether they will bring in money or increase the red figures. Will I turn into a "bottom line" businesswoman? Will I become like Silas Marner, keep a sack of gold coins under my bed and cackle with glee when I count them out every night? Where it will end? I don't know. But at the close of this festive day, I do know one thing. I am a bookseller now.

XXIV
The Return

In December Walter and I fly back to the States for our usual winter holiday season. While there, we feel almost as though we are leading two lives. We both become happily reabsorbed into activities with family and friends and Walter is drawn back into his clinical work as well as to weekly poker games with long-time cronies. At the same time, I'm planning events and publicity for the Griffin and gathering self-help and children's books for the coming year. It occurs to me during this enjoyable winter break that rather than having failed, as I sometimes feared before we began our venture in Portugal, I might actually have succeeded in both places.

When we return to the Algarve after the winter, I continue to ponder this idea because my work with the shop and the community's encouragement does indeed make me feel successful. And I wonder why having gone through something so uncomfortable as our first years in the house and so cumbersome as starting the Griffin should have strengthened my character. Perhaps because, while here, I have not only learned about Portugal, I also learned more about myself. What have I learned? That I am resourceful and can succeed in reaching a goal if I just don't give up. That my strengths are different from Walter's; the practical tasks didn't happen here unless I did them, yet I couldn't have done them without him. All in all I've learned that building a dream is hard slogging work. You just move things along a bit every day and later on, when you look back, what seemed like standing still was actually forward motion.

Our return is pleasantly free of the crises that awaited us after earlier winters. The house survived the winter in good order with the shop staying open half-days in the care of Pepper Wilson. Some weeks after Marvin and Pepper had performed at the shop's grand opening, Wendy mentioned that Pepper was looking for work and might manage the shop on a half-time basis during the Christmas season while Walter and I were away. At first I was reluctant, but I didn't want to stall the shop's gaining momentum by closing it for those weeks. Pepper came to train with me before we left and I was glad to find that she'd left her baby talk at home. She was happy to have the work and proved to be a quick study and an enthusiastic bookseller. Since we got back from Saratoga I have found Pepper to be a pleasant colleague. Her outgoing personality proves a real asset for stimulating sales. We work together compatibly and I schedule some overlap in our shifts so that we can discuss progress and exchange ideas.

The Griffin's income, however, is still not enough to continue to support Pepper's half-time salary. A few weeks after our return, Walter and I review sales accounts during lunchtime while the shop is closed and I sigh, "I'm afraid we'll have to give Pepper notice. The shop just can't afford her."

Walter makes me an unexpected offer. "What if I give you the amount Pepper earns each week? She's been a good worker and you two get along well."

I'm not sure what he means. "What about you, your shifts in the shop? There's not enough work for two people at the same time."

"No. I'm thinking that Pepper could replace me. The extra income is good for her and Marvin, and I'd like a chance to take some time off from the shop. I can afford it; don't worry. Finnegan Associates International is doing well, in Saratoga anyway." He smiles at me with a trace of pleading.

This feels like a huge change to me and I can't quite manage an answer. I nod and start to clear away the lunch dishes while blinking back tears of disappointment. Walter no longer managing the shop with me. The idea feels lonely. I have so hoped he would stay as enthusiastic about the Griffin as I am.

"You're doing a terrific job with the shop," Walter senses my dismay. "And you love it. It's always been mainly your thing, you know that; but it really isn't mine. I was glad to help you get going but now that Pepper has taken hold so well and the shop is humming along, this seems like a good opportunity for me to bow out a bit. I'll still be here to help in whatever you need. But I'd like a chance to keep my afternoons open."

I am still trying to get used to the idea. "What will you do with the open time?"

"Oh, a little gardening, a little golf, see patients, do some reading, maybe work on my article about alcohol consumption in various countries… whatever comes up."

Regretfully, I acquiesce. How can I refuse Walter's wish for more time to pursue his own interests, especially after he agreed to stay in Portugal longer just to let me have more time with the Griffin?

In April, we celebrate Walter's sixty-fifth birthday with a six-course dinner for two at an elegant Auberge in the mountain town of Santa Barbara de Nexe. The next day Walter sends a post card to his daughter, Kathy. "Now that I've reached the Big Six-Five, life is indeed much more interesting. My golf game improves; I speak Portuguese more fluently; I've had more requests to sing and play the piano at local restaurants; and my full-time custodian speaks to me softly and feeds me regularly." I smile at this little string of half-truths and murmur, "hear hear" in salute.

Though he no longer works half-days in the shop, Walter is always glad to listen or make suggestions when I want to talk about developing the Griffin, but as he said, the shop has always been mainly my thing. His main thing, since the rainy season ended, has become golf. He plays three or four times a week.

In truth, though he loves the game, golf really isn't enough for him. Short-term patients do appear, but they are few and most don't stay long enough to build the kind of therapeutic relationships that might enable them to get better. Despite his success at last year's military conference, no further word has come from the organizers. Walter rarely complains and continues to be good company but, though he doesn't say so, I feel that he is growing increasingly homesick.

In the next months I manage the Griffin with Pepper's help, and book sales climb steadily. By summer, I reach my goal of having the shop operate in the black, and can assume the expense of Pepper's part-time salary. She is a tireless promoter, going everywhere with a box of the Griffin's books in the "boot" of her car, and scouting the area for benefit luncheons, school book fairs and meetings that might provide a venue for sales. I too find ways to bring people into the shop. After pleas from a number of customers, I install a second-hand book section. This proves popular, earning extra income and bringing in more readers, many buying new books as well.

One day when I am at the sales desk, I am surprised to see Joost Roemer step into the shop. We've heard that Roemer Construction has hit hard times since the recent collapse of the region's building boom. Joost carries a briefcase and I notice that he has kept his good looks and his pleasing shy smile. I wonder if he is a new customer or if something else has brought him.

We shake hands across the sales desk. How are you, Joost?"

"I am well, thank you, but you have heard that we have closed the business?"

"No, I'm sorry." I haven't heard that their difficulties have gone so far. "What will you do now?"

"My father has gone back to Holland," Joost says, "and he has written a book. I am here to see if you would like to buy some copies to sell here in your shop." He slips a book out of his briefcase and hands it to me.

I take it from him, thinking what a funny turn-around that Joost should be here on his mission, after all the troubles we've had with his company—poor drainage, an electrical fire, the failed water pump, and inadequate heating. I glance through the pages of Jan Roemer's *Revelation Through Out of Body Experiences* and can't help feeling it's probably just as well that Jan has left the construction business. One would prefer a builder who concentrates on *in-body* experiences.

"Well, you see, Joost," I explain, "I don't buy books outright, but I'd be glad to take some of your father's books on consignment." When Joost looks puzzled, I described the system to him. He can leave some books with me; I'll pay afterwards for any that have sold and return those that haven't.

This is a new concept for Joost, one he does not find appealing. "No, I don't think so," he says. "I could not leave them unless they are paid for." He returns his father's book to his briefcase, we shake hands again, and he leaves. The odd interlude makes me realize how much has changed and continues to change around us. I can still picture the huge *Roemer Construçoens* sign that had attracted Walter and me on our first trip when we sought information about my mother's property. Now our house and shop are thriving and the Roemers are on their way out.

In June we receive exciting news; my daughters Julia and Helen are coming to visit. As a travel agent, Julia has flown to many spots around the world with ease. She made several trips with to Switzerland with us and also joined us on one of our early trips to Portugal. Now Walter and I look forward to showing her what we have built. I also especially appreciate Helen's willingness to make the long trip. That means a lot to me since she seldom travels and we haven't spent much time together in recent years. I'm excited at the prospect of being with her for two weeks, and see her visit as an opportunity for us to restore closer ties.

Walter and I drive to Lisbon on the afternoon before Helen's flight is scheduled to arrive. Our arrival coincides with Portugal's winning the world cup in junior football. All night, the entire city celebrates; young men drive their cars round and round waving banners, long streamers and Portuguese flags. People march and sing, beat drums, drink, dance and shout. From our balcony at *Nossa Senhora do Monte,* a small hotel high on a hill overlooking the city, we see the glowing lights and hear the celebration rising up from all neighborhoods. It goes on and on as though the city itself is roaring in triumph like a huge happy beast.

At seven the next morning we pick Helen up at Lisbon Airport. She looks tan and fresh and is nicely eager to "see stuff." After letting her sleep for a few hours, we three tour the city, stopping at the famous landmarks and strolling through the Alfama district with its steep narrow streets and colorful houses. The next day we drive to Sintra to show her both palaces, the eccentric nineteenth century Pena Palace on a hill, and the authentic eleventh century castle in the center of the city. Helen whizzes through all the sights with only mild interest. From a street vendor on the steps of the Sintra palace, I buy her a little brass and bead gismo like a miniature geodesic dome meant to be manipulated into various shapes. Unlike her polite reactions to landmarks and museums, her absorption in the little toy is intense and her mastery rapid, making me see again the quick and dexterous little girl of so long ago. We end our Lisbon stay with dinner at the Tivoli's rooftop restaurant and see the Castelo São Jorge's lights glimmering on the neighboring hill.

Overall, Helen finds Lisbon disappointing, just as we did when we first saw it years ago. She tells us she expected it to be all white, like the photographs of our villa, and is sorry to see the city so dingy and crumbling. Walter and I can easily understand, though by this time we feel affection for Lisbon's worn charms.

On the third day we drive down to the Algarve where Helen at last does see the white buildings she has expected. She likes our villa, enjoys perfecting her tan at our pool, and spends hours each day reading, a lifelong habit. I am glad that she seems interested and at ease in conversation with our friends at various gatherings and is always willing to go exploring with us. So many of her traits are familiar to me from her childhood—her keen powers of watching and learning--within three days she can lock the house, set the alarms, put dishes in their proper places, open and close the shop, and shelve books in the proper sections.

Her reticence is also familiar and we have to laugh at her deadpan answer to our question of what she thinks of Portugal. "Short, " she says, and in response to our puzzled expressions, she elaborates, "Everything is short. The mountains are short, the trees are short, even the people are short." A funny and odd assessment, but basically accurate. Trust Helen's ability to make us think by seeing things a bit aslant

One week later, on the afternoon of my birthday, Julia arrives with Holly, her colleague at the travel agency. Because both young women have toured northern Portugal before, now they fly directly to Faro where we meet them. During our time together, I spend my usual mornings working in the shop while the girls sleep late or lounge by the pool. In the afternoons, when Pepper is on shop duty, Walter and I gather up all three visitors and take them to our favorite places, inland to the Monchique Mountains, to Loulé for the markets, to Silves to see the castle, to the São Lourenço blue and white tiled church and to the *Centro Cultural*. We drive as far as Cap St. Vincent, and to towns all along the coast with their distinctive beaches and cliffs, fishing fleets, and special crafts. Helen buys two shirts as souvenirs. Julia and Holly scream with glee at the ceramic shops, buying bowls, plates and platters everywhere we go because every place has different designs and colors. Their enthusiasm makes me see the local wares with fresh eyes and I buy a few more plates myself. Sometimes, Julia and Holly return to a particular shop to acquire more crockery. By the time the two are ready to continue their vacation in Spain, their rented car is stuffed with wrapped ceramics and I have serious doubts that they will be able to walk into the Seville airport under their own power.

On our last evening together we have a farewell dinner by torchlight at one of the beach *barracas*. Over our meal of grilled prawns, Chicken Piri Piri and Sangria, we talk about the places we've visited in the past fortnight. Helen has been outwardly less ebullient than the others, but when Julia asks her what she liked best in Portugal, she answers thoughtfully that actually one has to experience all of it. That makes me feel good, as Walter and I have hoped to share our love of this country. Though each of the three girls has responded differently, all seemed to enjoy their visit.

Two days after Julia and Holly leave, we drive Helen back to Lisbon for her return flight. As we hug good-bye, she says that she plans to accumulate free air miles so that she can come to see us again next summer. Julia also spoke of hoping to return. I am touched and happy, but chagrined to realize that we may no longer be here in another year. But who knows? Life is full of unexpected twists and turns. We probably won't be able to sell the place quickly and there may well be opportunities for us all to return for visits in the future.

As Walter and I speed along the highway back down to the Algarve, I am at first a bit relieved to have a respite from all the touring, bustle and chatter but soon I feel hollow and sad that the girls are gone and we are all so far away from each other again.

Once our visitors are gone, we become once more thoroughly immersed in the activities of every day. We also enliven our daily routine by creating special events. During the midday period when the shop is closed to the public, I lead two writing groups, one every other week. After each session the participants browse along the bookshelves, often finding titles they want to buy. Wendy and Nigel use the Griffin every fortnight for play-reading evenings with a group of would-be thespians. This leads us to mount and publicize a series of theatrical performances attended by our customers as well as the actors' friends and acquaintances. Senhor Clementino's bookcases, ideal for displaying books during working hours, are easily rolled aside for these occasions. I buy fifty white plastic lawn chairs for seating our audiences, and Walter and I become adept at transforming the Griffin into a mini-theater. Pepper and Marvin give three performances in the lead parts of the play *Love Letters*. Their success inspires Robert Middleton, the gifted young actor, to mount a one-man show for two performances in which he appears as Charles Dickens reading aloud portions of his works. This proves so popular that he also recreates comparable appearances as Oscar Wilde.

While eagerly engaged by all these activities we know that our Algarvian time is drawing to a close. When we first contemplated living in Portugal, we gave ourselves five years to decide whether we would settle here permanently or eventually return home to the States. Our house fire brought us to a low point, but we learned within days that our immediate impulse to flee didn't easily or quickly translate into reality. Once in it, one cannot simply walk out on a dream. We decided to postpone our departure until after the opening of the shop. Then, once the Griffin was actually open, I fell in love with it and craved the day-by-day running of this enterprise that, with Walter's help, I had designed and created. I wanted the further satisfaction of establishing it within the community that I increasingly felt a part of. As always, Walter was generous, agreeing to delay our return to Saratoga for another year. Just as opening the shop was postponed several times, so in parallel fashion our return has also been postponed. As it is turning out, the undoing of our venture is taking almost as long as the doing. Everything takes longer than you think it's going to.

But this is the final year. As the months pass, just as I earlier tended to the practical tasks of getting us to Portugal, I now begin the work of transporting us home. Again, following Walter's dictum of one day at a time, one step at a time, I manage the details of our disengagement. I gradually acquire sturdy vacation furniture at second-hand villa sales, storing the pieces in the garage. Our goal is to sell the property as a unit—villa and shop—preferably to that nice retired couple we imagine as ideal buyers. That means a flourishing book business and an inviting house. Since the Wilsons are always searching for an inexpensive place to live and Pepper enjoys her work in the shop, they agree to our suggestion that they take up residence and stay on after Walter and I leave, with Pepper keeping the shop going, until the property sells.

Two months before our scheduled departure, we pack up and

send to Saratoga the antique furniture and art we inherited from Elke. We leave the bright curtains and all the kitchen ware in place, bring in the replacement furniture and, as a final touch, I hang colorful prints and pictures in every room, making the villa look light, inviting, and ready for viewing. Meanwhile I train Pepper in all aspects of the business and gradually reduce my own involvement. Our final event is a holiday " Reading Aloud" party in the shop to celebrate the coming Christmas season.

I contemplate the ending of our sojourn with keen regret at leaving my beloved shop. I also worry a bit that our decision not to stay here permanently might spoil the story I still hope to write. Then a question comes to me: Are there perhaps two stories inherent in our time in the Algarve? The first was going forth to create the villa and shop. The second is returning home. Each has had its own arc of development, with some overlap. As the outward-bound arc crested (as it did with the Griffin's opening) and leveled off before descending, the arc of returning began to rise in our thinking. If the circle of our going out and coming back could form the design, then might not everything be useful for my story?

I could gladly stay in Portugal longer, but it is different for Walter. He has done many good things here, seen patients, helped friends, assisted the psychiatric staff at Faro Hospital and even the national military, but ultimately his many idle hours and the language barrier have been a striking contrast to the needs and opportunities awaiting him in Saratoga every time he has returned to supervise his practice. Years ago, my career discouragement in the States was the main impetus for our move, now the dearth of opportunity in the Algarve for Walter is a primary reason for our return.

There are other reasons as well.

We had hoped that our five children and their families would come to spend vacations with us every summer, but the expense and the distance has proven too difficult to fit into their busy family and career schedules. Over time, we have missed them and our grandchildren too much to be contented with seeing them only during our winter trips home.

Also, we continue uncomfortable with the Algarve's health system, having heard stories of broken bones set without anesthesia and inadequate hospital care. Our preference for the familiar is probably unfair, but during last December, when I suffered extreme back pain from a herniated disk in my spine, I delayed surgery till our return to the States. Similarly, when our family physician in Saratoga diagnosed atrial fibrillation during one of Walter's stays, he was glad for easy access to heart specialists there.

In addition to these specific reasons, another is less well defined. We are tired of being expatriates. Though we've made many friends, to native Algarvians Walter and I with our different appearance, habits and history, are separate and visibly "other" and remain *estrangeiros*.

I remember my parents and their circle of friends in New York. Though their English grew steadily better during their ten years there, they clung to their affiliation with fellow émigrés, sharing memories and a common frame of reference. While they also gained many American friends, those didn't have that shared history. After ten years, Robert and Elke went back to Europe. I'm sure they benefited from their time in America—certainly the essential benefit of staying alive and out of concentration camps— but also acquaintance with American culture and ways of thinking that, on the whole, they liked. But they never fully belonged; the language, the customs, the tastes were too different. When Europe started to recover after the war, they went back to where they felt at home.

And so, Walter and I will also go back. Unlike my parents, we didn't flee to Portugal for safety, so that isn't a real analogy. But we have learned how we actually respond to living in a foreign culture. Doing so has been extremely interesting yet in the long run difficult and somewhat tiring. The small daily things take more effort, relationships formed in another language are too limited to be really satisfying, and we observe but don't take part in the national conversation about cultural and political issues. Gradually over the years we have come to feel the lack.

Despite these reasons, as the time draws near for us to leave, we both find ourselves with mixed feelings. We are truly sad to leave the Algarve and know we will miss our Vila Gilfinn, the site of our hopes, trials and triumphs. We are sorry also to leave the Griffin, which has brought us so many lively days. Hardest of all is saying good-bye to the many good friends who have brightened our lives. We comfort ourselves with hopes of seeing them again in the future, and turn with rising eagerness toward the new adventure of resuming our American lives.

XXV
Aftermath

In December of 1992 Walter and I concluded our sojourn in Portugal and returned permanently to our home in Saratoga Springs. Marvin and Pepper Wilson lived in our Vila Gilfinn while Pepper continued to manage the Griffin Bookshop. A year later the entire property was sold, regrettably not to our imaginary retired couple but to a villa management firm. Fortunately, a woman from one of my writers' groups joined Pepper as co-owner of the Griffin and together they arranged for its move to a new location on the EN 125, in the center of the town of Almancil.

Unlike Walter, I did not have a profession waiting for me in the States. Saratoga Springs was home, but it was also a big unknown for me. Walter was returning to his established practice, eager to expand it. I had no immediate plans beyond settling back into our house and community. The same question loomed that I had faced years earlier on the beach at Vale do Lobo. What, beyond daily living, would I *do* here?

But I was not the same person I had been then. I didn't feel dogged by failure; I was buoyed by success. I had designed, built, opened and operated a bookshop in a foreign country. More than that, I had built a productive and satisfying life there. No reason why I couldn't do the same here. At first I taught English at the local community college, once again trying to fit into a pre-existing slot. I could have continued, but this time I knew that I didn't want to. With starting the Griffin bookshop I had inserted a new wedge into a community's social and economic structure. Now, almost as spontaneously as the original idea for the bookshop, I found a new venture. I read an article about the University of the Third Age in France—a college-level program in which older adults alternated roles as students and teachers—and I thought, why not start something similar? I went to my former boss, the president of the college where I had worked earlier, proposed the idea of starting a learning in retirement program and, with his approval and some seed money, I became the founding director of the Academy for Learning in Retirement at Saratoga Springs. The Academy prospered and recently celebrated its twelfth anniversary. I also wrote and published a memoir of my having come to America as a child with my parents after we fled from Nazi Germany.

I could not have done these things without the confidence I gained during my years in Portugal. Odd that something so complex and difficult, with so many setbacks, should bring increased strength. I didn't feel strong at the time; I felt a series of crises and near-collapses. Compared to the mountain of hardships endured by real explorers of foreign climes—arctic cold, jungle heat, trackless wastes, hostile inhabitants—my small bookshop was a molehill indeed. But it was a hard-won accomplishment for me. Walter's encouragement repeatedly set me up on my feet, dusted me off, and urged me forward. Somehow, bit-by-bit, it got done and I grew stronger. Perhaps that says something in behalf of the often-maligned "geographic cure." I, for one, had to go away to gain the courage to thrive at home.

And Walter? He built up the practice that he loved. A while later, he took up an earlier dream and completed the doctoral dissertation he had left unfinished many years before. Both achievements brought him great satisfaction. He also continued to enjoy the memory of our Algarve years, and often introduced mention of Portugal into conversations with new acquaintances.

What was the place of this adventure in our lives? In separate ways, bringing our dream of Portugal into reality took us out of our accustomed ruts, good and bad, tossed us into new patterns, and enlarged our sense of who we were or could be. For Walter it brought the sense that he was not only an agent of change in others; he himself was capable of bold adventure. For me, it brought awareness that I was more than I had imagined, and that I could do almost anything I set my mind to. I learned that one can fail and still not *be* a failure, that persistence counts and that success feels wonderful.

But like failure, success is also temporary. Time passes, things change. In December of 2001 my dear Walter died of a brain tumor. I've always been grateful that during his final three months we had time to share our thoughts and express our love for each other. He felt that he had lived a good life, and left us with an unforgettable gift. When asked by his son if there was anything he wanted or anything we could do for him, Walter answered, "No, not really. All my dreams have come true."

The love of my family and support of my friends sustained me during the early painful months of grieving. Just as powerful was the sense that Walter was still with me, not in any supernatural way, but because he had been such a central presence in my life and given me so much love that I could still hear his voice and feel his belief in me.

One day I happened to remember how much he enjoyed the memory of our Algarve years. I recalled a dinner party in Saratoga when one long-time friend asked, "So, after all that upheaval did you make any money?"

"Not really, " Walter admitted. "The real estate market there collapsed while we were building and that lowered our selling price. Then, too, our air travel back and forth added to the costs, though otherwise we might have spent that on vacations." He paused for a moment to take a sip of his seltzer while thinking about how to sum up. Then he chuckled. "All in all, as far as we can figure, we didn't get rich but we pretty much broke even."

"Seems like a lot of trouble just to end up here where you

started." our friend said. "Do you ever regret it?"

Walter and I exchanged glances. I knew we were both thinking about all we had gained from our experience and how much we enjoyed our shared memories. Did we ever regret it?

"Never," Walter said and I chimed in, "Not even for a moment."

Recalling that moment made me unpack the carton that contained the journal I had kept during our years in Portugal. Together with letters from our children, my writing filled nine overflowing loose-leaf binders. My aim of writing a story of our adventure had been put aside after return to the States, obscured by all the activities of recreating a full life here. But the story was still there, waiting to be told. I started to read, to select highlights, and then to write and rewrite, feeling all the while that Walter was keeping me company.

Now the story is done and I am ready for new strivings and new goals. I still sometimes dream of Portugal, but am fortunate that I can rekindle the zest I found there, right in my own hometown.

As I write this, those friends in the Algarve who were expatriates there have scattered back to their home countries. Wendy and Nigel live in California; Ben and Kitty Edwards separated, with Ben continuing to live in the Algarve and Kitty returning to England; our Indonesian Dutch neighbors, Kurt and Dola Van Riin are in Holland living near their children; my Irish fellow language student, Fiona, returned to Dublin and later to London.

Our Portuguese friends have remained in the Algarve, except that our beloved Fernão, who introduced us to the Portuguese language, died several years ago. His wife Daphne and their children still live in the Algarve. It comforts me to know that the couple who first welcomed us and became our staunch friends, Mike and Odette Moreira, still own and manage the now enlarged *Pensão Bonita*.

Our former dog Caesar repeatedly escaped through the fence of Jumpers Pub and was eventually sent to a farm where he could run free. There, as far as I know, he lived happily ever after.

The Griffin Bookshop continues as a thriving literary center for travelers and international residents to this day.

In memory of my beloved husband
Walter John Finnegan
1926 - 2001